FORENSIC EXAMINATION
OF RUBBER STAMPS

ABOUT THE AUTHOR

Jan Seaman Kelly received her training as a forensic document examiner from George Lewis at the U.S. Postal Crime Laboratory in San Bruno, California. In 1993, she received her certification as a forensic document examiner from the American Board of Forensic Document Examiners (ABFDE).

Ms. Seaman Kelly has authored several published articles in professional journals such as the *Journal of the American Society of Questioned Document Examiners* and the *Journal of Forensic Sciences.* Her monograph, *Significant Dates of Typing Methods,* was published by American Board of Forensic Document Examiners in 1994.

Ms. Seaman Kelly began her term as President of the American Board of Forensic Document Examiners (ABFDE) in July, 2001. From 1994 to 1999, she served as a Director on the ABFDE Board of Directors and on the Executive Committee as Secretary from 1999 to 2001. Ms. Seaman Kelly is a Fellow in the Questioned Document Section of the American Academy of Forensic Sciences (AAFS) and a regular member of the American Society of Questioned Document Examiners (ASQDE).

FORENSIC EXAMINATION OF RUBBER STAMPS

A Practical Guide

By

JAN SEAMAN KELLY

Certified Forensic Document Examiner
American Board of Forensic Document Examiners

Charles C Thomas
PUBLISHER • LTD.
SPRINGFIELD • ILLINOIS • U.S.A.

Published and Distributed Throughout the World by

CHARLES C THOMAS • PUBLISHER, LTD.
2600 South First Street
Springfield, Illinois 62704

©2002 by CHARLES C THOMAS • PUBLISHER, LTD.

ISBN 0-398-07278-7 (hard)
ISBN 0-398-07279-5 (paper)

Library of Congress Catalog Card Number: 2002019185

With THOMAS BOOKS *careful attention is given to all details of manufacturing
and design. it is the Publisher's desire to present books that are satisfactory as to their
physical qualities and artistic possibilities and appropriate for their particular use.*
THOMAS BOOKS *will be true to those laws of quality that assure a good name
and good will.*

Printed in the United States of America
SR-R-3   .

Library of Congress Cataloging-in-Publication Data

Kelly, Jan Seaman.
    Forensic examinaion of rubber stamps: a practical guide / by Jan Seaman Kelly
        p. cm.
    Includes bibliographical references and index.
    ISBN 0-398-07278-7 -- ISBN 0-398-07279-5 (paper.)
    1. Rubber stamps--Identification. 2. Criminal investigation I. Title

    HV8077.5.R82 K45 2002
    363.25--dc21   2002019185

CONTRIBUTORS

Christine Cusack graduated magna cum laude from the University of Massachusetts where she earned a Bachelor of Science degree. Ms. Cusack studied the scientific examination of documents in private practice with Elizabeth McCarthy and Catherine Cusack. She has authored several articles on the subject of questioned documents with one being published by the *Journal of Forensic Sciences*. Memberships in professional organizations include the Questioned Document Section of the American Academy of Forensic Sciences and the Northeastern Association of Forensic Scientists.

James Green began his career in forensic document examination in 1988. He was the document examiner for the Eugene Police Department until his retirement in 2000. Mr. Green is a member of the American Society of Questioned Document Examiners (ASQDE), the Questioned Document Section in the American Academy of Forensic Sciences (AAFS), and the Southwest Association of Forensic Document Examiners (SWAFDE). Mr. Green operates a full-time private practice in Oregon.

A. Lamar Miller began working for the Alabama Department of Forensic Sciences after obtaining a pharmacy degree from Auburn University. He obtained his basic training in forensic document examination from Georgetown University. Mr. Miller is a Diplomate and past Director of the American Board of Forensic Document Examiners (ABFDE), a Fellow and past Chairman and Secretary of the Questioned Document Section in the American Academy of Forensic Sciences (AAFS), member and former Director of the American Society of Questioned Document Examiners (ASQDE), and a member of the Southeastern Association of Forensic Document Examiners (SAFDE). Mr. Miller has a private practice and lives in the Florida Keys.

Tobin A. Tanaka received his B.Sc. Degree in physics in 1990 and a diploma in meteorology in 1992 from the University of British Columbia, Vancouver, British Columbia, Canada. Mr. Tanaka was trained as a forensic document examiner by the Solicitor General Canada in Ottawa, Ontario from

1993 to 2000. Since 2000, he has been employed by the Canada Customs and Revenue Agency. Mr. Tanaka is a member of the Canadian Society of Forensic Science and the Society for Imaging Science and Technology.

To my husband David and my daughters Katie and Becca.

PREFACE

THE PURPOSE

Three years ago I embarked on a journey to research the manufacturing processes of seals and stamps. This research was spurred by the lack of contemporary literature to inform a forensic document examiner as to the manufacturing processes of rubber stamps, the types of normal and defect characteristics one could encounter when examining a stamp or its impression, and the recommended steps to be taken in the examination itself. Past literature included research papers by David Purtell, Maureen Casey Owens, A. Herkt, and Jay Levinson. Even though these works provide good information and are sound in research methodology, they are antiquated, ranging in age from 10 to 40 years from this writing.

The computer has been an integral part of stamp and seal manufacturing since 1985. With graphics software making it easier to duplicate artwork, the computer was a godsend for the local stamp makers because it made the various manufacturing processes of stamps using different materials affordable. For the forensic document examiner, the continued advancement of computer technology and its increasing use in stamp manufacturing opens a Pandora's box. The computer and scanner allow a stamp maker to scan a stamp impression for use as the artwork to produce a duplicate stamp. In the examination process, the forensic document examiner must be cognizant of the possibility of a duplicate stamp. As with all examinations, attributing proper weight to the defects in light of considering their source will allow the examiner to determine the likelihood that a duplicate stamp exists.

Technology has introduced new manufacturing processes and materials for use by the stamp manufacturer and maker in the production of stamps and seals. The purpose of this book is to inform the forensic document examiner of the various processes and how these processes can be identified and differentiated from each other in a forensic document examination. To insure accuracy in the information disseminated, the chapters were reviewed by the appropriate information sources. For example, Chapter 1 was reviewed by seal manufacturers Sal and Janet Cannizzaro and Ned Gibbons. Six stamp manufacturers and makers reviewed Chapters 2, 3, and 4 to ensure accuracy of information in describing the classifications, manufacturing processes, and characteristics of rubber stamps. Chapter 5, The Examination Process, was peer reviewed by forensic document examiner Brian Lindblom. Photographer Don Risi reviewed the information discussed by Lamar Miller in Chapter 6, and Chapter 7's discussion of inks was reviewed by Gary Werwa of Specialty Inks, Inc.

THE SCOPE

In our modern society, the seal will be found primarily on legal or government documents. A notarized signature, for example, is usually accepted as an authentic signature due to the presence of a notary stamp impression or seal. The rubber stamp's use spans the government and business aspects of our society. The industrial business setting uses stamp impressions for marking cartons as to contents or warnings such as "Fragile" or "This Side Up." Repetitive notices, such as "Past Due" or "Rush," are typically created with stamps in the office setting. Whether used in industrial or office settings, the rubber stamp assists the employee or owner in communicating a message in such a way that it allows for better time management and reduces business costs.

The scope of this book covers seals and rubber stamps for personal or office business use. Stamp making kits sold as novelty items or toys and minor manufacturing processes (past or present) that reflect a small percentage of the seal and stamp manufacturing market are not discussed. The majority of marking device cases (rubber stamp or seal) will involve a stamp or seal produced by one of the primary manufacturing processes. Therefore, the focus of this work is on the primary classifications of stamps and the mainstream manufacturing processes.

Rubber stamps used in the industrial setting are briefly discussed in Chapters 3 and 4. Stamps used in the industrial setting may be made of materials and ink formulas different from the more mainstream stamps due to the type of hosting surface and temperature conditions. The information disseminated in this brief discussion will let the examiner know that even though the same manufacturing process is involved as that used for the more mainstream stamps, the materials may differ and part of their examination may require further research into the specific purpose of the stamp.

The authors of the chapters have discussed in detail the history, manufacturing processes, and materials used in seals, stamps, and inks. Even though our objective was to be thorough in the discussion of these specific areas in the marking industry, the primary or mainstream processes are the focus. The photographs in this book reflect a realistic presentation of stamp shops and used stamp dies. The author did not clean any stamp die, but chose to leave the debris. The purpose of doing this was to give the reader a greater understanding of the appearance of a used stamp or seal die. Photographs also depict the position of the mold, die, or impression (right or wrong reading position) as viewed by the examiner in his or her analysis. My goal was to write a book that could be used as an instructional guide and reference by the forensic document examiner when confronted with a case involving a stamp, stamp impression, seal, or seal embossment.

THE PLAN

A firm foundation of knowledge has to be in place before the forensic scientist can conduct an objective examination. The book is divided by chapters in such a way as to guide the forensic document examiner through the manufacturing processes of seals and stamps. Chapter 1, authored by Christine Cusack, discusses the history and manufacturing processes of seals. Even though knowing the history of seals or stamps is not a requirement for the examination process, it provides information on the evolution of the seal or stamp from ancient history to its contemporary form and usage. The history also provides a time line of when certain manufacturing processes or materials became available. This information is worth its weight in gold if the case involves a disputed date.

I authored the next four chapters covering rubber stamps. Chapter 2 introduces the document examiner to the primary classifications of stamps and describes the characteristics that will assist the examiner in classifying a stamp submitted for examination. Chapter 3 is an in-depth study of the various manufacturing processes (mainstream) of hand, self-inking, and pre-inked stamps. Each manufacturing process is described in detail in an effort to assist the examiner in visualizing the process. Through visualization, the examiner can gain a better understanding of the normal characteristics and possible defects that provide clues in determining the specific process used to produce the submitted stamp or a questioned impression. Chapter 4 describes in detail the characteristics commonly observed on stamp dies categorized by materials in each manufacturing process as well as the listing of possible defects. Chapter 5 provides guidance to the forensic document examiner by suggesting an appropriate methodology of the examination process in a case involving a stamp to an impression comparison or an impression to impression comparison.

Chapter 6 discusses photography and the various techniques the forensic document examiner can use in photographing the stamp die or the impression. Lamar Miller discusses basic photography and offers suggestions as to its use in a stamp case.

James Green provides a general discussion of stamp inks and pigments in Chapter 7. Several stamp manufacturers who currently use stamp inks are changing to pigments. The Stampcreator Pro™ by Brother International, for example, uses pigments instead of inks. This chapter explains the difference between inks and pigments to assist the examiner in gaining a better understanding of stamp inks.

To assist the examiner in finding specific information quickly, several quick reference aids can be found in the Appendix. The first reference aid in the Appendix is derived from information discussed in Chapters 2, 3, and 4. From this data, Kimberly Kreuz created two reference tables that will assist the reader in determining the location of the desired information in this book. The charts are a quick reference using stamp classification and die material as the focal points in determining the type of manufacturing process. The second quick reference in the Appendix is a chronological listing of the significant dates in the history of seals and stamps. The Human Resource section is a complete listing of individuals in the stamp industry who contributed their knowledge to this book and can be found as the third quick reference in the Appendix. The purpose of this latter listing is to provide names of individuals who can provide information regarding seal or stamp manufacturing that may be of assistance to the inquiring document examiner. The fourth and final quick reference found in the Appendix is the Glossary that contains the terminology as defined by the marking industry. A great deal of miscommunication can be avoided if the forensic document examiner understands the marking industry terminology and uses it when seeking information about seals or rubber stamps from a manufacturer or maker.

J.S.K.

ACKNOWLEDGMENTS

To my husband David and my two daughters, Katie and Becca, I publicly thank you for the support, love, and encouragement you have given me during the last three years as I have worked on this book. The research and writing processes required to complete this work commanded a great deal of time and mental energy. I am fortunate to have had my family's support and I appreciate their patience and understanding.

David Kelly prepared several of the illustrations in this book as well as scanned all the photographs. His gift of time and computer wizardry made it possible for me to achieve my goal in making this book a complete guidebook for the forensic document examiner.

In addition to being blessed with a wonderful family, I am blessed with creative and gifted friends who offered their talent to assist me in achieving my goals. Special thanks to Karen Tucker Dunn and Cindy Risi for their contributions. Karen is another computer wizard who prepared some of the illustrations used in this book. Cindy accepted the responsibility of editor and critically reviewed the last few drafts. Both ladies have used their talents to assist me in past research and I am truly appreciative of their time and assistance.

Appreciation goes to those individuals who were gracious in the giving of their time to assist Christine Cusack during the research phase of the information gathering process for her chapter on seals. Those individuals are James Baturin of The Baumgarden Company of Washington, Michael Beaulieu of the Corporation Connection, Joseph Byrne of Ideal Seal Company, Janet and Sal Cannizzaro of Cannizzaro Seal and Engraving, John Delano of Make Your Mark, Ned Gibbons of A & A Marking Systems, Bruce Hale of Granite State Stamps, Inc., William Ryan of Millennium Marking Company, and Rex Tubbs of Engraving Connection.

I wish to thank Lori Aiken who assisted James Green by reviewing the draft of his Chapter 7 and assisting him in preparing the chapter for publication.

A note of appreciation to Jane Lewis, forensic document examiner in Wisconsin, and Heather Carlson, Oregon State Crime Laboratory, for their contributions to this work. Ms. Lewis conducted the thin layer chromatography tests and photographs on the ink samples discussed in Chapter 7. Ms. Carlson prepared the VSC 2000 images of the same inks tested by Ms. Lewis. Their contributions assisted Mr. Green in providing information discussing different aspects of stamp inks.

James Green conducted numerous interviews in his quest to obtain and verify information regarding stamp inks. Mr. Green and I would like to offer our appreciation to Charles Doty, Sue Fortunato, Larry Olson, Mike Suo, Thomas Sweet, Art Tracton, and Gary Werwa. These individuals graciously gave of their time and knowledge of inks to assist Mr. Green in his research.

Special thanks to Kimberly Kreuz, forensic document examiner in California, for her contribution in creating the two quick reference charts found in the Appendix. These two charts will be of great assistance to the document examiner in the initial stage of the rubber stamp examination.

Brian Lindblom, forensic document examiner with Document Examination Consultants in Ottawa, Canada, graciously gave his time to peer review the Examination Process chapter. A research project is not complete until it has undergone peer review. I felt Brian was perfect to conduct the peer review due to his experience in rubber stamp examinations. His input was of great assistance and I offer my deepest appreciation for his participation.

There are over 300 photographs in this work. I wish to express my gratitude to Sugar Knight and Michelle Garduno, photo processing technicians, who took the time to process the negatives to produce the highest quality print. I also extend my gratitude to Don Risi for his review of Chapter 6 on photography.

A project of this magnitude would not be possible without the contributions of those in the marking industry. A listing of all information contributors can be found in the Appendix. I also extend my appreciation to those individuals listed in the Human Resources section of the Appendix. However, there were a few individuals in the marking industry who took me under their wing and assisted with this project from the very beginning. Mollie Miller, owner of A-1 Rubber Stamp & Engraving, allowed unlimited access to her business and her wonderful stamp makers, Cliff Hughson and Kim Rowan. The information garnered from numerous interviews and repeated visits to the shop to observe the manufacturing processes provided the foundation for additional information gathering. William Collins of United RIBtype in Indiana; Cindy Thomas of U.S. Stamp/Identity Group, Inc. in Tennessee; Gene Griffiths of MDAI in Illinois; Eiji Yuki of Brother International in New Jersey; and Mike Mauro of M & R Marking Systems in Illinois were instrumental throughout this research project in assisting the authors in gathering information and reviewing the final drafts. My gratitude is extended to these individuals who gave their time toward this work and have made a significant contribution to forensic science.

I wish to extend my deepest gratitude to my contributing authors, Christine Cusack, Tobin Tanaka, Lamar Miller, and James Green. These document examiners displayed courage in agreeing to be contributing authors. Their contributions expanded the research and allowed more information to be disseminated to the forensic document examiner.

CONTENTS

FORENSIC EXAMINATION OF RUBBER STAMPS

Chapter 1

SEALS

CHRISTINE CUSACK

Wʜᴀᴛ ɪs ᴀ sᴇᴀʟ? A seal is an impression, a mark, or a device with a cut or raised emblem, symbol, or word which can be impressed in relief upon a soft tenacious substance, such as clay, wax, or paper to certify a signature or authenticate a document. Historically, seals preceded the invention of writing and once served as the standard in lieu of a signature. The principal purposes of a seal were (1) identification of the owner, (2) recording the nature of the object with which it was associated, and (3) prevention of unwarranted access to a container or document.[1] Today, the primary purpose of a seal is to convey the mark of authority and authenticate documents of some value or significance.

A HISTORICAL OVERVIEW

The history of seals has significance to forensic document examiners because it illustrates the impact of not only the importance but also the various incarnations of seals upon many a civilization. Equipped with a historical backdrop, the forensic document examiner brings not only a present-day fund of knowledge but a depth of understanding that otherwise would be vacuous.

Throughout the ages, seals have taken many shapes and forms; and the production, types, and function of early seals are found in most modern marking devices. To illustrate the historical progression, excerpts from *The Marking Story,* written by Karen Rivard and Thomas H. Brinkman, have been chosen.

"Some of the earliest seals date from the fourth millennium B.C. in Mesopotamia. One such ancient and popular seal was the cylinder. Cylinder seals were cut with metal implements known as gravers and generally were carved from stone and at times either gold, silver or glazed pottery. The size of cylinder seals ranged from 1/2 inch to 4 inches in length and the diameter was customarily one-fourth to one-third of its height. Cylinders were generally strung from a thong or a string and worn as either a wristband or a necklace" (Figs. 1.1A & 1.1B). "Their primary purpose was to safeguard and identify possessions or merchandise. Typically, small objects were placed in a jar, covered at the opening with a piece of cloth or animal skin and then bound at the neck with string. Thereafter, moist clay was packed around the neck of the jar and the cylinder seal was rolled over the clay. Larger objects were packed in mats and tied with a rope. The knot was covered with a thick layer of clay and rolled over with a cylinder seal" (Fig. 1.2).

"Ancient seals took other forms besides the cylinder. For example, the earliest Egyptian seals, dating from approximately 3000 B.C., were stamps in the form of a sacred beetle known as a scarab. The scarab was made of schist, soapstone or other soft material, engraved with hieroglyphics, and finished with a green or yellow tint. Scarabs were fitted with a string or wire to be worn on the finger or the wrist. Not unlike the cylinder seal, the scarab served as a model for seal design in other ancient societies. The scarab also served as the prototype for Greek and Roman seals known as signets. The first purely Greek signet seals are from 400 B.C. Many of these seals typically had the owners' portrait engraved on them. Because the signets were engraved in precious stones they became collectors items and today can be found in museums and private collections" (Figs. 1.3A, 1.3B, & 1.3C).

"Approximately 1730 B.C., new engraving methods began to emerge. Small cutting disks of various sizes and tubes with circular cutting edges were used with the bow-drill borer. The tube was used to cut circles and, when applied at an angle, crescents. The disks were used in an effort to execute the same intricate designs that had been carved by hand, but required the designs be reduced to combinations of straight lines. The new tool innovations, however, seem to have brought about a reduction in the quality of the carving. For example, the lines cut by a disk are wider and deeper in the middle than they are at either end. Another type of seal carving was created on an appliance similar to the potter's wheel. It was operated by foot and the iron cutting tools were kept in rapid rotation. This method produced results similar to those of the bow-drill.

"Approximately 350 B.C. lead, gold or silver bullae became prominent. With the introduction of the leaden bullae came a two-part matrix for making the seal impression. The device was a hinged tool with two flat, engraved circular impressions, one on each appendage and when pressed together would create a two-sided seal impression in the wax of lead. The term "Papal Bull" refers to the leaden bulla used by popes for hundreds of years. Sealing wax

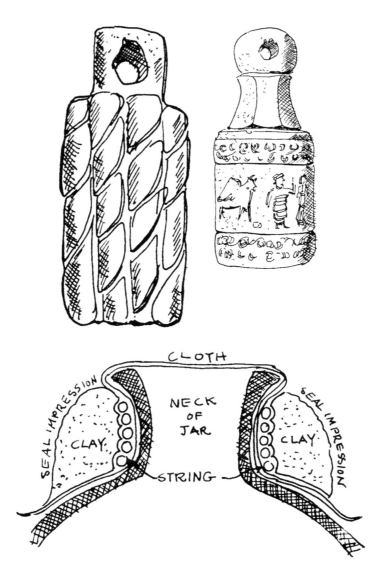

Figure 1.1A–B. (A) *Top left.* This cylinder seal is dated approximately 7th century B.C. (B) *Top right.* This cylinder seal is dated approximately 2750 B.C. These type of seals were the most popular in ancient times (Courtesy of Karen Rivard, Thomas Brinkman, and David Kelly).

Figure 1.2. *Lower center.* A section of the neck of a sealed storage jar is shown. The opening of the jar was covered with a piece of cloth or animal skin and then bound at the neck with string. Moist Clay was packed around the neck or the jar and the cylinder seal was rolled over the clay (Courtesy of Karen Rivard, Thomas Brinkman, and David Kelly).

became popular in the seventeenth century, and with it, personal seals for all who wrote letters.

"Historically, royalty, clergy, national and local government agencies and its officers as well as private citizens possessed seals. By the time the United States was formed, an official governmental seal had become a necessity. By

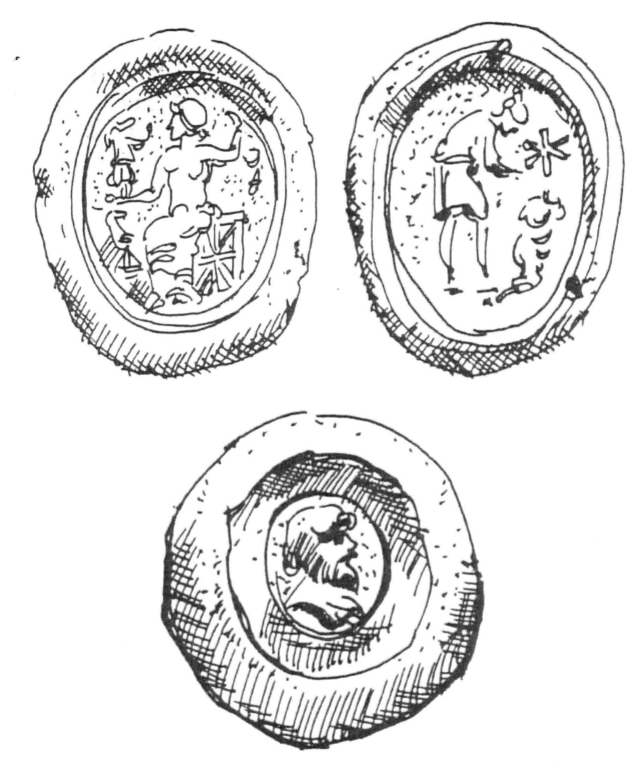

Figure 1.3A–C. Signet seals from 400 B.C. typically had the owner's portrait engraved on them and were made of precious stones. (A) *Top left.* This illustrates an impression from a Greek seal; (B) *Top right.* This impression is of an early Christian seal; and (C) *Lower center.* This impression is of Charlemagne's seal (Courtesy of Karen Rivard, Thomas Brinkman, and David Kelly).

example, a few hours after the Declaration of Independence was adopted on July 4, 1776, the Continental Congress appointed a committee to design a seal for the United States of America."

As time marched on, the demand for seals from government and commercial enterprises as well as private citizens increased the pressure to produce large quantities in a cost-effective manner. As a consequence of increased demand, the need for more efficient methods of mass production were conceived.

MANUFACTURING PROCESS

The practical application of the manufacturing process of seals to what forensic document examiners do may seem remote, but it is something we ought to know because it can assist us in knowing what we can and cannot do. There are currently four major techniques employed in the manufacturing of embossing seals. They are handpunched, mechanical, computerized, and laser.

Handpunched

The first technique is known by many names, handpunched being one; others are hand stamped or die sinking. As we know it, the technique became popular in the mid to late part of the nineteenth century and continues to this day, albeit to a lesser extent. Handpunched dies tend to be intricate, detailed artwork requiring unique skill and artistic faculty. Dies also require a significant amount of time to create compared to the more modern processes. There are few practicing artists today; Cannizzaro Seal and Engraving Company is one that offers distinctive, customized engraving to its clientele.

The process of creating a handpunched die is one wherein the engraver using case hardened steel stamps, sinks or punches the die by hand (Figs. 1.4 & 1.5). The act of punching the die displaces the metal thereby creating a smooth, rounded effect at the edges. The effect is apparent under high magnification, but it is not transferred onto the embossed impression. Steel stamps measure approximately 4 inches tall with a letter or a character such as a star or a triangle appearing in relief on the tip of the tool (Fig. 1.6). The size of the letter or character ranges from 1/32, 1/20, 1/16, 1/12, 3/32, 1/10, 1/8, 5/32, 3/16, 1/4, 5/16, 3/8, 7/16 to 1/2 (Fig. 1.7). The type style is either Gothic or Roman. The lack of standardization exemplifies this type of die. Although all dies are unique to varying degrees, a hand-stamped die bears the distinction of being more individual than other processes. Some elements that can distin-

 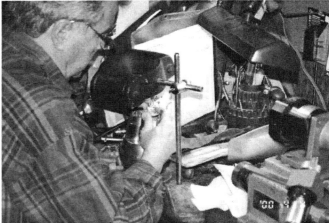

Figure 1.4. *Left.* Master die maker, Sal Cannizzaro, is shown creating a handpunched die. This technique is also known as hand stamped or die sinking and became popular in the mid to late 19th century (Courtesy of Christine Cusack).

Figure 1.5. *Right.* Master die maker, Sal Cannizzaro, is shown placing the final touches on a hand-punched die (Courtesy of Christine Cusack).

guish this type of die are the positioning of letters in relationship to the center and the border of the die, the irregular spacing between letters, the misalignment of letters, and the depth of each letter. For example, the depth of an "I" may be greater than a "W" due in large part to the variation in pressure applied by the die maker. The dies are typically made of brass; however, a die can be made of white metal.

Mechanical Engraving

The second technique is known as mechanical engraving or another common term is machine engraving. The equipment used in this type of engraving is best known as the "pantograph." In its earlier incarnation, the pantograph was used to engrave brass plates. However, during the mid-1950s, it was adapted for the production of dies (Figs. 1.8 & 1.9). The process was revolutionary for its time for it sped up the engraving process. Yet to some degree, it is still a manual operation and conceivably akin to the application of the bow-drill borer to seals. The process of creating a mechanically engraved die is one wherein an operator routes out the image on the die with a rotating tool called the cutter. The cutter, made of either high-speed steel or carbide, is located on one of the two pantograph tables. On the other table, a stylus is guided and controlled by an operator basically tracing over reverse set type slugs which are held in a type holder or over a prepared template. The template, made of paper, plastic, or brass, also reflects the graphic details the seal

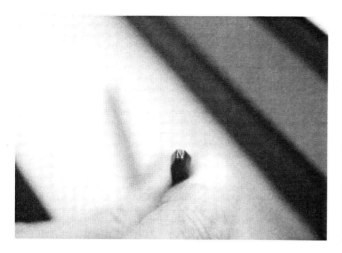

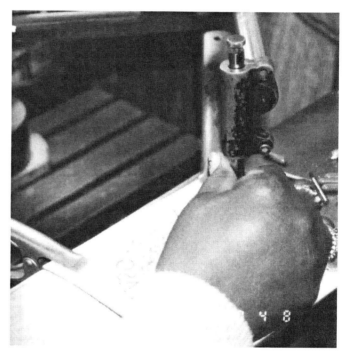

Figure 1.6. *Top left.* The letter "N" on the tip of a case hardened steel stamp is shown (Courtesy of Christine Cusack).

Figure 1.7. *Top right.* This illustrates case hardened steel stamps distributed by the now defunct Boston Enterprise, Allen Bros (Courtesy of Christine Cusack).

Figure 1.8. *Lower left.* Mechanically engraved dies are created by pantograph operators tracing over a prepared paper template (Courtesy of Christine Cusack).

Figure 1.9. *Lower right.* A pantograph operator is tracing over a prepared template. The carbide cutter located to the left of the template is routing out the image on the die (Courtesy of Christine Cusack).

will possess (Figs. 1.10A & 1.10B). Usually, the template is approximately four to six times larger then the actual engraved die (Figs. 1.11A & 1.11B). Once the letters and characters are engraved to the preferred depth, the die maker may be called upon to incorporate additional features that are not a part of the mechanical process; for example, the inclusion of what may appear to be a random mark or marks known as security features. In an attempt to replicate the die, an engraver may interpret the security feature as a defect in the die and thus may not reproduce it in the counterfeit die. The hand tools used to chisel the features are engravers' tools called gravers (Fig. 1.12). If the reader will recall gravers were utilized to cut cylinder seals. The gravers come in a wide variety of different points and widths. Some of the elements that essentially distinguish a mechanical die are standardized, such as the alignment and spacing. The depth of individual letters may differ, which is dependent on the individual die maker. The dies are made of either brass or white metal.

A variation on the two aforementioned techniques is an automatic "die sinking" machine known as the Automator. The device was conceived by David Klien and introduced to the market in the late 1970s by M & R Marking Systems. The automatic die sinking machine has a typewriter keyboard and as the operator depresses each type key, the machine stamps the proper characters into the die. The die sinking machine lived a short life because of the mechanical aptitude needed to set the die and to keep the machine operating. The equipment is still available; however, its wide spread use is not apparent. This device assisted the engraver with better alignment over hand-punching a die, but no proportional spacing existed; thus the "W" would take as much space as the "I." Also, the pressure could not be varied, hence the "W" would tend to be shallow and the "I" deeper.

Computerized Engraving

The third technique is best known as computerized engraving. By the early 1980s and as technology continued to improve a die could be engraved with the use of a computer. Dahlgren manufactured the first computerized engraving machine. Application was limited because the program was restricted to producing straight-line copy (a similar limitation also observed in the bow drill border of antiquity). Shortly thereafter, M & R Marking Systems and Dahlgren worked together to develop the "arc engraving" package. Basically, the computer program did all the work. The technology permitted die makers to engrave any die with any size character in any position (Figs. 1.13, 1.14, 1.15, & 1.16). As with the pantograph, the image is routed out with a rotating tool called the cutter. The cutter is also made of either high-speed steel or carbide, but it operates at a higher rate of speed than the pantograph (Fig. 1.17). Due to the rate of speed, the cutter is constantly doused with lubricating oil

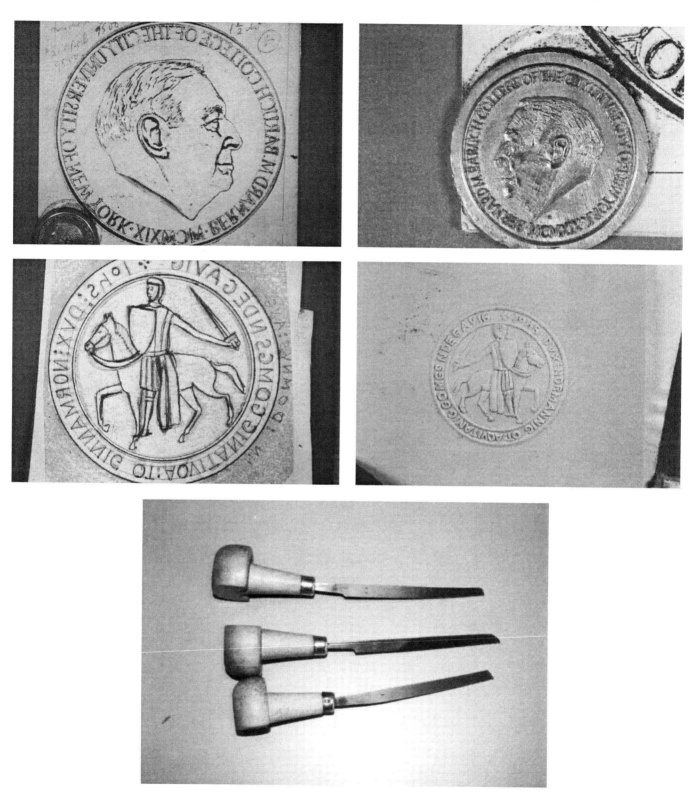

Figure 1.10A–B. (A) *Top left.* A paper template is prepared by the pantograph operator. The template may be made of paper, plastic, or brass and reflects the graphic details of the seal. (B) *Top right.* The lead counter produced from the paper template is illustrated in (A).

Figure 1.11A–B. (A) *Center left.* The paper template is usually four to six times larger than the engraved die. (B) *Center right.* The dry seal impression from the seal engraved using the paper template listed in (A) is shown (Courtesy of Christine Cusack).

Figure 1.12. *Bottom.* Hand tools used to chisel features into the seal are known as gravers. This photograph shows three gravers tools used by an engraver to produce a seal die (Courtesy of Christine Cusack).

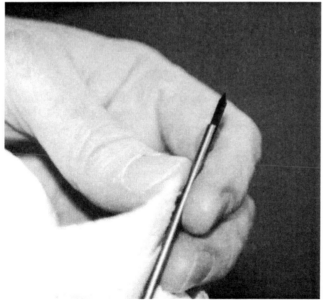

Figure 1.13. *Top left.* The Dahlgren Engraving System and computer used in the creation of computer engraved dies is shown (Courtesy of Christine Cusack).

Figure 1.14. *Top right.* Here is an example of a computerized engraving bed used in the computerized engraving technique (Courtesy of Christine Cusack).

Figure 1.15. *Center left.* Shown is a mechanism for securing dies of various sizes in the engraving bed (Courtesy of Christine Cusack).

Figure 1.16. *Center right.* This illustrates a housing for carbide or high speed steel cutter (Courtesy of Christine Cusack).

Figure 1.17. *Bottom.* A carbide cutter is used in the computer engraving machine (Courtesy of Christine Cusack).

that minimizes wear and tear and breakage. As with the mechanical engraving method, some of the elements that typify a computer die, such as the alignment and spacing, are standardized. Furthermore, because the cutter is controlled by air pressure, it tends to stay in contact with the die longer than other processes; thus the "W" tends to be deeper than the "I" and the right side of the cross stroke of a capital "T" tends to connect to the letter that follows. The dies are made of either brass or white metal.

Laser Engraving

The fourth technique introduced to the marketplace in 1989–1990 and the latest development in seal manufacturing is laser engraving. Although the laser engraver was initially marketed to rubber stamp manufacturers by 1993, the industry saw additional benefits to the laser engraver and introduced it to the trade. The laser engraving equipment is comparable to a laser jet printer. A print driver is integrated into a computer for the engraving system. The typesetting and page layout software package for the die and counter is called SOSET®. The graphic art software packages most commonly used individually or as an add on to SOSET® are CORELDRAW®, or ADOBE PrintShop®. Scanners are typically employed to import specialized artwork. The laser itself is a low-powered CO_2 beam of light that is focused in such a manner that it vaporizes material when directed onto a small area (Figs. 1.18, 1.19, & 1.20). The laser cuts the die from a sheet of plastic known as Delrin. It comes in two colors, black and white; dimensions; and depths. The laser is set to engrave to a specified depth. The Delrin is then placed into the laser system and the die is laser engraved and cutout. The counter is made simultaneously using a rubber stamp option that reverses and inverts the image while adding a shoulder to each character and feature. The shoulder is added to prevent tearing of the paper. Total die and counter engraving time for a standard seal is less than five minutes. Some of the elements that differentiate a laser die are the standardization of alignment, spacing, and depth of the characters. What differentiates it from the previously mentioned techniques is the die and counter are made of Delrin and the counter (which will be discussed presently) is formed simultaneously.

Regardless of the technique employed, the die traditionally is round but occasionally is rectangular in shape. The following table illustrates size, dimension, and composition currently available.

Size	*Shape*	*Composition*
1 5/8″	Round	White Metal
1 5/8″	Round	Brass
1 1/2″	Round	Brass

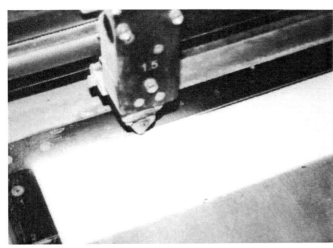

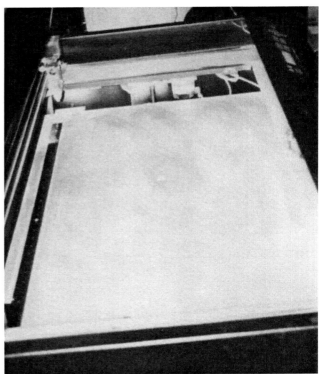

Figure 1.18. *Top left.* The Royal Mark Laser Engraving System is distributed by M & R Marking Systems (Courtesy of Christine Cusack).
Figure 1.19. *Right.* The bed of a flat bed laser engraver is shown. The flatbed CO_2 laser engraver is the most common laser used in the United States for marking industry applications (Courtesy of Christine Cusack).
Figure 1.20. *Lower left.* The flatbed CO_2 laser light beam (Courtesy of Christine Cusack).

2″	Round	Brass
2 1/4″	Round	Brass
1″ x 2″	Rectangular	White Metal
1″ x 2″	Rectangular	Brass

It ought to be noted that round brass dies measuring 2 1/2″ and 3″ were discontinued in the mid-1980s. However, inventories of these dies may still exist.

Figure 1.21. A laser engraved counter appears on the left with a laser engraved die on the right (Courtesy of Christine Cusack).

The die bears its image in intaglio and is commonly referred to as the female. The counter, known as the male, is born from the female and bears its image in relief. Until the introduction of laser technology, dies were made of brass or white metal; the counters of lead, Bakelite, or polystyrene. Laser dies and counters, as previously stated, are made of Delrin and formed simultaneously (Fig. 1.21). Of the modern countering techniques, lead was the first substance used to form counters. The lead counter is created by pouring molten lead into the pour holes in the base of an inverted seal press. The seal press is the mechanism which houses both the die and the soon to be formed counter. The brass die is thus wedged into the seal press and the flow of the molten lead against the face of the die creates the counter. This countering method is known as the lead splash.

About 1960, a compound invented in 1907 by Leo "Doc" Bakeleton was introduced to the marketplace. This compound, which came to be known as Bakelite, was thought to be a less hazardous way of forming a counter than the lead splash. To form the counter, the die and the Bakelite are placed into a vulcanizer. The Bakelite is heated and pressurized onto the die thus creating the Bakelite counter. By approximately 1987, a newer product and process for creating a counter was introduced. Best known as polystyrene, its use became widespread, displacing Bakelite as the most popular counter making material. Two primary reasons are responsible for this event: (1) Bakelite possesses dust particles which are potentially dangerous to one's health; and (2) the polystyrene counter is created with an injection molding machine, not a vulcanizer. The purchase price of the injection molding machine tends to be less than a vulcanizer and it is significantly easier to operate. Polystyrene is commonly distributed in pellet form. The pellets are placed into a chamber within the injection molding machine where they are heated to the melting point. The liquified polystyrene is positioned on top of the die and molded to form the counter (Fig. 1.22).

Unlike a lead counter, which is formed from the die within the structure of the seal press, a Bakelite or Polystyrene counter, as we have just learned, is not. The counter is affixed to a die holder with the aid of a product known as an adhesive wafer. The adhesive wafer is also used to attach both a laser die and counter to a die holder. The adhesive wafer is composed of paper and has a two-sided adhesive backer. Wafer thickness ranges from 5pt., 15pt., 20pt., 30pt., and 40pt. (Fig. 1.23). The brass or white metal die is pressed into a die holder under pressure (Fig. 1.24). The die holder, also known as a die clip, is the mechanism that houses the die and the counter. Once any kind of die or counter is properly mounted it is then inserted into a seal press (Figs. 1.25, 1.26, 1.27 & 1.28). Also, the depth of a Bakelite or polystyrene counter can vary, therefore an additional function of an adhesive wafer is to lift and compensate for any potential gap between the counter and the die holder. Thus, if the wafer were not inserted, then not only would the counter be unable to adhere to the die holder, but also the components would not be positioned to properly join.

Regardless of the manufacturing process, the die and counter are mounted in a seal press or placed into a die holder then inserted into a seal press. The first seal presses were heavy cast iron assemblies (Fig. 1.29). Quite often the presses were very decorative and shaped to look like a lion's head. Today most popular seal presses are hand-held pocket seals, desk seals made of steel, or electronic embossers.

Today, most dealers purchase dies from M & R Marking Systems, Millennium Marking Company, Stewart Superior, Louis Melind Company, and Consolidated Stamp Manufacturing. The dies typically have dashes or roped borders that are hobbed onto the die. Some are blank without any borders. For those dies without a border, it is the role of the dealer to engrave a customized border onto it. Without a border, the edge of the seal will tend to be acute and apt to tear the paper. The manufacturer also supplies the dealer with pre-stamped dies with commonly used nomenclature such as "Notary Public" or "Corporate Seal." The pre-stamped dies thereby reduce the amount of engraving required by the end dealer and potentially provide valuable information to the forensic document examiner.

Figure 1.22. The chamber of the plastic injection molding machine melts pellets of Polystyrene. The liquified material is positioned on top of the die and molded to form the counter (Courtesy of Christine Cusack).

THE EXAMINATION PROCESS

An understanding of the manufacturing process of dry seals permits the proper evaluation of class and individual characteristics. Although a die and its counter are made one at a time and by definition tend to be unique, there is one segment of the manufacturing process of brass and white metal dies that

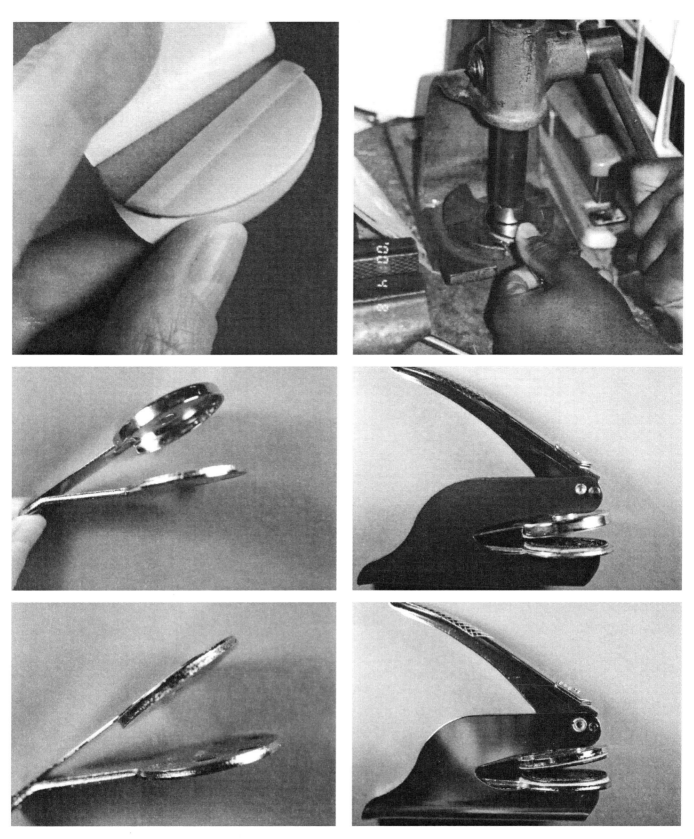

Figure 1.23. *Top left*. An adhesive wafer is wedged between removable protective coverings (Courtesy of Christine Cusack).
Figure 1.24. *Top right*. Assembly press mounts the female metal seal die to the die holder (Courtesy of Christine Cusack).
Figure 1.25. *Center left*. This illustrates a die holder for metal die (top) and a plastic counter (bottom). A brass or white metal die is noticeably thicker than plastic dies, thus requiring a mechanism to house and secure it (Courtesy of Christine Cusack).
Figure 1.26. *Center right*. A hand-held seal press for metal die and plastic counter (Courtesy of Christine Cusack).
Figure 1.27. *Bottom left*. This illustrates a die holder for Delrin dies and counters (Courtesy of Christine Cusack).
Figure 1.28. *Bottom right*. Shown is a hand-held seal press for Delrin dies and counters (Courtesy of Christine Cusack).

Figure 1.29. A desk seal press (Courtesy of Christine Cusack).

applies to many, but not all. As part of a production run, a die with a border, a state seal, a state name, a profession, or an official office is hobbed onto a die by a master mold (Figs. 1.30 & 1.31). If there is a defect in the mold or the mold is aging, then any abnormalities present in the master mold will appear on a batch of dies. This is a class characteristic which is defined as a feature or a defect specific to a production run rather than a specific die. It ought to be noted if the defect is not detected before a die from the batch is engraved, then the defect will appear in the counter.

An individual characteristic is a feature or defect that occurs through poor quality control in the engraving process or through use and abuse in the business setting. An example of an individual characteristic is any information specific to a particular die, for instance, a person's name. Accordingly, letter alignment, spacing and depth in relation to other parts of the die are unique

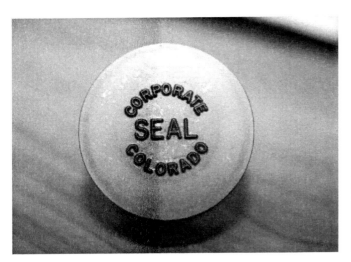 

Figure 1.30. *Left.* The front view of a corporate seal Colorado master mold. Note that no border appears on the Master Mold; thus, dealers may place a customized border on dies to prevent tearing of the paper (Courtesy of Christine Cusack).

Figure 1.31. *Right.* Another side view of a corporate seal Colorado master mold. The purpose of the tang on the backside of the mold is to anchor it to the hobbing machine (Courtesy of Christine Cusack).

to that die and its counter. Use and abuse of the seal is another type of individual characteristic. The life expectancy of brass or white metal dies is greater than lead or plastic counters; thus, the counters tend to wear much faster. If a replacement counter is made from the original die, then it is conceivable that a defect present on the die will be present not only on the virgin counter but subsequent counters. Furthermore, if a questionable impression is bold and crisp and a comparison impression is available, caution should be taken for both impressions may derive from the same die but from different time periods (Figs. 1.32 & 1.33). Another example of wear and tear occurs with the frequent application of a seal press over staples (Fig. 1.34).

Thomas Vastrick found in the course of his research:

> the most common individual feature observed was relative pressure variation within the impression. This characteristic can be caused by numerous features such as warping or unusual wear through misuse. The overall pressure exerted during the embossing process is also variable and can result in a great difference in appearance of the impression. Overall pressure is commonly the product of the person using the seal rather than the seal itself. Examinations of impressions made using various overall pressure of embossing revealed that relative pressure variation within the impression is both repetitive and identifiable.[2]

If the seal press responsible for creating the dry seal impression is available, an examination of the die and counter can be made to determine, to the degree the evidence will allow, the engraving process. Upon close inspection

Figure 1.32. *Top left.* Here is an impression from a Harrington Hotel Co., Inc. die and the original counter (Courtesy of Christine Cusack).
Figure 1.33. *Top right.* Also shown are the impression from the same Harrington Hotel Co., Inc. die and a new counter made from the die (Courtesy of Christine Cusack).
Figure 1.34. *Lower center.* This illustrates damaged lead counter by repeated application of the seal press over staples (Courtesy of Christine Cusack).

of a brass or white metal die, different engraving techniques produce certain features. For example, if a letter or character is hobbed or handpunched into a die, it will tend to have a smooth, sunken appearance; whereas, if it has been machine or computer engraved, tool marks in the form of a circular pattern appearing in the trough or grooves in the side walls of a character may be observed (Figs. 1.35, 1.36 & 1.37). It ought to be noted that these features are not transferred to the embossed impression. Due to standardization within the industry and the routing tools used to create mechanical and computerized dies, it is virtually impossible to distinguish between the two manufacturing processes.

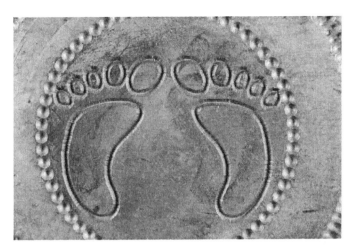

Figure 1.35. *Top left.* A hobbed and computer engraved die; the hobbed portions are the rounded impressions that encircle the computer engraved toes and feet. Note the smoothness to the hobbed portion of the die and the grooves on the side walls on the toes and feet (Courtesy of Christine Cusack).

Figure 1.36. *Top right.* Sample of hand stamped letters and hand engraved artwork are illustrated (Courtesy of Christine Cusack).

Figure 1.37. *Lower center.* A sample of computer engraved letters and artwork are shown (Courtesy of Christine Cusack).

Apart from the smooth, sunken appearance in the die, there are features which can be evaluated and tend to individualize handpunched dies from mechanical or computer engraved dies. They are the positioning of letters in relationship to the center and the border of the die, the irregular spacing between letters, the misalignment of letters and the depth of each letter.

The dates of introduction of the four major manufacturing techniques can be helpful toward dating a document. As previously discussed, laser dies are made of Delrin and not brass or white metal. And the laser counter is also made of Delrin and not lead, Bakelite or polystyrene. As a consequence, the laser die and counter can be easily differentiated from the other processes. If the laser seal is available, then it can be helpful in terms of dating a document. The laser engraving technique came on the market in 1993. Therefore, if a questioned document is dated prior to 1993 and the dry seal impression both from the disputed and known exemplars is identical, then it can be deduced that the document is not authentic.

The examination of a dry seal impression is best viewed from the reverse side of the page because the details tend to be clearer; however, it ought to be examined from both sides. The use of side lighting and, if available, a VSC, to enlarge the impression tends to be a very effective method of evaluating an impression.

The sequence of handwritten, typewritten, or printed matter on a document can provide valuable information toward authentication. When a dry seal is placed over material already on a document, the impression will tend to be uniform and consistent with the areas with no intersection. However, when a dry seal impression is made before the handwritten, typewritten, or printed matter some of the following features may be displayed:

- Evidence of flattening of portions of the dry impression;
- Evidence of ink deposit at the base of the near side of a raised character;
- Evidence of unnatural change in the direction of the writing line or the type print;
- Evidence of a break in the writing line over an embossed area (Fig. 1.38).

Finally, it may also be beneficial to review the following list to collect additional data that may prove helpful toward authenticating a document.

- Obtain a copy of the dry seal order form;
- Check with the manufacturer regarding the manufacturing process and compare it to the seal;
- Obtain samples of the dry seal impression from the manufacturer and compare it to the questioned impression;
- Check with government agencies to verify dates of incorporation, commission, or registration;
- Check with the Marking Device Association International for seal specifications and changes in specifications. The MDAI publishes a Manual of Official and Require Seals. It is also involved in Operation Bogus; an acronym for Block Orders to Generate Unauthorized Stamps/Seals. The MDAI works closely with the Forensic Document Laboratory of the INS to combat counterfeit stamps and seals.

Quite often the authenticity of a document is based upon a confluence of factors the examination of a dry seal being one. To determine whether a dry

Figure 1.38. Evidence of ink deposit between the "u" and "s" and break in the writing line appear as well as unnatural change in the direction of the writing line in the "a" (Courtesy of Christine Cusack).

seal is authentic in most instances requires a comparison dry seal impression. If a comparison dry seal is not available, then access to the actual seal press can be helpful not only to create comparison impressions, but also to evaluate the manufacturing process. Finally, the dry seal impression itself as well as other aspects of the document need to be taken into consideration to evaluate the authenticity of a questioned document.

REFERENCES

1. Rivard, Karen & Brinkman, Thomas H.: *The Marking Story.* Evanston, IL: The Marking Device Association, 1968, p. 14.
2. Vastrick, Thomas W.: The examination of notary seals. *Journal of Forensic Sciences:* (27): 899–911, 1982.

Chapter 2

CLASSIFICATIONS OF
STAMPS

STAMP CLASSIFICATION IS BASED upon the location of the ink media used to ink the stamp die. Hand stamps, self-inking stamps, and pre-inked stamps are the three primary classifications that a forensic document examiner will most likely encounter. Hand stamps and self-inking stamps are dependent on an outside ink pad whereas the die of a pre-inked stamp contains the ink. Automatic stamps and hot stamping are two additional classifications discussed in this chapter.

All classifications of stamps can be purchased from a major manufacturer or a local stamp maker. Major manufacturers such as Millennium Marking, U.S. Stamp/Identity Group, and M & R Marking Systems manufacture and distribute machines and materials to the local stamp shops. A local stamp shop, such as A-1 Rubber Stamp & Engraving, has employees with the expertise to use several manufacturing processes to produce the stamps they sell to customers who range from large businesses to private individuals (Fig. 2.1). The majority of local stamp shops are family owned and the employees are very knowledgeable about all areas of stamp manufacturing.

In every forensic document examination, the examiner is confronted with the question of whether the questioned material came from the known material. To answer that question, the document examiner should be equipped with the knowledge of the class and individual characteristics of the submitted material. If the rubber stamp suspected of producing the questioned impression is submitted for examination, the examiner needs to recognize through visual examination the class characteristics of each classification, including the general appearance of the ink reservoir, the stamp mount, and the container housing the die.

Figure 2.1. This family owned A-1 Rubber Stamp & Engraving is a local stamp shop in Las Vegas, Nevada can make vulcanized rubber, photopolymer, and flat die stamps.

HAND STAMPS

The wood-mounted hand stamp and the steel-framed self-inking stamp are the oldest types of stamps in the hand stamp classification.[1] The hand stamp differs from a self-inking stamp as it is dependent upon a separate ink pad. Prior to the mid-1970s, vulcanized rubber was the only material used for the hand stamp. Since the late 1970s, laserable rubber and photopolymer have been introduced as acceptable materials for the die. Until 1981, the only method available to attach the die to the stamp mount was to glue the die onto a moulding mount or a knob handle mount (Fig. 2.2).

The die in hand stamps manufactured before 1970 was vulcanized rubber mounted on a wood mount with a handle. The more expensive rubber stamps of that day had additional features of a rubber cushion and a title.[2] The cushion functions as the support for the die to provide even impressions (Fig. 2.3). Whether a cushion was used or the die was mounted directly onto the wood mount, the die was glued onto the mount by hand. In 1981, Gene Griffiths developed a double-sided, self-adhesive strip providing the stamp maker with a second method of attaching the die to the die plate.[3] Both the self-adhesive cushion and the non-adhesive red rubber cushion are attached to a wood mount.

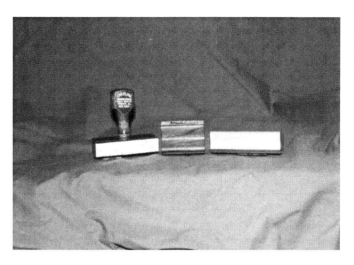 

Figure 2.2. *Left.* The mount for the hand stamp will either be a knob handle mount or a molded mount. The ink source is separate and not contained in the die or mount.
Figure 2.3. *Right.* Shown here is a cushion with a dipple surface. The cushion supports the die to provide even impressions.

The material used as a mount for hand stamps prior to 1983 was wood. Bruce Powell, an Ohio stamp maker, revealed his prototype of a plastic mount in the mid-1970s. In 1983, Jeff Lovely, a stamp maker from Tacoma, Washington, introduced a plastic mount as an alternative to the wood. In 1988, Gene Griffiths of Gregory Mfg. Co. and Len Sculler of M & R Marking Systems each introduced their own plastic mount at the Montreal Marking Device Trade Show. The mount is referred to as a plastic mount and is made of expanded, extruded PVC that has a blowing agent added to it. The wood design is either hot stamped or ink printed on the PVC.[4] The forensic document examiner will discover that there is no limit to the size of the mount used for hand stamps. The larger hand stamp dies are mounted on a wood mount called a rocker mount. The rocker mount differs from the standard mount because its surface is curved instead of the traditional flat surface (Fig. 2.4). The curved shape allows the impression to be made evenly as the stamp is rolled onto the surface. For standard vulcanized rubber dies, the rocker mount has the red textured cushion and the die is glued to the cushion by hand. If the stamp uses ribbed-back dies, the rib mat will be glued to the rocker mount.

The index, also called the title, contains the text of the stamp die and will be secured on the wood mount with a plastic cover. As a rule, one of the original impressions made from the stamp is used as the index.

A few stamp businesses display their name and address on the handle of the wood mount. This information will direct the document examiner to the seller or manufacturer of the hand stamp (Fig. 2.5).

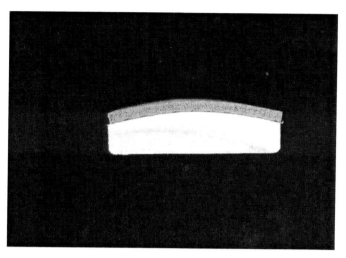

Figure 2.4. *Left.* Illustrated is a side view of a rocker mount. The mount base is curved to accommodate larger stamp dies.

Figure 2.5. *Right.* Stamp maker's name may be displayed on the side of the plastic container of the self-inking stamp or the handle of the hand stamp. The index is secured under a plastic cover on the side of the hand stamp. The title or index is produced from one of the first impressions made from the stamp die.

SELF-INKING STAMPS

The self-inking stamp, also called a self-inker, is a stamp that has the stamp die and the ink source in one container. The plastic self-inker was developed by Trodat in the early 1970s with a mechanism similar to that of the mechanical metal self-inker used in the early 1900s.[5] The plastic self-inker has grown in popularity to the point that the majority of vulcanized rubber or photopolymer stamps will be in a plastic self-inker and not on a wood or plastic mount.

The plastic self-inker is a plastic box containing a die plate that rotates inside and seats against a miniature stamp pad allowing for repetitive stamping. A cushion is not used in a self-inker and the die is secured onto the die plate by a double-sided adhesive strip. Generally, the outside of the plastic box will bear the name of the manufacturer and the stamp maker may also be displayed (Fig. 2.6). The index is usually positioned on top of the plastic container secured by a plastic cover.

Self-inking stamps are not limited to a plastic container and can be in a variety of sizes and shapes. Several stamp manufacturers market self-inking stamps as pocket stamps or as part of a writing instrument. If the self-inking stamp is housed in a pen, the stamp is located in the upper part of the pen's cartridge and the die is either vulcanized rubber or photopolymer that rests against its stamp pad when not in use. The stamp die housed on a writing

Figure 2.6. Here are examples of various plastic containers by different manufacturers housing self-inking dies. The 2000 Plus Printer marketed by COSCO, Stamp-Ever by U.S. Stamp & Sign, IDEAL by M & R Marking Systems and Compact by Louis Melind are trade names used by these manufacturers. The manufacturer is the supplier of the containers and other stamp materials to the local stamp maker. The manufacturer may be able to provide an investigative lead to the identity of the stamp maker by providing the names of the local stamp shops that purchase proprietary products such as plastic self-inker containers.

instrument's cartridge can contain a text of 30 characters per line with a maximum of three lines.

The mechanics of the plastic self-inker housing and its operation actually assists the person in making impressions that have even ink coverage. However, since the self-inker is operated by a human, it is possible to make impressions that lack even ink coverage.

PRE-INKED STAMPS

A pre-inked stamp is the only type of stamp that has the ink saturated in the die, eliminating the need for a stamp pad. The PermaStamp marketed by S.C. Johnson Wax Company was the first gel stamp released in the early 1960s.[6] Pre-inked stamps gained acceptance and were readily available in the 1970s.[7]

The pre-inked stamps of the 1990s can have a die with a high relief or a flat die with little or no relief, depending upon the material used for the die. High relief dies are made of gel or foam-type material that absorbs and retains ink. The die of the pre-inked stamp is glued directly onto the die plate of the stamp mount and does not use a cushion or self-adhesive strip. The container housing the die can be plastic or metal, with or without a visible handle, and usually has a cover to protect the die (Fig. 2.7).

Figure 2.7. *Left.* Pre-inked stamp containers come in a variety of shapes. The container may or may not have a knob handle, but all containers will have a cover to protect the die.
Figure 2.8. *Right.* U.S. Stamp's ThermalVision® flat die stamp (thermal process) and Brother International Corporation's Stampcreator Pro flat die stamp (light burst process) containers.

Pre-inked stamps with a low relief or no relief die made their debut in the mid-1990s.[8] The low or no relief dies are made of different materials depending upon the manufacturer. In addition to a flat surface die, another characteristic these stamps share is that the ink exits the die only through micropores in the print area. The background, or non-print area, is dry to the touch and free of ink. The flat die pre-inked stamps are housed in a plastic container similar in design to those used on the high relief die stamps (Fig. 2.8). The size of the container is dependent upon the manufacturer. For example, Brother's Stampcreator Pro 2000 dies are available in eleven sizes, while the Millennium's MaxLight dies are available in ten sizes.

AUTOMATIC STAMPS

Automatic stamps, also called electronic stamps, are multi-purpose machines that can stamp number, date, and clock-time combinations on documents. The employer's time clock is an example of an automatic or electric stamp. Automatic stamps can be found in all facets of the business sector. These machines utilize various printing processes in the production of a stamp impression.

HOT STAMPS

The stamp business name on the handle of a wood mount and the wood appearance on the extruded plastic stamp mounts are examples of hot stamping. The document examiner encounters examples of hot stamping when examining documents prepared for mass distribution requiring a custom imprint, such as business cards, napkins, pens, or match covers. The process of hot stamping is similar to iron-on transfers and does not involve ink as the image's color is derived from melted plastic. Impressions created by a hot stamping machine have a slight indentation. Hot stamping is also a very popular method of stamping by amateur and professional stamp artists.

REFERENCES

1. Jackson, Coy: Starting a business from scratch. *Marking Industry Magazine, 95* (11): 18–21, 2000.
2. Purtell, David J.: The identification of rubber stamps, Presented at Seminar No. 4, the Royal Canadian Mounted Police, Crime Detection Laboratory, May 1956.
3. Griffiths, Gene. Executive Director of Marking Device Association International.
4. Ibid.
5. Ibid.
6. Kreeger, Cindy: More pre-inked stamp history. *Marking Industry Magazine, 95* (4): 20, 1999.
7. Jackson, Coy. Starting a business from scratch. *Marking Industry Magazine, 95* (11): 18–21, 2000.
8. Kreeger, Cindy: More pre-inked stamp history. *Marking Industry Magazine, 95* (4): 20, 1999.

Chapter 3

MANUFACTURING PROCESSES
OF STAMPS

IN THE PREVIOUS CHAPTER, we discussed the primary classifications of rubber stamps and identified them as hand, self-inking, or pre-inked stamps. Within each classification, there are several manufacturing processes utilized to make the die for the stamp. As we will discuss in this chapter, referring to all stamps as rubber stamps is a misnomer as numerous materials are used to make the stamp die and it is the material chosen for the die that determines the manufacturing process. Some materials are well-suited to only one manufacturing process, while other materials can be used in two or more processes. For example, the pre-mix gel used for gel stamps is made using the vulcanization process and does not lend itself to the laser engraving, while vulcanized rubber can be used in the vulcanization and the laser engraving processes.

This chapter will discuss the main manufacturing processes including vulcanization, laser engraving, ultraviolet, light burst technology, and the thermal printer. It is important for the document examiner to keep in mind that more than one process may be used to manufacture a stamp. For example, a pre-inked stamp made of salt-leached rubber undergoes the vulcanization process prior to laser engraving. In order to identify the manufacturing process used in making the stamp, the examiner must have the actual stamp. As a rule, examining only the impression will not reveal definitive evidence as to the identity of the manufacturing process. Of course, there are a few exceptions to this rule and these will be discussed in Chapter 4.

The history of each manufacturing process and the steps that take place within each process in the production of a stamp die will be discussed in this chapter to aid the document examiner in understanding the evolution of each process.

VULCANIZATION

History of Vulcanization

Goodyear to Post-Civil War

The vulcanized rubber stamp had its historical beginning in the kitchen of Charles Goodyear who accidentally dropped some rubber mixed with sulphur on top of a hot stove in 1839. He discovered that instead of turning into a gooey mess, the rubber "cured" and was still flexible the next day. Goodyear called his discovery "vulcanization" after the Roman god of fire, Vulcan.[1] Goodyear applied his invention to the world's first vulcanized rubber overshoes in 1843. Upon receiving his patent in 1844, Goodyear's vulcanized rubber overshoes were manufactured by the Samuel J. Lewis Co. of Naugatuck, Connecticut.[2]

While Goodyear applied his invention of vulcanized rubber to the latest footwear, Jonathon C. Walker of Colcord, New Hampshire obtained the first U.S. patent for a hand stamp in 1843.[3]

Mr. Walker's patent described a rocker-bottom style wooden stamp with felt covers (Fig. 3.1).

In 1844, Horace Wells, a dentist from Hartford, Connecticut, patented anesthesia after a successful experiment of directing one associate to administer nitrous oxide while a second associate extracted one of Well's teeth.[4] Well's discovery created a boom in the dentistry field as teeth were being extracted painlessly, creating an increased market in false teeth.

Prior to vulcanization, dental bases were expensive as they were made from gold and difficult to make. With the advent of vulcanization, dentists were making dental bases from vulcanized rubber set in plastic molds. The vulcanized rubber simplified the process, and virtually every dentist had a small, round vulcanizer, called a "dental pot," in his office. The dental pot vulcanizers would be used to make rubber stamps 20 years later.[5]

Prior to 1864, stamp impressions were made by metal printing stamps which were also called mechanical hand stamps and preceded rubber stamps by six to eight years. B.B. Hill is considered "the father of the hand stamp" and operated one of the first mechanical hand stamp companies, B.B. Hill's Brass Wheel Ribbon Ticket Dater.[6] The Civil War created a demand for hand stamps when revenue stamps issued by the Union were required on all business papers, i.e., checks, notes, drafts, bills, etc. Mechanical hand stamps were used to mark these documents to meet the government's requirement that the revenue stamps be canceled with a notation of the date and the name of the person canceling them.

Figure 3.1. A rocker bottom style stamp patented by Jonathon C. Walker in 1843 is illustrated (Courtesy of Karen Rivard, Thomas Brinkman, and Karen Tucker Dunn).

The Inventor of the Vulcanized Rubber Stamp

From historical accounts, there is no single inventor credited with the invention of the vulcanized rubber stamp. Several individuals laid claim to inventing the first rubber stamp, but a written and objective record does not exist.[7] The three individuals who have received recognition in the early 1900s either in the form of an article in a stamp trade magazine or a declaration made at a stamp convention were Henry C. Leland, L.F. Witherall, and James Orton Woodruff. Since there isn't an official record of the true inventor, the claims of all three will be discussed.

Henry C. Leland was credited with inventing the first vulcanized rubber stamp in the June 1910 *Stamp Trade News* article entitled, "The Invention of the Rubber Stamp."[8] Mr. Leland's story begins with his travels as a salesman for a metal-dating and cancellation stamp company in 1863. During one of his travels, a broom manufacturer suggested that it would be beneficial to have a stamp that could be rolled on a broom handle to print a label.

While working at a print shop, one of Leland's first attempts at making a vulcanized rubber stamp was to set up a type form and make a plaster-of-paris cast of it. He then placed soft rubber bands from an old printing press on the cast and applied heat using a flatiron. This first attempt at vulcanization was successful and encouraged Leland to experiment using the dental pot as the vulcanizer. According to Leland, he had produced the first vulcanized rubber stamp and was preparing a patent for his process when a relative stole his information and sold it to a third party.

A paper presentation by L.F. Witherall of Knoxville, Illinois at the 1916 Chicago Stamp Convention provides the second claim to inventing the rubber stamp.[9] In his presentation, Witherall claimed his discovery came in 1866 while working as a foreman for a wood pump manufacturer. Identification markings were made with brass or copper stencils and paint. This marking process proved difficult in stenciling the pumps as the paint would run creating blotches on the pumps. Witherall decided he would try to correct the problem by cutting stencils out of thin rubber sheets. As he looked at the letters he had cut out of the thin rubber, he wondered if he could use the letters instead of the stencil to make the identification markings on the pumps. Witherall cut more letters out of thicker rubber, glued them to a bedpost, rolled the bedpost on a leather ink pad, and pressed the inked letters onto the pump making a good impression.

Witherall not only claimed to have invented the first rubber stamp using his bedpost, he even claimed to have made the first vulcanized rubber stamp using a dental pot in a Chicago dentist office. According to Witherall, after purchasing a vulcanizer, he entered into different partnerships setting up a factory to make rubber stamps. His business soon became financially strapped when the Dental Rubber Syndicate demanded that Witherall pay ten dollars per pound royalty in addition to the three dollars per pound he was already paying for the flesh-colored dental rubber. The combined royalty fees destroyed his business and placed Witherall in financial ruin.

The individual who most in the marking industry credit with inventing the vulcanized rubber stamp is James Orton Woodruff of Auburn, New York.[10] Between 1864 and 1866, James Woodruff observed rubber letters mounted on a curved wooden block being used to print identifying information on washtubs. While studying the impressions, Woodruff speculated whether the rubber letters could be vulcanized in a vulcanizer to create smaller stamps.

Woodruff enlisted the assistance of his uncle, a dentist by the name of Urial Woodruff. The two Woodruffs experimented using the dental pot as the vulcanizer and produced a few good quality stamps. James Woodruff set up a factory with his modified version of the dental vulcanizer which is described as follows, "made of boiler iron that was about 18 inches in diameter by 24 inches high, which was placed upon a stove. From the ceiling above the vulcanizer was suspended a tackle which was used to place and remove the heavy top and flasks."

Post-Civil War to Today

Handset moveable type has been around since its invention by Johann Gutenberg in the 1400s and was referred to as hand-set type, printer's foundry type, or foundry type.[11] The use of metal type is categorized as hot type and was initially used in the manufacturing process of stamps at the beginning of the 20th century.[12] The individual type was raised and arranged on a composing stick in the mirror image of the desired text on the stamp die. Numerous designs and sizes of foundry type were available and the printer's preferences tended to identify the stamp maker who made the stamp.

The materials used for the first molds of vulcanized rubber stamps were made of a solution of plaster-of-paris or clay placed over the metal type form. Once dried, the mold held the rubber while it was being vulcanized in the vulcanizer pot. Stamp gum was placed on the mold and an iron plate was placed on top of the rubber. The mold plate and the iron plate were tightly clamped together forcing the stamp gum into the mold plate while it was cooking. It was then placed into the boiler of the vulcanizer where it would be in direct contact with steam until the rubber cooked.[13]

In the 1930s, stamp makers began replacing the handset moveable type with the Linotype and the Ludlow. For those stamp makers who could afford the expensive machines, the Linotype or the Ludlow allowed them to typeset five to ten times faster than hand-setting type. As a result of the introduction of the Linotype and the Ludlow, new type was cast for every stamp and the problem of uneven character height from worn foundry was eliminated.[14]

A clay mold was used for the handset or hot metal type prior to 1940. The stamp maker would mix plaster and pour it into a frame that held the type. After he squeezed the excess out, the stamp maker would allow the plaster to bake and harden. Then the mold was removed from the type hopefully without cracking the mold. The matrix board appeared in the mid-1940s simplifying this process by eliminating the time-consuming and frustrating process of making the clay mold.[15]

The Warner 46 vulcanizer was sold in the 1950s and 1960s to budding stamp entrepreneurs. Warner Electric Company of Chicago manufactured this machine that allowed the stamp maker to begin his small business in his own kitchen. The Warner 46 had the unique feature of a reversible chase. The type was set in the chase, one letter at a time, heated and compressed with a matrix to form the mold. The matrix mold and rubber were placed together on the other side of the chase, inside a recessed cavity designed for molding rubber. A single heated platen at the top of the machine cured both the matrix and the rubber.[16]

The most commonly used method in the manufacture of vulcanized rubber stamps from early 1900s to late 1970s was the Ludlow or Linotype machine. By 1999, very few stamp businesses used a Ludlow or Linotype machine. Most stamp makers disposed of these machines making room for the photopolymer machine and the latest laser technology.

HAND AND SELF-INKING STAMPS

Prior to vulcanization, stamp dies were carved by hand using various materials including wood and ivory. Vulcanization of rubber is one of the oldest traditional manufacturing processes and employs heat and pressure to the material to form the die of the stamp. Handset type is a predecessor of the Ludlow and Linotype machines. The use of handset type declined as stamp makers chose the Ludlow or Linotype in making lead casts from hot metal type. Use of the Linotype is almost nonexistent and the Ludlow is quickly following the same path to extinction as the contemporary stamp maker chooses the use of cold type over hot type in the manufacturing process. The document examiner will encounter vulcanized rubber stamps made from hot type since a few stamp makers still use the Ludlow, and to a lesser extent, the Linotype. Because hot metal type is still used, this section of the chapter will describe the vulcanization process using the Ludlow and Linotype.

Different materials are subjected to the vulcanizing process in the production of stamp dies. Dies made of raw rubber and laserable rubber used in hand and self-inking stamps are vulcanized as well as the foam and powder and the pre-mixed gel for pre-inked dies. No matter what type of material is used, the vulcanizing process will follow the same steps using a matrix board as the negative and vulcanizing the material using heat and pressure to produce a die with a high relief.

The Ludlow

The process is the same for the Ludlow and the Linotype, except the Ludlow requires the stamp maker to load the type with the appropriate spaces on a composing stick (Fig. 3.2). The Linotype, also called a "line casting machine," uses a keyboard similar to a typewriter to direct the placement of the type slugs and spacers onto a composing rack, thereby eliminating hand setting each individual piece.

The Ludlow process utilizes a slug-cast composition which is hand–set and begins with the placement of the individual typeface matrices and spacers on a composition stick (Figs. 3.3A & 3.3B). The composition stick will hold only one line of text and the individual typeface and spacer had to be centered or positioned by the stamp maker. In 1964, Ludlow introduced the self-centering stick that promised to save time because the stick automatically centered the line of type.[7] The composing stick is then locked into a caster (Fig. 3.4), and molten metal, usually lead, is forced into the type character to form the type slug, a solid piece of flat metal, which has a raised printing surface or relief (Fig. 3.5). The type is removed from the composing stick and returned to the

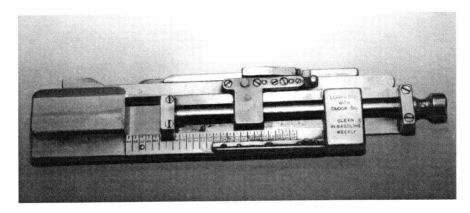

Figure 3.2. A composing stick used in the Ludlow type setting process to hold type matrices.

Ludlow storage system for future use. A text of more than one line requires the stamp maker to use several composing sticks; otherwise, after the type slug of each line is made, the stamp maker must empty the composing stick and add the required characters to compose the next line of text.

The type slugs are placed in a chase (a metal plate with metal bars locked in place) in order to secure the type slugs and wood cuts (Fig. 3.6). One chase can hold various sizes of type slugs and wood cuts that the stamp maker needs to make into vulcanized rubber stamps (Fig. 3.7). The metal bars are tightened to eliminate movement of the type slugs during the vulcanizing process (Fig. 3.8). The matrix board, a thermoset material, is cut to cover the chase and coated either with silicone, oil similar to W/D 40, or a light dusting of powder, such as talc or de-tack powder (Fig. 3.9). The light coverage of talc or oil on the matrix board makes it easier to separate the type slugs from the matrix board after removal from the heat press. The matrix board is placed on top of the secured type slugs in the chase and both are placed in the heat press where they are subjected to timed heat and pressure. Through vulcanization, the matrix board usually hardens to 90 durometer and will bear the impression of the type slug that acts as the negative for the vulcanized rubber stamp. Once the matrix and type slug are separated, the matrix is placed on a metal plate with a handle and the type slug is returned to the molten metal pot to be melted (Fig. 3.10). The raw rubber gum is placed on top of the matrix board (Fig. 3.11) and aluminum foil is placed on top of the gum (Fig. 3.12). The thickness of the foil determines the size of the relief of the die. The matrix board and rubber setup are then placed into the vulcanizer which uses heat and pressure to squeeze the rubber into the crevices of the matrix board leaving a positive impression of the desired stamp on the rubber (Fig. 3.13). The metal sheet is removed from the heat press and the matrix and rubber are separated (Fig.

Figure 3.3A–B. (A) *Top left.* Here a stamp maker removes type from the Ludlow storage drawer and (B) *Top right.* places it in the composing stick.

Figure 3.4. *Lower left.* The composing stick is locked into a caster where molten metal is forced into the type character to form the type slug.

Figure 3.5. *Lower right.* The type slug, a single piece of metal with a raised printing surface, slides onto the receiving tray and is picked up by the stamp maker.

3.14). The sheet of rubber has been vulcanized and bears the raised die (Fig. 3.15). The matrix can be used as the mold for duplicate rubber dies of the same text as the matrix is now cured and will not soften with additional heat.

The final step is to cut the rubber die from the rubber sheet and trim it for mounting as a hand or self-inking stamp (Figs. 3.16A, 3.16B, 3.16C & 3.16D). Trimming of the rubber is achieved either by hand trimming or by a cutter.

Figure 3.6. *Top left*. The type slug is arranged in the chase by the stamp maker.

Figure 3.7. *Top right*. A chase can hold numerous jobs consisting of various sizes of type slugs and wood cuts.

Figure 3.8. *Center left*. Tightening the metal bars in the chase secures the type slugs preventing movement during the vulcanizing process.

Figure 3.9. *Center right*. The stamp maker dusts the matrix board with powder to prevent the matrix board and the type slug from sticking together after vulcanization.

Figure 3.10. *Lower left*. Lead type slug is returned to the vat of molten metal to be melted for reuse.

Figure 3.11. *Lower right*. The vulcanized matrix is placed on a metal plate with the text facing up. Raw rubber is placed on top of the matrix board.

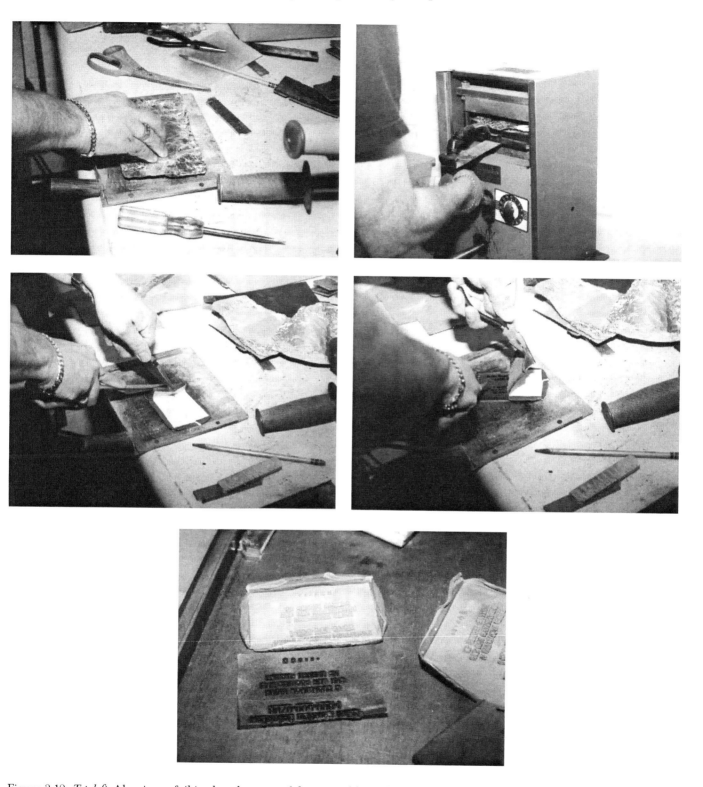

Figure 3.12. *Top left.* Aluminum foil is placed on top of the raw rubber. Thickness of the stamp relief is determined by the number of aluminum foil sheets used.

Figure 3.13. *Top right.* The metal plate with the matrix board and raw rubber covered with aluminum foil is placed in the vulcanizer and subjected to heat and pressure.

Figure 3.14A–B. *Center.* Upon removal of the metal plate from the vulcanizer, the vulcanized rubber is separated from the matrix board.

Figure 3.15. *Lower center.* The vulcanized rubber bears the raised die that will be used to make the stamp.

Figure 3.16A–D. (A) *Top left*. The die on the vulcanized rubber is trimmed using scissors, knives, or scroll saws. (B) *Top right*. The stamp maker cuts a wood mount to fit the rubber die. (C) *Lower left*. The vulcanized rubber die is mounted on the stamp mount. Attachment is achieved with a self-adhesive cushion attached to the wood mount. (D) *Lower right*. Once the handle has been attached to the wood mount, the stamp maker inks the die and makes an impression. One of the first impressions made from the finished stamp will be used for the index (title).

The Linotype

Tobin A. Tanaka

The invention of the Linotype was a savior to those in the printing and rubber stamp industry. Rather than having to painstakingly place every letter of a font by hand into a chase, an entire line was line cast as a single block of metal.[18] When using perforated tape, common to telex machines of the era,

Figure 3.17. Charles Smith of Carolina Marking Devices types the text for the die using the keyboard of the Linotype (Courtesy of John B. Houston).

speeds of up to 15 lines per minute could be achieved. This is a remarkable speed considering the machine was physically producing the lines in cast lead.[19]

The keyboard of the Linotype machine may make the use of the machine appear easy (Fig. 3.17). That was not the case, as the Linotype operator was responsible for ensuring that the keypunching was performed accurately and, more challenging, that the clarity of the "slug" was high. The complexity of the Linotype machine with its combination of electro-mechanical controls with hydraulics and electronics required extensive training for proper operation.[20] Lead was the starting material for the slugs, which was deposited as a lead bar nicknamed lead "pigs" into a melting pot (Fig. 3.18).[21] The lead pigs were lowered into the heated melting pot and automatically melted at the correct rate. When the temperature of the melting pot was not sufficient, the characters on the resulting slug lacked clarity. When examining the characters, they would appear to be fuzzy with a lack of defined lines.

Linotype machines were equipped with different font sizes. The selection of type styles and fonts was limited when compared to the electronic fonts seen today. But, unlike electronic fonts which are not physically cast into lines, the Linotype machine used magazines which were hydraulically positioned. From these magazines, the characters and spacers forming a mold for a line were positioned onto an assembling elevator. This line was then delivered to

Figure 3.18. Mr. Smith is hanging the lead pig which is then lowered into the Linotype's melting pot (Courtesy of John B. Houston).

the casting area where the hot lead was formed around the characters and spacers to form a line (Figs. 3.19A, 3.19B & 3.19C). The result was a lead cast bearing the desired die text in wrong reading position (Fig. 3.20).

Accurate timing of the hydraulic clutches and transfer mechanics was critical.[22] Mistimed motions of any of the components would result in a product of unusable quality, if any product at all. Mechanical tolerances on some of the delicate components were approximately 0.001, astounding considering the thermal gradients and vibration that the machine endured. To further complicate matters, the operator would have to define the spacing between characters and words, commonly referred to as justification. Another term the marking device industry uses when referring to the arrangement of characters on a line is "quadding." This spacing would also have to be centered, left justified, or right justified depending on the application. Knowledge of the spacing required along with the general high learning curve needed for successful

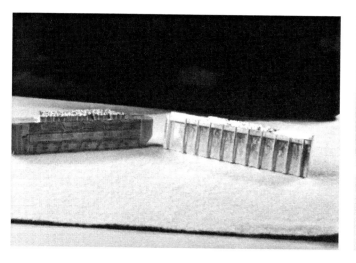

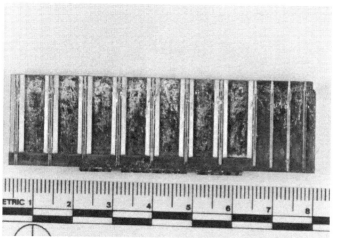

Figure 3.19A–C. The Linotype and Ludlow slugs differ in appearance. (A) *Top left.* The Ludlow slug is on the left and the Linotype slug is on the right. Both sides of the Ludlow slug are smooth. (B) *Top right.* One side of the Linotype slug is flat. (C) *Lower left.* The other side of the Linotype slug has slats (Courtesy of Tobin Tanaka).

Figure 3.20. *Lower right.* The lead slug from the Linotype and Ludlow will contain the type high (relief) text in the wrong reading position (Courtesy of Tobin Tanaka).

operation of the Linotype machine meant that most operators were experienced printers who learned their craft through an apprenticeship program.

The remaining steps of vulcanizing rubber using the Linotype mirrors the process using the Ludlow or any other hot type process. To prevent shadowing, lines with a small amount of text were ground down on the edges (Fig. 3.21). Once the stamp maker finished grinding the edges of the lead cast, it was placed on top of the matrix board (Bakelite) and both were then placed in the vulcanizer to create the die text. After the matrix board is made, the lead cast

Figure 3.21. Shadowing is prevented by grinding down the edges on lines with a small amount of text (Courtesy of Tobin Tanaka).

is melted and used for future lead casts. Upon completion of vulcanization, the matrix board will bear the die text in right reading position. The raw rubber would then be placed on top of the matrix board and placed in the vulcanizer for the required application of heat and pressure to produce a vulcanized rubber die.

The Merigraph

The Ludlow and Linotype machines are two forms of hot type used in the manufacture of vulcanized rubber stamps. As discussed earlier in this chapter, these two machines used lead slugs formed from molten metal and metal type. The Merigraph Process is a cold type method replacing the Ludlow and Linotype in the production of vulcanized rubber stamps. Mr. John B. Houston of Carolina Marking Devices, Inc. states that there are customers who prefer natural rubber stamps. This cold type method allows the stamp maker to continue to supply his customer with a vulcanized rubber stamp. He further states that very few stamp shops use this method.[23]

The Merigraph Process is a hybrid of the vulcanization and ultraviolet processes. The Merigraph Process begins in the same manner as the ultraviolet process by using a computer to prepare the artwork for the negative and curing the polymer plate to produce a "board" slug of the text. The polymer board slug is approximately 95 durometer in hardness and replaces the lead slug from a Ludlow or the line cast from a Linotype machine when vulcanizing the text into the Bakelite matrix board. The relief on the Merigraph polymer plate is higher than that found on the lead slugs. However, the difference is nominal in the impression in the Bakelite. The vulcanization process is utilized when the Merigraph plate is placed on top of the Bakelite and both are placed in the vulcanizer. Through the vulcanization process, the relief type on the Merigraph plate instead of a lead slug will be pressed into the Bakelite forming the impression. Upon completion of the Bakelite's vulcanization, the Merigraph plate is removed and the Bakelite bears the impression of the stamp text in right reading position. Raw rubber is placed on top of the Bakelite and both are placed in the vulcanizer to complete the vulcanization process.[24]

FACSIMILE SIGNATURE STAMPS

Tobin A. Tanaka

Before the advent of the ultraviolet process, some manufacturers of rubber stamps used a method involving the use of a zinc cut to produce the text on a stamp die including facsimile signature stamps. The process of producing a zinc cut involved several steps that could affect the quality of the final product.

The process began with the signer choosing the signature from several signature samples to be used for the facsimile signature stamp. All specimen signatures were produced as a camera-ready image. "Camera ready" meant that the signatures were executed with dark colored ink on plain white paper (no background lines). Dark colored ink on a white background resulted in a high contrast between the signature line and the background. It was recommended that the signer use a roller ball or a fountain pen with proper ink flow to ensure that a solid line was put on the page. Ballpoint pens were not recommended due to the skipping and improper operation of the ball point in the steel housing on faulty pens.

In some instances, the signature specimen(s) provided were not the ideal camera-ready image. Specimens may have been written on lined paper, or with a light colored blue ink from a ballpoint pen, or on tinted paper. Any of these factors would affect the production of the zinc cut. The manufacturer who was quality conscious would detect these potential problems and request the signer to re-submit his or her signatures using the proper materials. A zinc cut could then be made once a camera-ready specimen signature was ready. Unless a rubber stamp manufacturer had numerous orders for facsimile signature stamps, most zinc cuts were made by engraving companies who provided services to the stamp-making industry.

The selected signature was photographed onto a negative using a graphics camera. If an engraving company was providing the zinc cut, the stamp man-

Figure 3.22. Finishing nails are commonly used to secure a zinc cut to a wooden block (Courtesy of Tobin Tanaka).

ufacturer would receive a proof whose appearance was similar to a blueprint instead of a negative. The proof was made by applying printers' ink to the zinc cut, placing a sheet of paper on top, then running a roller on a rail system over the paper. Defects in the zinc cut image would then be visible. If the quality did not meet the engraver's standards, another zinc cut would be made from the graphics available or the engraver would request submission of better graphics. The resulting zinc cut bore a positive relief in the signature area similar to that on handset or Linotype. For rubber stamp manufacturers, the zinc cut was nailed onto a wooden block with finishing nails (Fig. 3.22). The height of the zinc cut was made to be type high corresponding to 0.918 inches. "Type high" was the standard height for Linotype, handset type, and zinc cuts. This standard height allowed the same chase to contain any combination of handset type, Linotype, and zinc cuts.

Once the stamp manufacturer received the zinc cut, the process of manufacturing the facsimile stamp is the same as the vulcanization of raw rubber as described earlier in this chapter.

Casey-Owens reported in 1978 on two methods of facsimile signature production with one method involving the carving of the rubber by hand to form the stamp and the second method involving the hand carving of wood to form the woodcut, allowing any number of stamps to be made.[25] In both methods, the original signature is traced onto transfer paper, a thin, almost transparent waxy-finished paper. The stamp maker traced the signature using either a copying pencil or a hectograph-type carbon paper which was used to transfer the tracing to the dampened piece of rubber or wood by applying pressure. The signature would transfer in reverse onto the wood or rubber.

The wood is carved adjacent to the outline of the signature by hand using a fine gouge. The outline is enlarged, possibly by a second engraver, who outlines the area in an outward direction using a courser gouge. According to Casey-Owens, the carving is far enough away from the signature line that the remaining unwanted wood can be removed by a mechanical router. The finished woodcut can be used for printing or as a matrix to mold additional rubber or metal stamps.[26]

Casey-Owens reported a third method of producing facsimile signatures that involves mechanical reproduction by use of a routing machine with a pantograph control to trace the signature. The pantograph is guided by hand and the rubber die produced by this method could be used to make numerous stamps.[27]

Purtell reported the carving method for rubber began with copying the signature on a piece of paper with hexograph ink and transferring it to the rubber. Then the rubber was cut away from the lines by hand, leaving the signature in reverse relief.[28] Because it used rubber instead of wood, only one stamp could be made from this carving method.

PRE-INKED STAMPS

History

Pre-inked stamps are the most expensive stamps on the market. Their introduction into the stamp market was slow due to the manufacturing expense. The 1950s ushered in an era of manufacturers experimenting with a gel type substance to make pre-inked stamps. By mid-1990s, pre-inked stamps became one of the major classifications of stamps and the forensic document examiner will encounter pre-inked stamps made of a variety of materials and manufactured in a variety of ways.

NCR and Barry Green patented the salt-leached technology in the 1940s. NCR used this technology to manufacture pre-inked cash register dies and pre-inked price marking stamps.[29]

A patent was issued in 1957 to Harry Leeds and John Levey for manufacturing products with microporous resinous structures.[30] S.C. Johnson & Sons, Inc. acquired the patent and intended to use the technology of the microporous material called "Porelon," an abbreviation of "pores" and "nylon," for developing new products such as "automatic marking devices, writing instruments, self-lubricating bearings, cosmetics and toiletries, bandages with built-in medicaments, rollers and plates for printing equipment, cigarette filters, dry batteries and waterproof sheeting that permit the passage of air" (*The Jonwax Journal,* 1959).[31] The company developed this technology and marketed the Perma-Stamp Pre-inked Stamps and Porelon Ink Rollers.

By 1960, rubber stamp manufacturers throughout the United States and overseas had received training on the manufacturing process of gel stamps and sold them under the name of Perma-Stamp (Figs. 3.23A, 3.23B & 3.23C). Due to licensing agreements and patents, the number of gel suppliers, such as S.C. Johnson Wax Company, were limited. However, the company was the first to market the pre-inked gel stamp. The company eventually overcame the problems of each gel batch reacting differently and the gel's susceptibility to heat and humidity. Once the problems were resolved, the gel stamp was a popular stamp to market due to its ability to stamp multiple images with each image being a quality impression.[32]

While S.C. Johnson Wax Company was refining their gel stamp, Swedpoint, a Swedish company, developed an adjustable mount. An adjustable mount is crucial to a gel stamp as it will compensate for the individual stamping the impression, thereby providing the best impression possible.[33]

The application of the salt-leached process to pre-inked stamps was accidentally discovered by Shachihata in 1964 while the company was working on a new nib for markers. The pre-inked stamps from Shachihata were released in 1968 and were manufactured using the salt-leached process with a plastic die mount.[34]

A pre-inked stamp made of a cushion-type foam and gel-type ink mounted on a mount with spring feet was marketed in 1965 (Fig. 3.24). Bankers & Merchants of Chicago named their pre-inked stamp the Faymus Stamp and offered a free pre-inked stamp that made an impression of red lips in their *NewsWeek* and *Times* advertisements. The stamp was eventually phased out.

Wilsolite Corporation developed a manufacturing system using synthetic rubber and salt for pre-inked stamps in the mid-1970s.[35] This development allowed small to medium stamp companies to make their own pre-inked stamps as it simplified the process. Prior to the use of salt-leached rubber, the gel systems of the 1960s and 1970s took two days to produce a full form in one color. This newer process took only one day and allowed the stamp maker to make a full form in different colors.[36]

In 1989, Dave Hedgecoth discovered a method of self-stabilization for pre-inked gel. He discovered that a special series of solvents could be heated to a point of doubling the size of the cells, which would allow his all-gel material to be self-stabilized in 15 minutes. Mr. Hedgecoth currently has two patents on

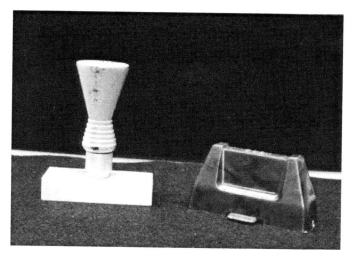

Figure 3.23A–C. (A) *Top left.* Shown here are pre-inked stamps from the early 1960s. The stamp on the right is a Perma-Stamp. (B) *Top right.* The cover of the Perma-Stamp. (C) *Lower center.* The die of the Perma-Stamp is a pre-mix gel.

manufacturing pre-inked stamps with laser engraving and one patent with mechanical engraving.[37]

Pre-Mix Gel Dies

Gel stamps are expensive to produce, and therefore, they are made by only a few companies. The majority of local stamp makers order the pre-mixed gel stamps from a manufacturer.

One method of manufacturing gel stamps uses a pre-mix gel, which is a mixture of liquid plastic and ink that has the consistency of paint. Some stamp mak-

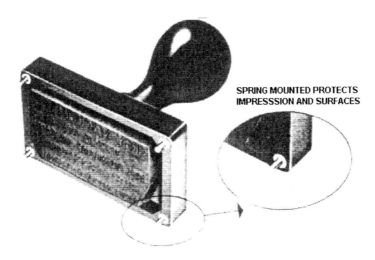

SPRING MOUNTED PROTECTS
IMPRESSSION AND SURFACES

Figure 3.24. The Faymus Stamp was a pre-inked stamp with a mount supported on spring feet (Courtesy of *Marking Industry Magazine* and David Kelly).

ers refer to the pre-mix gel as a slurry inked gel with the ink encapsulated in the pores of the gel. Whether the material is referred to as a pre-mix gel or a slurry inked gel, the mix uses an oil base ink that is microencapsulated in the gel.[38]

The process begins with preparing a hard polymer plate using a mat negative to make the image of the stamp die. A concentration of "release spray" is applied to the polymer plate prior to placement on the matrix board. Once the polymer plate is placed on top of the matrix board, it is covered and molded with heat and pressure using the vulcanizer.[39] Once it has cooled, the polymer plate is removed from the matrix board leaving the stamp images formed on the matrix board.

The matrix board is in the chase and the stamp maker rubs pre-mix gel into the crevices of the matrix board, making sure the mix covers all the print area. An air bubble can occur if the maker fails to rub the gel evenly and adequately into all the crevices on the matrix. An overfilling of pre-mix gel is applied to the chase which is then covered with release material to speed stabilization. Once the release material is in place, the chase is secured with the chase lid and placed in the vulcanizer. When it first comes out of the vulcanizer, the gel mold has a consistency similar to brownies fresh from the oven, i.e., vulnerable to cracking and breaking if not handled gently. The gel mold requires at least one hour of cooling time to reach its full strength.[40]

After cooling, the gel slab is removed from the chase and the excess ink is blotted off. Some manufacturers have an additional step of placing the gel slab in a Stabilization Oven for 15 minutes and when removed, excess ink is once again blotted off. The process of blotting out the excess ink, sometimes with a paper towel, will continue until all the excess ink has been removed. Damage can occur to the gel slab during this process if the maker did not allow enough cooling time prior to the excess ink removal. Once the excess ink has been removed, sealer is applied to the back of the gel slab and once it air dries, the slab is ready to be cut and mounted as a pre-inked stamp.

Foam and Powder Dies

A combination of nitrile-butadine (NBR) foam and powder has been used as die material for pre-inked stamps since 1980. The vulcanizing process of this material involves the use of a pre-formed slab and the powder version of that same slab material. In addition to NBR, PVC can also be used for the foam (slab) and powder.

A photographic negative of the desired stamp text is made and exposed onto either a Rigilon or Merigraph plate. Introduced in 1980, the Rigilon plate is a photopolymer plate that can be used to create a Bakelite mold (Figs. 3.25A, 3.25B & 3.25C).[41] The Rigilon plate is then washed to remove residue around the letters or text of the stamp die leaving the text in relief and in the wrong reading position. Wrong reading position is defined as placement of the negative in a position where it is backwards and cannot be read left to right. The Rigilon plate is placed on top of a matrix board and subjected to heat and pressure through vulcanization. The Bakelite mold will reflect the text in right reading position. Once the text has been molded into the matrix board, the powder is rubbed into the face of the matrix board and then packed into the cavities that form the printed text. A thin layer of powder is then applied to the mold making sure the entire area is covered.[42]

The matrix board is sandwiched between a metal plate and the pre-formed foam slab. The bearer bars are secured and release paper is placed over the matrix board and bearer bars. A second metal plate is placed on top and the entire unit is placed in the vulcanizer. Once the vulcanizing process is complete, the material is removed from the vulcanizer and allowed to cool to room temperature.

Unlike pre-mix gel stamps, the foam and powder stamps have to be inked once the dies have been cut. The stamp will not be trimmed as close to the die, leaving an excess background which functions as the ink source for the die. The foam and powder stamps are inked by placing the dies face down in a container of ink and leaving them submerged in the ink for approximately 30 minutes before removing and placing on several sheets of paper towels. The stamps are fully inked and should remain face down on the paper towels to drain the excess ink. Once the excess ink has been drained, the dies are ready to be glued to the stamp mount as a pre-inked stamp.[43]

Figure 3.25A–C. (A) *Top left.* Rigilon plate is used as the negative in forming the text on the Foam and Powder pre-inked dies. The text of the die is in wrong reading position. (B) *Top right.* The text of the die is vulcanized into the Bakelite mold in the right reading position. (C) *Lower center.* The final step is to fill the crevices of the text in the Bakelite mold with powder, lay the pad of the same foam material on top, and place in the vulcanizer. The finished stamp die will reflect the text in wrong reading position.

ULTRAVIOLET (PHOTOPOLYMER)

History

Photopolymer was invented in 1960 and entered the stamp industry for use in the manufacturing process of stamps in the early 1970s. Prior to this process, the only die material used as a die for a facsimile signature stamp was vulcanized rubber using a zinc or magnesium cut prepared by an engraver as the negative.[44]

Phototypesetting machines were used by the larger rubber stamp companies in the mid-1970s to make the photopolymer stamps. This was an expensive process because the photopolymer machine required black and white artwork to be transferred to a negative. Therefore, the stamp company had to have a darkroom and a graphic arts camera to generate the film negative that would be used in the phototypesetting machine.

Manufacturing photopolymer stamps was simplified in the early 1980s when an improvement in the process enabled the photopolymer machine to make its own negative in the open light without the need for a graphic arts camera or darkroom. This simplification increased the availability of photopolymer stamps as it allowed the medium and small stamp companies to enter that area of the market by manufacturing photopolymer stamps in-house.[45]

Since 1985, with the introduction of desktop publishing, the computer has been used in the manufacturing process of the photopolymer stamp.[46] Phototypesetting machines, for the most part, were retired to the closet to gather dust. With the addition of the scanner, all stamp companies, whether large or small, could produce a photopolymer stamp in any design as well as produce a good quality facsimile signature stamp. By 1999, half of the stamps made in the United States were photopolymer stamps.[47]

The Ultraviolet Process

Photopolymer is a photosensitive soluble plastic or resin that polymerizes (hardens) when exposed to ultraviolet light. Photopolymer can be in the form of a sheet or a clear, viscous liquid resembling the consistency of honey (Fig. 3.26). Photopolymer must be stored out of direct sunlight and indoor light as it is the exposure to ultraviolet light that cures or hardens the photopolymer making it a useful material for a stamp die.

The first step is to make a negative for the photopolymer stamps. The vast majority of today's stamp makers use a scanner and computer to make the negative instead of camera equipment. With standard digital image software, the computer operator can scan an original or a copy of artwork and signatures (Fig. 3.27). If the image needs retouching, the operator can remove defects in the image's print area. In the case of signatures, light pen pressure can cause a broken line or non-print area in the die due to that particular area lacking the necessary density for an adequate amount of polymer to form the stroke. To prevent that from occurring, the computer operator will add thickness to the signature's stroke line to provide the density necessary for the poly-

Figure 3.26. *Left.* Photopolymer is a photosensitive soluble plastic or resin that hardens when exposed to ultraviolet light. The liquid polymer has the consistency of honey and is stored out of direct sunlight and kept in protective containers.

Figure 3.27. *Right.* Kim Rowan of A-1 Rubber Stamp & Engraving scans the artwork to be used for the text of the stamp die. Software such as CORELDRAW® allows the computer operator to retouch or repair defect areas in the art or signature. Once the artwork is acceptable, the operator prints a negative using a laser printer.

mer to adhere onto the die. If Mylar® is used as the negative, the computer operator will thicken the line prior to printing the image on the Mylar using the laser printer. If the negative is a sheet of vellum, the operator can thicken the stroke by making multiple generation photocopies of the signature until the desired thickness is achieved. As any seasoned document examiner knows, the line in a print area thickens with each copy generation due to increased deposits of toner with each additional generation.

Scanned signatures usually need to be reduced in size to fit on the stamp. If vellum is used, the operator uses the reduce function of the photocopier to achieve the desired size. If Mylar is used, the operator can reduce the signature size using the computer software.

Once the type has been printed on a sheet of vellum using the laser printer, a film negative is required for the ultraviolet process. Even though the negative can be generated using professional camera equipment and a darkroom, the majority of stamp makers use contact negative film that can be used in open daylight. This type of film processes only when it is exposed to ultraviolet light (Fig. 3.28).[48]

The processed negative is placed on the bottom glass plate of the photopolymer machine so the metal bearer strips are facing upward. The negative is placed on the glass in the "right reading" position. Right reading is defined as the copy is in the correct reading position with the film's emulsion side fac-

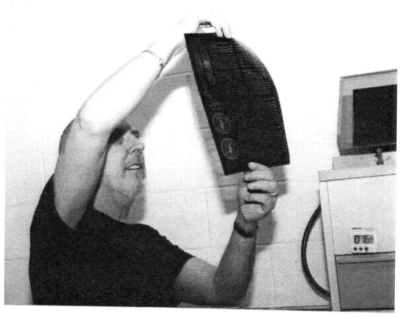

Figure 3.28. Cliff Hughson of A-1 Rubber Stamp & Engraving inspects the negative looking for defects or bad spots in the print area.

ing up. Cover film of plastic Mylar covers the negative to separate it from the liquid polymer (Figs. 3.29A & 3.29B). Pressure is applied to smooth the film and to remove air pockets or creases (Fig. 3.30). A border is placed around the edge of the plate area using foam stripping tape with the corners open to allow excess polymer to escape (Fig. 3.31). The foam stripping tape, also called damming tape, resembles window insulation tape. Liquid polymer is poured onto the plate and allowed to spread until it is flush with the foam stripping (Figs. 3.32A & 3.32B). It is during this stage that air bubbles may occur. The air bubbles must be removed from the print areas of the image (Fig. 3.33). If allowed to remain, the air bubble creates a non-print area on the die which may be reflected in its impression. Most photopolymer machines are equipped with a device to remove the air bubbles, but a straight pin or paper clip is just as effective.

The substrate is a film that the polymer sticks to. One side of the substrate film is smooth and one side is rough. The rough side of the substrate film is placed directly on top of the liquid polymer (Fig. 3.34). The tint of the substrate determines the color or tint of the polymer die and can be yellow, pink, milky white, or clear. The top glass is placed on top of the substrate with metal bearer strips. Clamps are fastened on each end of the glass plates to secure them together (Fig. 3.35). The stamp maker allows five minutes for the poly-

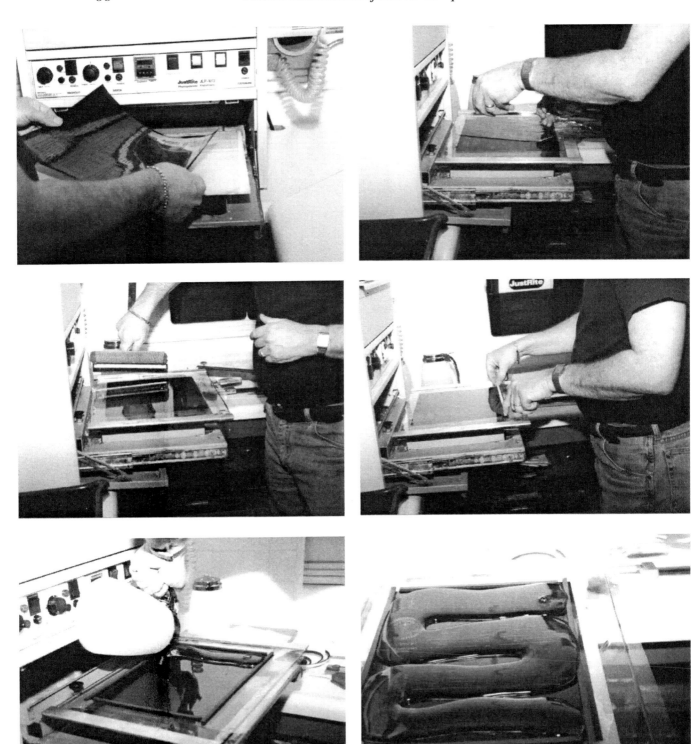

Figure 3.29A–B. (A) *Top left.* The negative is placed on the glass in "right reading" position and (B) *Top right.* covered with cover film made of Mylar®. The plastic cover film acts as a barrier between the negative and the liquid polymer.

Figure 3.30. *Center left.* The stamp maker smooths the film removing wrinkles and air pockets.

Figure 3.31. *Center right.* Foam stripping tape, damming tape, is placed around the edge of the covered negative.

Figure 3.32A–B. (A) *Lower left.* Liquid polymer is poured onto the plate. (B) *Lower right.* The liquid polymer is allowed to spread until it is flush with the damming tape.

mer resin to settle and flow out through the open corners of the foam strip frame.

For liquid polymer, the first exposure to the ultraviolet light is the back exposure. The back exposure builds a solid base for the stamp images, bonds the substrate to the photopolymer material, and dictates how much character depth (relief) will be on the stamp.[49] The amount of exposure time is crucial to the development of a good quality stamp. A back exposure time that is too long will cause less polymer resin to build images resulting in a smaller relief. A proper back exposure time averages between 22 and 30 seconds to create a background that is one-third of the total thickness of the finished plate. Once the back exposure is complete, the clamps are removed and the glass is turned over in preparation for the second ultra-violet exposure (Fig. 36).

The second ultraviolet light exposure is called the front exposure and directs the light through the negative to harden the resin only where the light hits, forming the characters on the die. The front exposure averages 120 to 140 seconds and will harden the characters deep enough to attach to the background. An excessive front exposure will cause the characters to widen and fill in.

Upon completion of the timed exposure, the cover film is removed from the photopolymer plate (Fig. 3.37). Four different methods can be employed to remove excess photopolymer during the washout phase using water and a biodegradable detergent (Figs. 3.38A & 3.38B). If the polymer is submerged into a washout tank, the excess is removed by either the autobrush, the auto-jet, or the ultrasonic method. The plate is then removed from the wash and rinsed with water to remove excess polymer and detergent. If the machine is not equipped with its own washout tank, the stamp maker will remove the excess photopolymer by hand using water and a soft hand brush.[50] After completion of the washout, the relief (printed area of the die) is fully formed and the photopolymer sheet is soft. To be used as a stamp die, the photopolymer must be hardened. This is achieved through a post-exposure of ultraviolet light which hardens the exposed polymer. The hardened polymer sheet is given a final rinse (Fig. 3.39), and is ready to be cut and trimmed for mounting as a hand or self-inking stamp.

LASER ENGRAVING

History

Laser, acronym for Light Amplification of Simulated Emission of Radiation, is a technology with numerous applications in a myriad of industries.

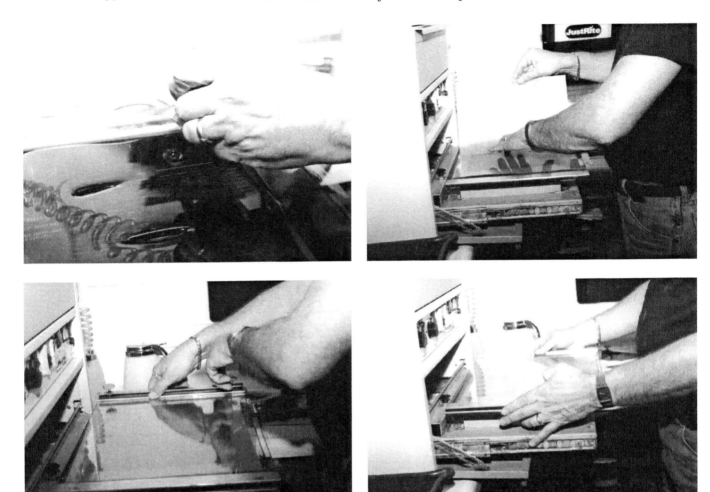

Figure 3.33. *Top left.* An air bubble is removed from the photopolymer by the stamp maker. Failure to remove the air bubble will cause a non-print area on the die.
Figure 3.34. *Top right.* Substrate is placed rough side down on the photopolymer. The photopolymer sticks to the substrate film.
Figure 3.35. *Lower left.* Metal clamps are fastened on each end of the glass plates.
Figure 3.36. *Lower right.* Upon completion of the back exposure, the metal clamps are removed and the glass plate is turned over in preparation for the front exposure.

Lasers are used for cutting, welding, holding, surgery in medicine, marking in industry, and manufacturing of stamps.[51]

The groundwork for laser technology began in the United States in the 1960s and the 1970s. In the 1980s, Europe became the leader in high-power lasers after years of research and development.[52]

Laser technology entered the stamp industry for use in the manufacture of stamp dies in the early 1990s and has grown steadily as the cost of purchasing

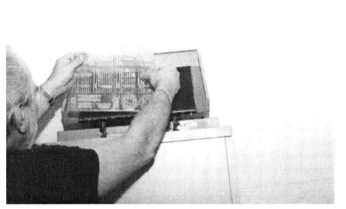
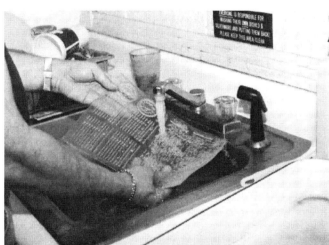

Figure 3.37. *Top left.* Upon completion of the timed back and front exposures, the cover film is removed from the photopolymer plate.

Figure 3.38A–B. (A) *Top right.* The photopolymer plate is placed into a wash filled with water and biodegradable detergent. The photopolmer plate is then removed and rinsed with plain water. During the wash process, loose photopolymer or print areas that lack adequate density will fall off. (B) *Lower left.* Cliff Hughson checks the polymer sheet to make sure the excess and loose polymer has been removed.

Figure 3.39. *Lower right.* After post exposure, the photopolymer is given a final rinse. The individual dies on the photopolymer plate are now ready to be trimmed and mounted.

a laser continues to decrease and the quality of the materials used for the stamp die continues to increase. Lasers were initially used by stamp makers whose business included production of signage such as nameplates. With the advent of OSHA, ADA, and other laws requiring increased use of signage, the laser proved to be a valuable tool to produce these type of products in a timely manner.[53]

There are two main types of lasers used in marking applications. The laser used for engraving rubber or synthetics is the CO_2 laser which uses an active mixture of carbon dioxide, helium, and nitrogen oxide. The second type of laser is the Nd:YAG laser that uses a rotated crystal to produce the laser beam and is used for engraving metals such as brass or aluminum.[54]

The CO_2 laser engraving system used for stamp engraving is sold as a Class 1 enclosed unit and uses a laser that has between 25 and 100 watts of power. The wattage affects the speed of the engraving, not the quality. The lower wattage units allow small and medium stamp businesses to enter the laser stamp market since the price of owning a laser engraver increases with the amount of wattage.[55]

In the manufacture of rubber stamps, the flatbed CO_2 laser is the most common type used in the United States. A rotary laser can also be used and is more commonplace in Europe. Louis Melind, a U.S. manufacturer in Illinois, uses a rotary laser to produce rubber stamps.

Laser Engraving Process Using the Flatbed Laser

The laser engraving process can be used in the manufacture of hand, self-inking, and pre-inked stamps. In hand and self-inking stamps, the dies can be made of raw rubber, laserable rubber, and photopolymer. In pre-inked stamps, the foam and powder material as well as the salt-leached rubber can be used in the laser engraving process. The laser engraving process is the least complicated of all the manufacturing processes and is considered user-friendly for the stamp maker.

The laser engraving process utilizes a computer that is at least a 100 MHz Pentium with a 32MB of memory, a print driver for the engraving system, and a graphic arts software package, similar to CORELDRAW® or ADOBE PrintShop®.[56] The step of making a negative of the artwork is eliminated since the artwork will be displayed on the computer screen.

Once the artwork is completed, the die material, referred to as a slab, is placed on the table of the flatbed laser (Fig. 3.40). Numerous stamps can be engraved in various sizes and differing text on one slab. The laser engraver operates in a similar fashion as the laser printer in that the laser beam transfers a beam of light through the mirrors and lens to the rubber material (Fig. 3.41). The focal length changes the size of the laser beam at the burn point. For example, a two-inch focal length has a beam size of .005 while a one and one-half inch focal length has a beam size of .003. A shorter focal length is typically used on the less powerful machines.[57]

The laser beam vaporizes or burns away the background (non-print area) leaving characters that form the stamp die. A relief die is left with a back-

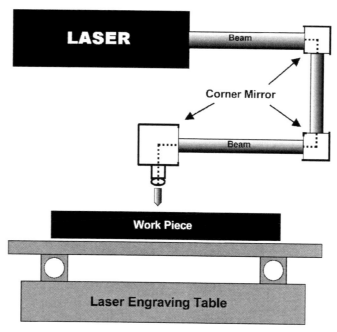

Figure 3.40. This drawing illustrates low the laser beam bounces off of the mirrors to the lens which directs the beam to vaporize or burn away the background area of the rubber slab (Courtesy of Diane C. Bosworth and Karen Tucker Dunn).

ground that has small, disconnected lines, representing the burn path of the laser beam. The disconnected laser lines are caused by the laser firing many times during the engraving process. The measurement of the number of times the laser fires per inch is referred to as the PPI, acronym for "pulses per inch," which is set by the driver.[58]

The smoothness or the depth and appearance of the burn lines can be affected by the dpi that is set in the driver, application of the engraver's power at a higher speed, less power at a slower speed, and controlling the ramping. Ramping has to do with reducing the laser power as the beam reaches the edge of the character.[59] The application of any of these factors will affect the smoothness of the background, but not the depth of the relief.

The dies can be cut from the slab either by hand or by the laser engraver. Prior to inking, any dust or other contaminant should be removed from the die. This can be done by hand or by using a vacuum system.

Inking is the next step. If the die is for a hand or self-inking stamp, the die is trimmed and mounted. If the die is for a pre-inked stamp, the die must be inked prior to mounting. One method of inking is to immerse the dies in ink allowing time for total ink saturation. Removal of excess ink is achieved either through blotting out the excess or allowing the excess to drain out of the die.

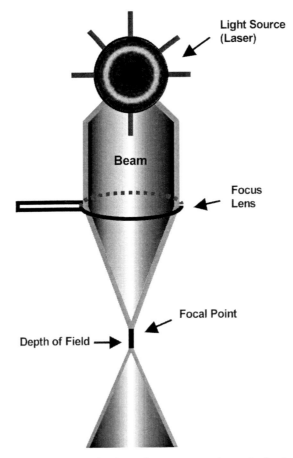

Figure 3.41. This drawing illustrates the laser beam going through the focus lens for the focal point and depth of field (Courtesy of Diane C. Bosworth and Karen Tucker Dunn).

A second method of inking a pre-inked die is to use a vacuum system. The vacuum system removes air surrounding the die so ink will impregnate it ensuring a proper ink load. The excess ink is removed by a vacuum die compress unit and the die is ready to be mounted.[60]

Salt-Leached Rubber

The use of salt-leached rubber for pre-inked stamps saw a resurgence in popularity in the mid-1990s with the introduction of laser engraving. The laser engraving of salt-leached rubber, also called salt-leached foam, is similar to that of the laser engraving of laserable rubber.

The salt-leached rubber is natural rubber that has salt dispersed throughout the material. Prior to shipping the material to the stamp maker, the manufacturer places the salt dispersed rubber in a wash bath for a couple of days to remove the salt. The dispersion and removal of salt from the rubber is done by the manufacturer. The stamp maker receives the material in a slab form that is ready for laser engraving. Upon completion of the laser engraving of the salt-leached rubber, the slab of rubber is then placed in a vacuum where ink is vacuumed into it providing equal absorption of ink throughout the material. Once the ink absorption has been completed, the sheet of salt-leached rubber is removed, the dies are cut from the sheet, and mounted as pre-inked stamps.

Laser Photopolymer

Stewart Superior Corporation introduced Merigraph laser polymer in 1998 and is the only manufacturer that currently markets laser polymer. The manufacturing process begins with the polymer in a liquid state and exposing it to ultraviolet light for curing to create a sheet of polymer that has a 40 durometer hardness.[61] The sheet is then distributed to the requesting stamp maker who can laser the polymer on a 25 watts or above laser engraver.[62] The stamp maker laser engraves the desired text making the die and cuts the die from the sheet for mounting as a hand stamp or self-inking stamp.

Laser Engraving Process Using the Rotary Laser

The rotary laser is similar to the flatbed laser in that both use the light from a laser beam to burn or vaporize the background of the stamp, leaving only the relief of the die. However, there are a few important differences that will be described in this section.

Laserable rubber is the primary stamp die material that can be rotary laser engraved. It is important to note that salt-leached rubber can also be engraved using the rotary laser. Currently, only one company in the United States uses the rotary laser for stamps and the material of choice is laserable rubber. The laserable or salt-leached rubber is taped to the drum of the rotary laser instead of laying flat on a tabletop. While the drum spins at a high rate of speed, the laser is moving sideways in small increments right to left vaporizing the background of the stamp die.[63] Keeping these notable exceptions in mind, the steps in the manufacturing process using a rotary laser engraver are the same as those listed in the laser engraving.

LIGHT BURST TECHNOLOGY

History

One of the latest processes to be developed for use in stamp manufacturing is light burst technology using a Xenon flash. This process was first introduced in Europe in 1996 by Unigraphics and then in the U.S. in 1997 by U.S. Stamp & Sign.[64] Brother International Corporation followed with the release of their unit, the SC-2000 Stampcreator Pro™ in November 1998.[65] Millennium Marking entered the light burst technology stamp market by releasing the MaxLight in November 1999.

The ease of use and compact size of the light burst process or thermal heat process machines are popular choices for non-stamp businesses to enter the stamp market. For example, OfficeMax® and Brother International Corporation entered into a partnership in January 2000 that would allow OfficeMax to offer custom designed pre-inked stamps "while you wait" to its customers by placing Brother's SC-2000 Stampcreator Pro in 700 of its stores.[66] In all likelihood, more partnerships will follow as well as an increase in beginning stamp entrepreneurs operating a stamp business from their homes.

Light Burst Technology Process

As discussed in the last section, there are three stamp manufacturing units that use the light burst or Xenon Flash process. Each manufacturer differs in the use of the material for the die and the steps taken to produce the stamp in their unit. Due to the differences in material and the function of the units, the three manufacturers' light burst process will be discussed individually.

FlashStamp® uses foam-type material for the die. The process begins by using computer software to make a film positive of the stamp text. The positive is placed on the platen of the FlashStamp Machine, which is freestanding and not connected to the computer. The FlashStamp foam is placed on top of the film and the lid is closed. The machine exposes the foam to an intense "flash" of light and pressure to seal the background of the foam. Once removed from the machine, the foam is inked followed by the blotting out of excess ink. The dies are then cut into individual dies and mounted for pre-inked stamps.[67]

The Stampcreator Pro from Brother uses material made of microporous rubber for the die. This machine is the only light burst unit connected to a personal computer or Macintosh. The image of the stamp is created using software that accompanies the system. A positive image is created using thermal transfer printing to an acetate cover sheet that the machine positions over the printing die of the stamp. The Xenon flash seals all the micropores on the die except the printing portion, which is covered by the positive image of the cover sheet.[68] The ink is packed in a plastic bag in the base of the stamp and is released by attaching the stamp handle. It takes approximately 15 minutes for the stamp material to absorb the ink at which time it is ready for use.[69]

The MaxLight System by Millennium Marking Co. allows stamp makers to use their own software and laser printer to typeset the text of the die onto vellum in 300 to 1200dpi (Figs. 3.42A & 3.42B). The stamp maker uses at least a 300 dpi laser printer to print the desired artwork or text on the MaxLight vellum sheet. The prepared vellum is the film positive designed for one time use that is trimmed and placed over the porous foam. Clear cellophane tape secures the film positive to the unexposed porous foam (Fig. 3.43). With the film positive in position, the covered foam is placed inside the Light Burst Unit and secured in the chamber using the unit's pressing screw (Fig. 3.44).

The cover of the MaxLight Light Burst Unit is placed over the chamber and the number of light bursts required is based on the size of the foam pad (Fig. 3.45). The porous foam rubber pad is a silicone based foam coated with carbon. The light burst flash causes a chemical reaction in the carbon coating creating heat which seals the uncovered areas of the pad.[70] Upon completion of the light burst exposure, the tape holding the film positive is removed from the exposed foam (Figs. 3.46A & 3.46B). The foam pad bearing the text of the stamp die is placed in a trim ring eliminating the need to glue the die to the mount (Fig. 3.47). Once the trim ring has secured the die, the ink cartridge is placed into the trim ring on the back of the exposed foam (Figs. 3.48A, 3.48B & 3.48C). The stamp mount is snapped over the trim ring and the ink will penetrate the foam in one or two hours (Figs. 3.49A & 3.49B). Once the ink has penetrated the foam, the stamp is ready for use as a pre-inked stamp.[71]

Millennium released a second generation MaxLight Ultra Exposures, on January 1, 2000. The revised unit replaces the acrylic plate with a glass platen that allows the stamp maker to produce numerous stamps of various sizes in one production run (Fig. 3.50). The original MaxLight Light Burst Unit uses one intensity setting of numerous light bursts to seal the background of the porous pad. The MaxLight Ultra Exposures Unit features an adjustable intensity setting for the light burst. As a result, it is able to use a single light burst with an intensity setting based on the size of the production run in order to seal the background of the porous pad.

The process for the MaxLight Ultra Exposure light burst unit differs from the original in the steps to produce a pre-inked stamp. The vellum with the artwork is placed face down on the glass platen. Mylar is placed on top of the artwork followed by the unexposed porous pad (Fig. 3.51). The materials are sandwiched between the glass platen and a metal sheet (Fig. 3.52). Once the

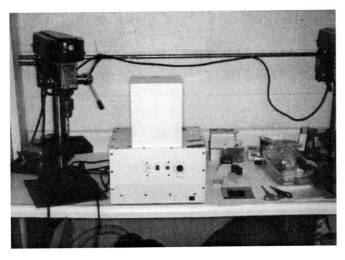

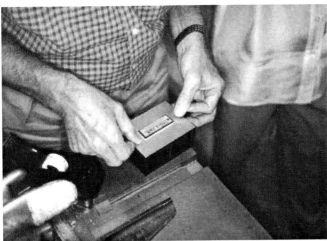

Figure 3.42A–B. (A) *Top left.* The MaxLight System is a standalone light burst unit. It is the only unit thus far that is not connected to the computer. (B) *Top right.* The exposure chamber of the MaxLight System is accessible once the cover is removed.

Figure 3.43. *Lower left.* The stamp maker uses cellophane tape to secure the film positive bearing the desired artwork to the porous pad.

Figure 3.44. *Lower right.* The unexposed foam pad covered with the film positive is placed in the exposure chamber of the Light Burst Unit.

metal sheet is in place, the unit's lid is closed and a rollbar attached to the sides of the unit is brought forward by the stamp maker causing the light burst to discharge (Fig. 3.53). The lid is then opened and the material is removed. Upon exposure to the single light burst, the micropores in the pad are sealed with the exception of the text. The process of mounting and inking the die remains the same as that used in the original MaxLight Light Burst Unit.

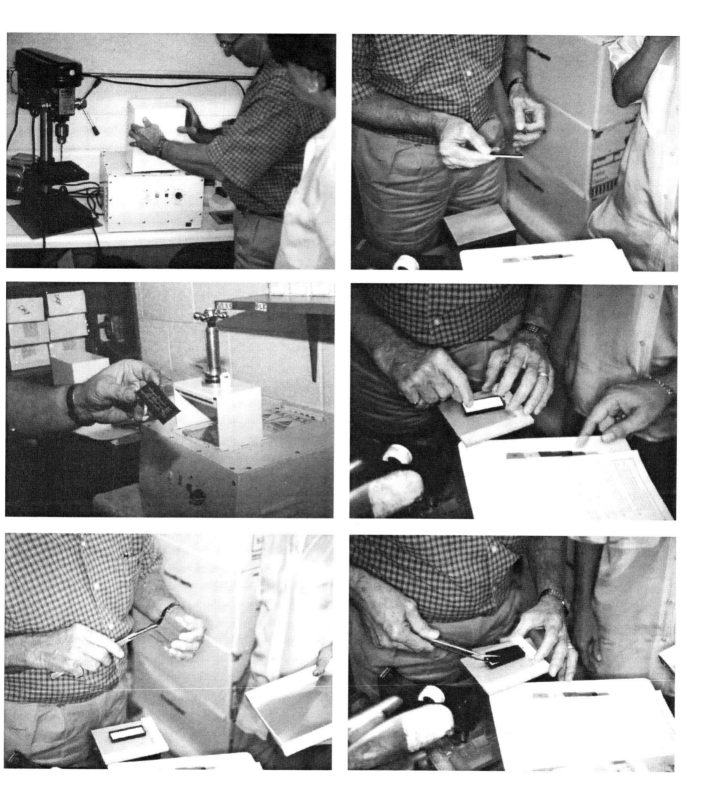

Figure 3.45. *Top left*. The cover is placed over the exposure chamber and a set number of light bursts are fired to seal the exposed areas of the porous pad.

Figure 3.46A–B. (A) *Top right*. The exposed pad is removed from the light burst chamber and the tape is removed. (B) *Center left*. The text on the exposed die is white prior to inking.

Figure 3.47. *Center right*. The exposed die contains the desired text and the background is sealed. The exposed die is placed in the trim ring of the mount base. This eliminates the need to glue the die to the mount since the trim ring will hold the die securely in place.

Figure 3.48A–B. (A) *Lower left*. The ink cartridge is stored in an air tight packet. (B) *Lower right*. Once the exposed die has been secured, the stamp maker opens the packet containing the ink cartridge and places it on top of the pad. (C) Using a blunt instrument, the stamp maker applies pressure to the pad. This insures that the ink cartridge is in contact with the exposed pad.

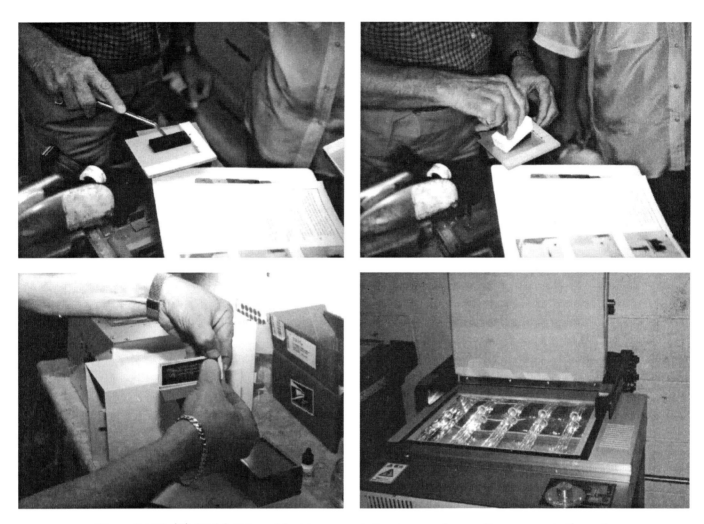

Figure 3.48C. (C) *Top left.* Using a blunt instrument, the stamp maker applies pressure to the pad. This insures that the ink cartridge is in contact with the exposed pad.

Figure 3.49A–B. (A) *Top right.* The stamp mount is snapped into place over the trim ring. (B) *Lower left.* The stamp maker checks to make sure the mount is secure.

Figure 3.50. *Lower right.* The MaxLight Ultra Exposures Unit is the second generation light burst unit marketed by Millennium Marking. This unit uses just one light burst that can be set at varying intensities to seal the background of the porous pad.

THERMAL PRINTER

History

The thermal printer process entered stamp die manufacturing in 1996 with Brother International Corporation's release of the SC-300 followed by U.S. Stamp & Sign's ThermalVision® Printer in 1998 and the Stamp Printer by Trodat in 1999. Brother International discontinued the SC-300 in mid-1999 and

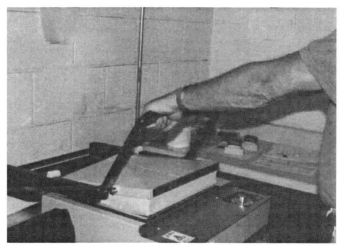

Figure 3.51. *Top left*. The stamp maker places the vellum with the artwork directly on the glass platen. The Mylar is then placed on top of the vellum followed by the unexposed pad.
Figure 3.52. *Top right*. A metal plate is placed on top of the materials and the lid of the unit is closed.
Figure 3.53. *Lower center*. The intensity of the single light burst used to seal the exposed areas of the pad is determined by the size and/or number of pads on the glass platen. The single light burst is triggered when the roll bar on top of the lid is brought forward by the stamp maker.

replaced it with a higher dpi unit, the SC-900, released in August 1999. All four units produce a low or flat die stamp that can be made within minutes.

Thermal Printer Process

U.S. Stamp's ThermalVision® Printer and Trodat's Stamp Printer are the same machine that produce pre-inked stamps using microporous rubber (salt-leached foam) for the die. The stamp maker typesets the text into a PC-com-

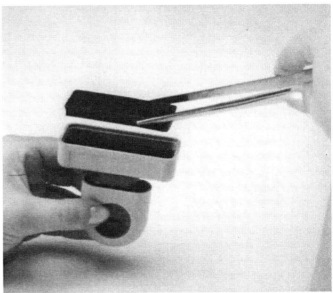
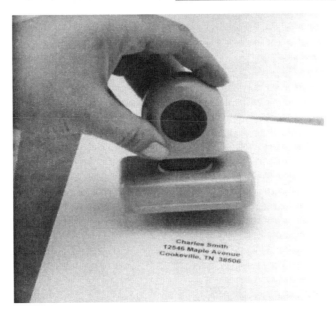

Figure 3.54. *Top left*. The ThermalVision is attached to the computer. The stamp maker typesets the text into a PC-compatible graphics program that instructs the ThermalVision to print the text (Courtesy of Cindy Thomas).

Figure 3.55A–B. (A) *Top right*. The pre-inked die is loaded onto the machine's pallet which is fed through the machine. (B) *Center left*. The thermal head seals the background of the die allowing ink to print only where there is text or graphics (Courtesy of Cindy Thomas).

Figure 3.56A–B. (A) *Center right*. The pre-inked die is removed from the machine's pallet and glued onto the mount. (B) *Lower center*. The stamp is ready for immediate use (Courtesy of Cindy Thomas).

patible graphics program and the program is instructed to print to the ThermalVision® Printer or Stamp Printer machine (Fig. 3.54). The pre-inked die is loaded onto the machine's pallet which is fed through the machine (Figs. 3.55A & 3.55B). Unlike the other thermal units and the light burst units, these two thermal printers do not use a sheet of positive film that is placed on top of the die material. As the pallet goes through the machine, the thermal head seals the background of the die allowing ink to print only where there is text or graphics. The die is then removed from the pallet and glued onto the mount (Figs. 3.56A & 3.56B).[72] Since the die used for these two printers is pre-inked, the stamp is ready for use.

The SC-300 PC is connected to a PC or MAC to create a disposable pre-inked stamp. Brother classifies this stamp as disposable because it cannot be re-inked. The ink is contained in the stamp pad which is a spongy material wrapped with polyester film. The text is typeset on a PC or MAC which instructs the SC-300 to print the text. The text or graphic of the die is created on the stamp pad by the thermal print head perforating the pad creating a silk screen image that allows the ink to exit in the image area only.[73]

HOT STAMPING PROCESS

Hot stamping uses heated type holders containing type-high foundry type or commercially prepared dies. The type or logo to be printed is a reverse image and is loaded into the type holder by the stamp maker who then secures it in the hot stamping machine with set screws. Once the type is electrically heated to the desired temperature, the hot type is pressed against a strip from a roll of plastic and an image in right reading position is melted onto the document or desired item. The plastic is used to create the impression instead of ink. The wood veneer of the mount and handle of a hand stamp is an example of hot stamping. The hot stamping design gives the handle and mount a wood appearance even though they are not made of wood, but expanded extruded PVC.

REFERENCES

1. Miller, Joni K. & Thompson, Lowry: *The Rubber Stamp Album.* New York, Workman, 1978, p. 10.
2. Connecticut Rubber Group: History Information dated 5/17/99 posted on website www.rubber.org/subdiv/ctrg/index.htm.

3. Rivard, Karen and Brinkman, Thomas H.: *The Marking Story.* Evanston, IL, The Marking Device Association, 1968, p.23.
4. Ibid.
5. Ibid.
6. Miller, Joni K. & Thompson, Lowry: *The Rubber Stamp Album.* New York, Workman, 1978, p. 10.
7. Ibid, p. 11.
8. Ibid, p. 14.
9. Ibid, pp. 11-12.
10. Ibid, pp. 12-13.
11. Casey, Maureen, A.: The individuality of rubber stamps. *Forensic Science International, 12:* 134–144, 1978.
12. Murphy, George: Century of progress. *Marking Industry Magazine, 95* (4): 26, 1999.
13. Casey, Maureen, A.: The individuality of rubber stamps. *Forensic Science International, 12:* 134–144, 1978.
14. Jackson, Tom: The millennium remembered. *Marking Industry Magazine, 95* (4): 15, 1999.
15. Murphy, George: Century of progress. *Marking Industry Magazine, 95* (4): 26, 1999.
16. Jackson, Tom: The millennium remembered. *Marking Industry Magazine, 95* (4): 15, 1999.
17. Jackson, Tom: The millennium remembered. *Marking Industry Magazine, 95* (4): 14, 1999.
18. Tanaka, H. & Tanaka, N. Interview.
19. Mergenthaler Linotype Company brochure 138. 04-566-15M.
20. Tanaka, H. & Tanaka, N. Interview.
21. Houston, John B.: President of Carolina Marking Devices, Inc., Charlotte, NC.
22. Mergenthaler Linotype Company Hydraquadder brochure. 760.125.1-D-10X.
23. Houston, John B.: President of Carolina Marking Devices, Inc., Charlotte, NC.
24. Ibid.
25. Casey, Maureen A.: The individuality of rubber stamps. *Forensic Science International, 12*: 134–144, 1978.
26. Ibid.
27. Ibid.
28. Purtell, David: The identification of rubber stamps. Presented at Seminar No. 4, the Royal Canadian Mounted Police, Crime Detection Laboratory, May 1956.
29. Kreeger, Cindy: A comparison of pre-inked stamp processes: gel laser, flashstamp[R] and thermal. *Marking Industry Magazine, 94* (8): 18–21, 1999.
30. Ibid.
31. Ibid.
32. Beagely, Karen and Wettlaufer, Ward: The history of pre-ink production. *Marking Industry Magazine, 94* (8): 22–25, 1999.
33. Ibid.
34. Kreeger, Cindy: More pre-inked stamp history. *Marking Industry Magazine, 95* (4): 20–23, 1999.
35. Beagley, Karen & Wettlaufer, Ward: The history of pre-ink production. *Marking Industry Magazine, 94* (8): 18–21, 1999.
36. Ibid.
37. Kreeger, Cindy: More pre-inked stamp history. *Marking Industry Magazine, 95* (4): 20–23, 1999.
38. Mauro, Michael. M & R Marking Systems. Piscataway, NJ.
39. Video of M & R Marking: Pre-Mix Gel

40. Mauro, Michael. M & R Marking. Piscataway, NJ.
41. Jackson, Coy: Starting a business from scratch. *Marking Industry Magazine, 95* (11): 18–21, 2000.
42. Lowrance, Kenny: Superior Rubber Stamp & Seal Co., Wichita, KS.
43. Lowrance, Kenny: Superior Rubber Stamp & Seal Co.
44. Murphy, George: Century of progress. *Marking Industry Magazine, 95* (4): 26, 1999.
45. Ibid, p. 28.
46. Ibid, p. 28.
47. Griffiths, Gene: Executive Director, Marking Device Association International.
48. Louis Melind Company. An introduction to manufacturing methods for rubber stamps and imprinting plates, undated.
49. Newger, Don: Louis Melind Company. Onarga, IL.
50. Hazen, Tony: Stewart Superior Corporation. Laporte, IN.
51. Berghammer, Willy: The European laser market. *Marking Industry Magazine, 95* (3): 24–26, 1999.
52. Ibid.
53. Griffiths, Gene: Executive Director of the Marking Device Association International. 1999 Interview.
54. Berghammer, Willy: The European laser market. *Marking Industry Magazine, 95* (3): 24–26, 1999.
55. Bosworth, Diane: Laser engraving: to buy or not to buy. *Marking Industry Magazine, 94* (11): 28–30, 1999.
56. Ibid.
57. Collins, William: Vice President of Operations of United RIBtype. Fort Wayne, IN.
58. Bosworth, Diane: Owner of Access Business Solutions, Inc., Hudson, WI.
59. Collins, William: Vice President of Operations of United RIBtype. Fort Wayne, IN.
60. Ibid.
61. Han, Michael. General Manager. Stewart Superior Corporation. Laporte, IN.
62. Cox, Andre: A new laserable polymer material. *Marking Industry Magazine, 95* (3): 46–48, 1999.
63. Newger, Don: Louis Melind Company, Onarga, IL.
64. Kreeger, Cindy: A comparison of pre-inked stamp processes: Gel, laser, flashstamp[R] and thermal. *Marking Industry Magazine, 94* (8): 18–21, 1999.
65. Yuki, Eiji: Product Manager of Stamp Marking Devices. Brother International Corporation. Interview at Comdex, 1998.
66. Brother International Corporation. News release. *Marking Industry Magazine, 95* (6): 41, 2000.
67. Kreeger, Cindy: A comparison of pre-inked stamp processes: gel, laser, flashstamp[R] and thermal. *Marking Industry Magazine, 94* (8): 18–21, 1999.
68. Jackson, Tom: A new pre-inked system bursts onto the scene. *Marking Industry Magazine, 94* (8): 35, 1999.
69. Kelly, Jan Seaman: Flat die stamps: a new technology from brother. *Journal of the American Society of Questioned Document Examiners, 1* (2): 82–87, 1998.
70. Antonio, Ernie. Sales Manager. Millennium Marking Company. Elk Grove Village, IL.
71. Millennium Marking Co. News release. *Marking Industry Magazine, 95* (9): 39, 2000.
72. Kreeger, Cindy: A comparison of pre-inked stamp processes: gel, laser, flashstamp[R], and thermal. *Marking Industry Magazine, 94* (8): 18–21, 1999.
73. Kelly, Jan Seaman: Flat die stamps: a new technology from brother. *Journal of the American Society of Questioned Document Examiners, 1* (2): 82–87, 1998.

Chapter 4

CHARACTERISTICS OF STAMP DIES AND THEIR IMPRESSIONS

IN CHAPTER 2 WE DISCUSSED the classifications of stamps and in Chapter 3 the manufacturing processes of stamps. This chapter will discuss the materials used in each manufacturing process, characteristics of the stamp die based on material, characteristics of the impressions, and any anomalies or defects that can occur either from the manufacturing process or from wear and use.

The classifications of hand stamps and self-inking stamps were discussed in Chapter 2. As you may recall, the only difference between a hand stamp and a self-inking stamp is the placement of the ink source, i.e., the hand stamp uses a separate ink pad while the die and ink pad are in the same container of the self-inking stamp. Both use the same materials for the stamp dies and for that reason, will be grouped together in this chapter.

VULCANIZED RUBBER DIE STAMPS

Characteristics of a Vulcanized Rubber Stamp Die

While conducting research for this book, the author discovered differing terminology between forensic document examiners and members of the stamp manufacturing industry when describing the various parts of the stamp die. Members of the stamp industry refer to the non-print area of the die as the "background" and the term "shoulder" as the foundation or base of the characters of the stamp die.[1] Herbertson refers to the non-print area of the die as the "mat" and for the shoulder, coined the term "riser" to describe "the transition between the printing surface and the lower supporting mat."[2] The differing terminology has been included in order to assist the document examiner in maintaining an understanding of the various areas of the stamp die and in recognizing the area discussed in the available literature.

The die of a vulcanized rubber stamp is opaque and can be any color. A vulcanized rubber stamp can be classified as a hand stamp or a self-inking stamp, but never a pre-inked stamp. Raw rubber, also called molding rubber, is used for vulcanizing and can be used in laser engraving. However, most manufacturers prefer to use laserable rubber for the laser engraving process and use the molding rubber for vulcanization since its chemical makeup has flow agents that allow it to be molded into the nooks and crevices of the embedded image in the matrix board.[3] The die is type high, i.e., has a high relief, and the background of the vulcanized rubber die is smooth and free of any lines. The arrangement of the characters on each line of text is made by the stamp maker in combination with the preference of the customer. Quadding or justification are two terms commonly used when referring to the arrangement of the characters.[4] The three types of quadding are: right quadding (justification), center quadding (justification), and left quadding (justification). As a rule, the line text produced by the Linotype will be center justified because it tends to produce an even impression across the entire length of the stamp. The shoulder is wider at the base than at the top and the outline of the character is even (Fig. 4.1). With magnification, the side view of the shoulder (riser) may have an uneven baseline and a rough texture that resembles the side of a steep mountain.[5]

If individual type (Ludlow or handset) was used to form the text of the die, the outline of the type slugs may be present around the grouping of letters forming the word (Fig. 4.2).

Characteristics of a Merigraph Processed Vulcanized Rubber Stamp Die

A vulcanized rubber stamp manufactured using the Merigraph Process, a sheet of photopolymer with a hardness of 95 durometer, is used instead of Linotype or Ludlow type matrices to make the die text in the Bakelite mold may have one or two distinctive characteristics not found on the dies manufactured using the hot type method. Outline of individual metal slugs will not be present in the Merigraph Process since it is a cold type method and does not use metal type. The individual character produced by the Merigraph Process has a round shoulder, a wider base than that found on a Linotype or Ludlow character, and an irregular outline of the character (Figs. 4.3A, 4.3B & 4.3C). Detailed designs or artwork can be created since the negative is prepared on the computer in the Merigraph Process and the stamp maker is not limited to a set design of letters or numbers as in the hot type processes.

Figure 4.1. *Top left.* ABFDE text on a vulcanized rubber die is produced from a lead slug using the Ludlow.

Figure 4.2A–B. (A) *Top right.* Outline of the individual type may be present on the die if it was produced from a hot type manufacturing process using handset type or Ludlow type. (B) *Lower center.* The outline of the character is straight and has a square-edged shoulder that is wider at the base than at the top.

Characteristics of a Vulcanized Rubber Stamp Impression

Impressions produced by a vulcanized rubber stamp will be influenced by the type of paper, the size of the stamp, the interaction of the ink to the paper, and the individual making the impression. The type of ink, the type of paper, and the material used for the die of the stamp work in concert with each other and affect the quality of the impression. The making of a stamp impression is as individualized as handwriting. An individual tends to use the same 'technique"

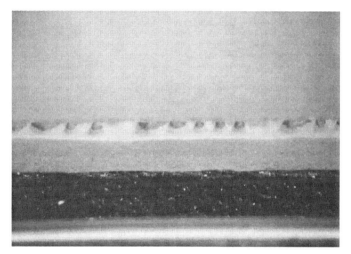

Figure 4.3A–C. (A) *Top left.* A vulcanized rubber die produced using a Merigraph polymer sheet instead of metal type is used to form the stamp text into the Bakelite mold during vulcanization. The characters on the rubber die produced from the Merigraph material differs from those produced from hot type in that the outline of the character is irregular and the side view of the dies reveals round-edged shoulders as shown in Figures 4.3B *(top right)* and 4.3C *(lower center)*.

when making an impression. The two most common causes of a less than perfect stamp impression involve the mechanics of stamping, i.e., failing to hold the stamp correctly creating an uneven impression and hitting the surface with the stamp using too much force causing the stamp to bounce (Fig. 4.4).

The printing characteristics of the vulcanized rubber stamp are similar to the letterpress (relief) printing method. In a properly stamped impression on 20-pound paper, the forensic document examiner will observe the following characteristics (Figs. 4.5A & 4.5B):

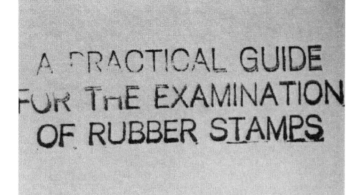

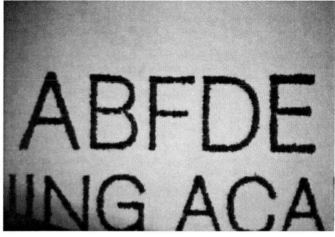

Figure 4.4. *Top left.* This is an impression from vulcanized rubber hand stamp. The shadowing or doubling of a few characters and the printing of the outline of the lead slug were caused by the stamper using too much force during the stamping process. The excess force caused the stamp to bounce while producing the impression (Courtesy of Lamar Miller).

Figure 4.5A–B. (A) *Top right.* This is an impression produced by a vulcanized rubber die manufactured using the Ludlow. Figure 4.5B *(lower center)* is an impression made by a vulcanized rubber die manufactured using the Merigraph process. Even ink coverage with intermittent patchy areas and a ring of ink outlining the character is a characteristic commonly observed in impressions produced by vulcanized rubber dies (Courtesy of Lamar Miller).

- Even ink coverage.
- Ring of ink outlining the individual letter may be observed. This is due to the relief of the print area squeezing the ink out to the edge of the ink line. This effect may not be visible in heavy impressions.
- An absence of an indentation in the ink line.
- Rounded beginning and ending of letters.

- Ink filling in sharp angles and intersection point of two lines.
- Some patchy areas may be observed. This could be caused by combination of factors including the vulcanized rubber die, the ink media, or the type of paper.

Potential Defects on a Vulcanized Rubber Stamp Die

- Vulcanization of the raw rubber requires a set timed exposure to heat and pressure. If the timing is off in either step, it will affect the stamp die. Overheating the rubber can harden the print area of the die causing cracks in the die and decreasing the thickness of the background of the die. Subjecting the die to less than adequate heat and pressure makes it difficult for the stamp maker to separate from the matrix board causing distortion in the print character on the die (Figs. 4.6A & 4.6B). The background of the die is not as pliable as a rubber stamp that received the proper heat and exposure.
- Compromised materials can affect the quality of the die and its life span as a functional stamp. For example, the raw rubber used for vulcanization has a shelf life and if used when it is old, will cause defects such as cracking.
- Air bubbles can occur in the raw rubber if air pockets are present in the material. If exposed during the vulcanization process, the air pocket creates an air bubble (Figs. 4.7A & 4.7B).
- Air bubbles can also occur in one of two steps during the manufacturing process of vulcanization and will cause a non-print area if it is located on the die (Figs. 4.8A & 4.8B). If air is trapped when the matrix board is placed on top of the type slug and then vulcanized, the air bubble is present in the matrix board and every stamp made from that matrix board will have the air bubble in the die. Since multiple stamps can be made from the matrix board with the air bubble, the air bubble would be considered a class characteristic. Air bubbles can also occur during the second step of vulcanization when air is trapped during the positioning of the raw rubber on top of the vulcanized matrix board prior to placement in the heat press. The air bubble will be present only on that one stamp die, therefore, making it an individual characteristic.
- Improper trimming of the background. If the stamp maker cuts the background too close to the print area of the die, part of the slug outline may print due to insufficient support to hold that part of the die in place during stamping (Figs. 4.9A & 4.9B). If too much background is left, the edge of the background may print during the stamping process and be present in the impression.
- Wear on the type. Wear can cause excess rubber or "fins" to appear on the die which will print if located in the print area of the die. Breakdown of the

Figure 4.6A–B. (A). *Top left.* This is a separation of vulcanized rubber from the matrix board after being subjected to less than adequate vulcanization. (B) *Top right.* This is an example of a vulcanized rubber die reflecting the distortion caused by inadequate vulcanization of the rubber.

Figure 4.7A–B. Air bubbles in vulcanized rubber are caused by air pockets present in the material prior to vulcanization. Figure 4.7A *(lower left)* is a side view of the die and 4.7B *(lower right)* is the top view of the background of the die. Numerous air bubbles tend to be present if the source is material compromised by air pockets.

corner of the walls on the type can cause rubber "fins" to appear in the impression (Figs. 4.10A, 4.10B & 4.10C). Casey-Owens reported that type set too loosely is another cause of "printing fins."[6] Wear and continual use can also cause part of the type matrice to not print because the edges of the type have been worn off or the middle has been worn down to the point of being concave instead of flush (Figs. 4.11A, 4.11B, 4.11C & 4.11D).

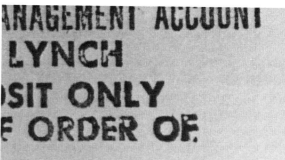

Figure 4.8A–B. (A) *Top left.* This is an example of an air bubble on the printing area of the die. Its source could be an air bubble in the matrix board or air was trapped between the matrix board and the natural rubber prior to the rubber's vulcanization. (B) *Top right.* Air bubble creating a non-print area in the impression (Courtesy of Lamar Miller).

Figure 4.9A–B. (A) *Lower left.* The background was trimmed too close to the "R" causing the bottom of the slug outline of the "F" and the "R" to print as shown in 4.9B *(lower right).*

- Type face damage from constant use and handling. The opportunity for type face damage is greater in the type used for the Ludlow and handset because the type is handled by the stamp maker (Figs. 4.12A & 4.12B).
- Misalignment in the line of text. If the misalignments are large, the source will either be handset type or the Ludlow. The large misalignments will jam in the Linotype machine.
- Typographical errors as a result of the stamp maker misspelling the text. As a general rule, this type of error or defect would be detected during the

Figure 4.10A–C. (A) *Top left*. The type matrice used to make the lead slug of the second "E" created a fin on the bottom. In 4.10B *(top right)* a photo demonstrating the fin on the lead slug "E" was transferred to the embedded image on the Bakelite. In 4.10C *(center left)* a photo is shown of the fin appearing on the rubber die whose text was created from the Bakelite mold.

Figure 4.11A–C. (A) *Center right*. The "I" in this lead slug is concave as a result of long term use of the type matrice. (B) *Lower left*. The concaved image is transferred to the Bakelite mold, which is then transferred to the die shown in 4.11C *(lower right)*.

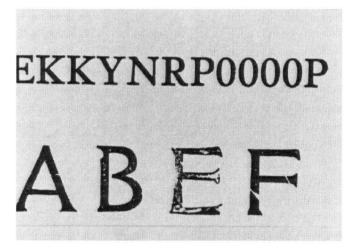

Figure 4.11D. (D) *Top left.* The index of the hand stamp bearing the impression made from the die containing the concaved character. Because the lead slug of the "I" is recessed deeper than the surrounding characters, it creates a non-print area in both the "I" and the "M" (Courtesy of Lamar Miller).

Figure 4.12A–B. (A) *Top right.* This is an example of damaged type face caused by constant use and handling. (B) *Lower center.* The damaged typeface is reflected in the stamp impression (Courtesy of Tobin Tanaka).

proofreading process. However, mail order and Internet stamp businesses are subject to this type of error because the customer has mistyped or misspelled the word. These type of orders are definitely a WYSIWYG.

- Insufficient use of lead spacers. Spacers provide spacing between lines of text to insure proper alignment.
- Improper assembly of the chase. The slugs must be tightly secured to eliminate movement during the vulcanization process. To eliminate movement

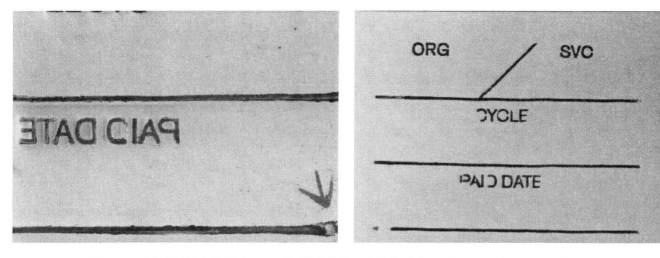

Figure 4.13A–B. (A) *Left*. Defects in the "P," "A," and "D" of "PAID" on a vulcanized rubber die were caused by crushed type. (B) *Right*. Non-print areas in the impression from the defects in the die are shown (Courtesy of Lamar Miller).

of the cast line or lead slugs, the stamp maker will tighten the metal bars bracing the last type slug in the chase.

* Crushed type will create a non-print area in the die (Figs. 4.13A & 4.13B).
* Improper mounting of the die to the die plate. If the die is not aligned parallel to the sponge rubber edge of the mount, the impression will be crooked.
* Poor adhesion of the rubber die to the die plate could result in a portion of the rubber die being distorted as pressure is applied during stamping.
* Dirt and debris on the die can create a non-print area.

Potential Defects on a Vulcanized Rubber Stamp Die Typeset on a Linotype

In addition to the above listed defects, stamp dies produced using the Linotype may exhibit additional defects. The document examiner should keep in mind that if the defect is a result of a malfunctioning Linotype machine, the defect will be common to all the cast lines produced from that machine. The additional potential defects using the Linotype machine are as follows:

* If the heat is not set properly on the Linotype, the type slug will bear areas of pitting and can also cause the character to be fuzzy in appearance. The proper setting should be at 537 degrees (Figs. 4.14A, 4.14B, 4.14C & 4.14D). The defect was caused by underheating at 500 degrees.

Figure 4.14A–D. (A) *Top left*. Pitting of Linotype is slug caused by setting the Linotype at 500 degrees instead of the proper setting of 537 degrees. (B) *Top right*. The pitting and cracking is transferred to the Bakelite mold. The damage to the type is transferred to the rubber die 4.14C *(lower left)* with the end result of the impression containing non-print areas in 4.14D *(lower right)* (Courtesy of Lamar Miller).

- Defective cast lines. The cause may result from errors made by the Linotype operator or from a malfunctioning Linotype machine.
- Improper grinding of the edges of long lines with little text. Stamp makers often grind the outer edges of these long lines to prevent background impressions from printing.
- Errors in spacing resulting in an improper center quad line.

Characteristics of a Vulcanized Rubber Facsimile Stamp

Hand carving was an integral part of the process in the production of a facsimile signature stamp prior to the photopolymer material and the ultraviolet process. For a hand carved stamp, the engraver must carve a series of strokes to capture the appearance of lines naturally crossing when written by a pen. It is very difficult, if not impossible, to achieve the effect of a continuously written crossing line. As a result, all of the gouge cuts appear to be directed from outside points toward the crossing area. The examiner may observe the additional characteristics including unevenness of line edges, unevenness of line thickness, and difficulty of tapering beginning and ending strokes.[7]

The facsimile signature stamp produced from a zinc cut will have a smooth background on the vulcanized rubber die. The signature has a high relief with the outer edges uneven and may even appear to have gouge marks (Figs. 4.15A, 4.15B & 4.15C).

Potential Defects on a Facsimile Signature Stamp Made from a Zinc Cut

The manufacturing defects that can occur in the production process of facsimile signature stamps made from a zinc cut will be the same as those observed in the vulcanized rubber manufacturing defects.

Characteristics of a Laser Engraved Vulcanized Rubber Stamp Die

A few stamp manufacturers may choose to laser engrave the image of the stamp die onto vulcanized rubber instead of using hot type. Since laser engraving adds a step to the production of a vulcanized rubber die, the characteristics of the die remain the same as listed above with the exception of having a smooth background. If the die has been laser engraved, the background will have lines embedded in the background, a telltale sign of laser engraving.

Potential Defects on a Laser Engraved Vulcanized Rubber Die

The defects that can occur during the manufacturing process of a laser engraved vulcanized rubber die are considerably fewer than with a vulcanized rubber die. Printing fins from excess rubber are non-existent from the laser engraving process. Defects that could occur are:

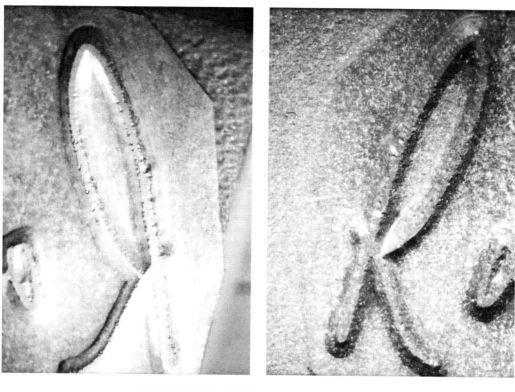

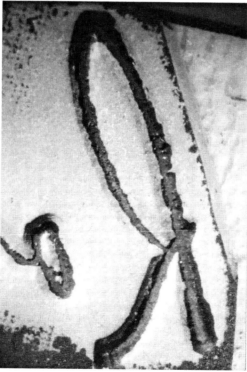

Figure 4.15A–C. (A) *Top left*. This is a zinc cut of a facsimile signature. Note the gouge marks along the character outline and that the character is in wrong reading position. (B) *Top right*. The gouge marks are duplicated in the Bakelite mold (right reading position) and the vulcanized rubber die (wrong reading position) as shown in 4.15C *(lower center)*.

- Air bubbles are still possible if they occurred during the vulcanization process.
- Defects caused by compromised materials.
- Improper trimming of the background can still occur.
- Poor adhesion of the rubber die to the die plate could result in a portion of the rubber die being distorted as pressure is applied during stamping.
- Poor shouldering of the die caused by the laser cutting too much of the rubber background, leaving a shoulder that is too narrow to adequately support the die for an even impression.[8]
- Failure to horizontally align the stamp onto the die plate during gluing will create an impression out of alignment of the baseline on the hosting material.
- Dirt and debris on the die or print area of the stamp.

RIBBED BACK RUBBER TYPE

History

Ribbed back rubber type has been available since the 1940s. It is used for product identification, date coding, general marking applications and can be found in stamp kit sets located at your local office supply store. United RIB-type, Base-Lock, Shoreline, and Griplock are the major manufacturers of ribbed back type who market this type of stamp in kit sets and customized ribbed back rubber stamps for industrial use.

The traditional molding process for ribbed back rubber type uses a master matrix. A cast is made using a master mold, master matrix, and rubber. The elements are vulcanized and the ribs and type are formed in a single cast.[9]

In the late 1990s, most of the major manufacturers started using lasers to "etch" ribbed rubber type. If laser engraving is used, it most likely is applied to the logos and not the individual type of the ribbed back rubber. The ribs and a solid face are cast using the traditional method creating a slab of rubber. The slab of rubber is laser engraved to produce the type.[10]

Characteristics of a Ribbed Back Rubber Stamp Die

Ribbed back rubber type can be made of natural rubber, Buna, PVC, and silicone. Each material has specific applications based on its tolerance to heat or chemical applications. For example, ribbed back rubber type made of natural rubber is for general use and is inked with a water-based ink, whereas silicone is the material of choice for thermal ink transfer printers due to its high heat tolerance.

Figure 4.16. *Left*. A "logo" is a term used for ribbed back rubber type that is a single line of characters molded into one piece.

Figure 4.17. *Right*. This is an example of a self-inking ribbed back rubber stamp using a cylindrical mount. This type of mount is commonly found in industrial settings.

Ribbed back rubber type can be an individual segment of rubber bearing a single character that is arranged on a ribbed (grooved) base mount with other characters to form the die of the stamp, or it can be in the form of a single line of characters molded in one piece called a "logo," which is placed in the grooved mount to form the die of the stamp (Fig. 4.16).[11] The base mount can be flat, rocker bottom, or cylindrical and can be made of rubber, metal, or plastic (Fig. 4.17).

The major manufacturers of ribbed back rubber type follow industry standards for thickness and baseline alignment. Therefore, the ribbed type of one manufacturer will, in most cases, fit the grooved or ribbed mount of a second manufacturer. Due to these strict standards of measurement, it is difficult for small manufacturers to mold ribbed back rubber type because the master molds are very expensive, and the complex molding methods employed require near-perfect conditions in order to achieve the proper alignment and thickness. The industry standard for minimal thickness of ribbed rubber type is .210 inches (± .003).[12]

The forensic document examiner will not be able to determine the manufacturer of a ribbed back rubber stamp from the type size or type style. Due to the competitive nature of the industry, the manufacturers tend to duplicate each other's type size and type style. The industry's standard type size is between 1.59mm (1/16th of an inch) and 28.8mm (15/16th of an inch).

A ribbed back rubber stamp comprised of individual characters will be longer than the same text on a logo or a die manufactured with a different material. This is due to the size and spacing of the individual characters. Each individual character is guillotined from a single cast producing uneven segments since the characters vary in width (Fig. 4.18). Even though the individual segments are guillotined, they are still connected by the seam of the rib. The examiner will observe uneven rubber in the area surrounding the seam when a segment has been pulled off or separated from the strip. Kerning of the letters is used to decrease the space between the cut letters allowing them to set as close as possible to each other. In a single strip, the guillotining may not be a straight line as it may cut so close to the character that the cut line follows the outline of the character.

If the stamp is composed of text using individual segments of ribbed back rubber type, horizontal alignment should be even as the ribbed base mount securely holds the individual segments in place. If a letter is observed to be out of vertical alignment, the letter has been placed in the ribbed mat upside down. The manufacturers designed the characters such as the "I," "N," and "O" to be misaligned vertically if placed on the mat upside down which is reflected in the impression (Figs. 4.19A, 4.19B, 4.19C & 4.19D).

Segmented ribbed back rubber type can be purchased in a kit set as a hand stamp or a self-inking stamp. The set will contain the various characters, appropriate stamp pad, mount with ribbed base mat (for the hand stamp), and tweezers. The tweezers are used to place the individual characters onto the ribbed mat.

Characteristics observed on the die and the mat will provide clues as to the identity of the manufacturer. For all manufacturers, the characters that form the die of the ribbed back rubber stamp are set in relief and the guillotining of some of the segments will appear uneven. The guillotining of the individual rubber segments is done by hand, not by a machine. The cut line may not be straight due to kerning. Due to these two influences, the individual character is not centered in its mat. The cut line of a few segments may appear to curve or follow the outline of the character causing an absence of the background on the one side while the other segments may be surrounded by excess background (Fig. 4.20). The appearance of the curved cut is caused from the type being pressed tight to the side of the blade distorting the rubber prior to cutting. After cutting, the rubber returns to the original shape giving the appearance of a curve in the cut.[13]

United RIBtype uses several different materials to meet specific applications. Natural rubber is for general purpose use and can be gray or red in color with a standard hardness of 55-durometer. A softer durometer setting is available at 30-durometer. Buna is a synthetic rubber, black in color, and recommended for use with oil-based inks. The standard hardness of Buna is 50-durometer, but can also range from 30-durometer to 90-durometer. PVC is a

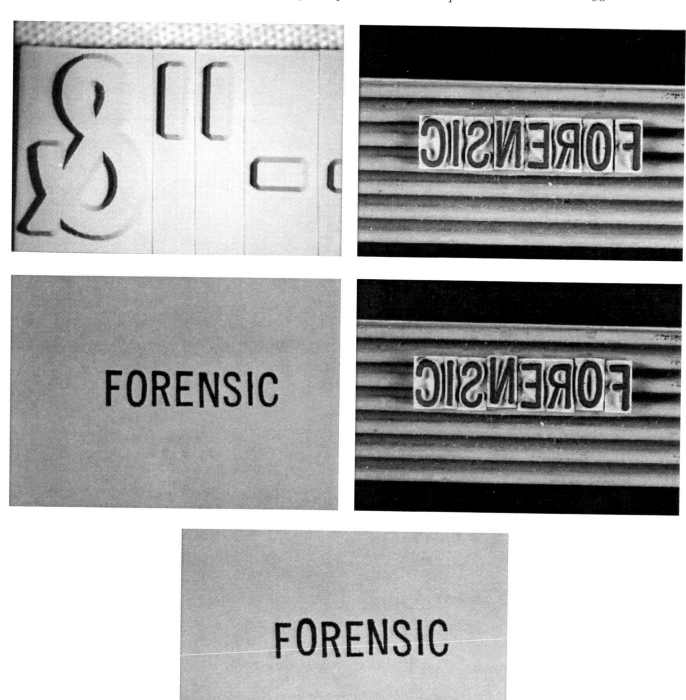

Figure 4.18. *Top left*. Individual characters of ribbed back rubber are guillotined. The segments are uneven because the characters vary in width.

Figure 4.19A–D. (A–B) *Top right* and *center left*. Proper placement of individual segments on the grooved (ribbed) mount and its impression are shown. (C) *Center right*. Improper placement of the "O," and "N" segments on the grooved mount causes a horizontal misalignment of those two characters that is reflected in the impression (D) lower center.

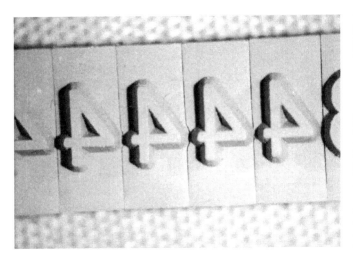 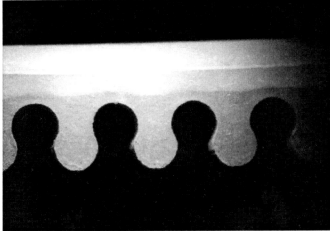

Figure 4.20. *Left.* The guillotine cut is curved between the two "4"s. The process of cutting the rubber into individual segments involves pressing the type tightly against the blade distorting the rubber prior to cutting. After cutting, the rubber returns to its original shape.

Figure 4.21. *Right.* Side view of a rib manufactured by United RIBtype will be round with the seam flush with the rib. The rubber may be in two colors.

flexible plastic material that has greater durability for some applications. PVC is green in color and suitable for the vulcanization process only, not laser engraving. Silicone will be either white or blue in color and its application is for use with thermal ink transfer printers because of its high heat tolerance.[14]

The rib direction on the back of the type and the mat is horizontal unless the customer specifically requests the rib direction to be vertical. The rib will be round with the seam flush with the rib, and may be a different color than the rib characters (Fig. 4.21). The back of the rib mat will not list the manufacturer name.

Microscopic examination of the United RIBtype rubber that has been vulcanized reveals a textured mat. The middle to upper portion of the shoulder and the face of the characters have a smooth surface. Shiny crystals, resembling salt, appear sporadically on the mat and the face of the characters (Fig. 4.22). These crystals are remnants of the crystal talc that covers the matrix board during the manufacturing process to prevent the vulcanized rubber from sticking to the matrix.[15]

Microscopic examination of the United RIBtype rubber that has been laser engraved reveals laser burn lines of varying depths on the background (Fig. 4.23). The shoulder has a smoother appearance than other stamps that have been laser engraved. The lines are very subtle and this subtleness is due to United RIBtype controlling the ramping. The edge of the character is almost straight when the ramping is turned off.[16] Natural rubber and Buna rubber can be vulcanized or laser engraved, while PVC and silicone lend themselves only to vulcanization. Crystal talc is present on the laser engraved rubber but in a lower concentration than that found on the vulcanized ribbed back rubber.

Base-Lock is another large manufacturer of natural rubber or Buna ribbed back type. Base-Lock also markets ribbed back rubber in the company name of Sta-Tite. The most notable characteristic that separates Base-Lock from other manufacturers of ribbed back rubber is that the Base-Lock name is etched in the master mold, and therefore, appears on the back of the rib (Fig. 4.24). Another characteristic with regards to the rib is that Base-Lock's rib is round with the seam protruding above the rib (Fig. 4.25).

Base-Lock uses two processes in the manufacturing of ribbed back rubber. The primary process used by Base-Lock and Sta-Tite is vulcanization using lead type. The outline of the lead slug is evident and the examiner can observe the outline using magnification. If lead type was used, the background, shoulder and face of the character may be mottled due to concentrated areas of talc.

The second manufacturing process of Base-Lock uses the hard polymer as a master matrix. This type of process will not have the outline of the lead slug. Microscopic examination will reveal a background with a smooth surface with a small amount of shiny crystals on the background, shoulder and face of the die of the stamp.

Gripline is the product name of the ribbed back rubber manufactured by Superior Marking Products of Chicago. The type is currently manufactured in Canada using the etched master method, which leaves an image where the character is surrounded by its own outline.

The end of the Gripline rib is shaped like a triangle with a square base (Fig. 4.26). The background, shoulder, and face of the die have a smooth surface that is relatively clear of any debris such as talc crystals.

Shoreline is the final manufacturer to be discussed. Shoreline uses natural rubber that is gray in color with a hardness of 50 durometer. Shoreline also manufactures a deep base-lock (ribbed back) stamp that has a deeper relief. This type of stamp is made of natural rubber, orange in color, and has applications in industrial settings. Shoreline specializes in letter or alphabet kits and one or two line text on the die. It is rare for Shoreline to produce a logo ribbed back stamp.

Shoreline rib has a pointed end shaped like an arrow, but the base is not square like the Gripline rib (Fig. 4.27). The manufacturer name is not etched on the rib mat.

Microscopic examination reveals the outline of the lead slug on the rubber segment, which is the classic characteristic of the Ludlow (Fig. 4.28). The background and shoulder have a textured appearance. Shoreline applies baby powder to aid in the separation of the vulcanized rubber from the matrix board.

Figure 4.22. *Top left*. Shiny crystals observed microscopically on the United Ribtype die are the remnants of crystal talc that is applied to the matrix board prior to vulcanizing the rubber.

Figure 4.23. *Top right*. Light laser engraving lines can be observed on a United RIBtype logo. The depth of the laser engraved lines is determined by ramping. The shoulder of the characters on this laser engraved United RIBtype logo is smooth because of controlling the ramping function of the laser engraver (Courtesy of Lamar Miller).

Figure 4.24. *Lower left*. The name "Base-Lock" can be observed in the grooves of the ribbed back type manufactured by Base-Lock (COSCO) (Courtesy of Lamar Miller).

Figure 4.25. *Lower right*. The side view of a rib manufactured by Base-Lock is shown. The end is round with a protruding seam.

Potential Defects on Ribbed Back Rubber Stamp Die

Vulcanization is part of the manufacturing process of all ribbed back rubber including laser engraved stamps. Heat and pressure are used to "cure" or vulcanize the raw rubber. Defects caused by air bubbles, too much residual

Figure 4.26. *Top left*. This is a side view of a rib manufactured by Gripline (Stewart Superior). The end of the rib is a triangle shape with a square base and shoulders.

Figure 4.27. *Top right*. The side view of a rib manufactured by Shoreline is shown. The end of the rib is shaped like an arrow.

Figure 4.28. *Lower center*. Shoreline uses the Ludlow in the manufacturing of their ribbed back rubber type. The slug outline may be present on the individual rubber segments.

powder or talc on the die, and a compromise in the materials will have the same appearance on the ribbed back rubber as they do on the more mainstream vulcanized rubber stamps. However, due to the physical structure of the rib, the following are additional defects that may be present:

- Excess rubber on the seam area of the rib mat may cause misalignment of the letter which would appear as a horizontal misalignment in the impression.
- Break in the Bakelite mold can cause a failure of a clean separation of the vulcanized rubber from the mold (Fig. 4.29).

Figure 4.29. *Left.* Excess rubber surrounding the outline of the "H" was caused by a crack in the Bakelite mold. The rubber failed to cleanly separate because of the defective mold.
Figure 4.30. *Right.* The vulcanized rubber separated prematurely from the Bakelite mold due to poor type setting.

- Poor type setting in the Bakelite causing the vulcanized rubber to prematurely separate from the mold (Fig. 4.30).

LASERABLE RUBBER STAMPS

History

The history of laserable rubber is rather scant. Common sense dictates that laserable rubber would have entered the marketplace in the 1990s with the increased popularity of the use of lasers in the manufacture of stamps.

The Material Safety Data Sheet lists the chemical name for laser rubber as polyisoprene compound and it differs from raw rubber in that laser rubber does not have the flow agents to allow it to mold into the crevices of a matrix board.[7] Laser rubber is vulcanized by the stamp manufacturer and shipped to the local stamp businesses where it is ready for placement on the laser for stamp die production. Local stamp businesses can purchase non-vulcanized laser rubber and vulcanize it themselves prior to producing the stamp die with the laser.

Figure 4.31. This is an example of laserable rubber with the die laser engraved on a flatbed laser. Laser burn lines are apparent on the background and the shoulder of the character.

Characteristics of a Laserable Rubber Stamp Die Engraved on a Flatbed Laser

The laserable rubber can be red or grey in color and is subjected to vulcanization prior to placement on the laser table. The print area of the die is produced using the laser engraving process and the background reflects the telltale signs of the laser, i.e., burn lines left by the laser beam as it vaporized the background of the slab leaving only the relief of the die. Under magnification, the laser lines are disconnected and aligned vertically and/or horizontally to the die, which has a high relief (Fig. 4.31). The laser fires many times during the engraving process causing the disconnection of the laser lines. The measurement of the number of times the laser fires per inch is referred to the PPI, acronym for "pulses per inch," which is set by the driver.[18] The laser lines can be observed on the shoulder of the printed character or letter, but do not extend onto the face or top of the printed area of the die. The width of the laser lines is dependent upon the dpi of the artwork, therefore, it is an adjustable characteristic. The number of laser lines observed on the stamp's background increases as the dpi of the artwork increases. Other factors that affect the smoothness of the background are the amount of power used, the speed of the engraving, and ramping. The face of the print area of the die will be smooth and free of lines or marks. The edge of the background may contain characteristics of being cut by the laser using the vector cutting feature or manually cut by the stamp maker. Once the die is cut and trimmed, the die is mounted for use as a hand stamp, a self-inking stamp, or a dater.

Characteristics of a Laserable Rubber Stamp Die Engraved on a Rotary Laser

A laserable rubber stamp engraved on a rotary laser has a few characteristics that are unique to a rotary laser. The Louis Melind Company in Onarga, Illinois is currently the only company in the United States that uses a rotary instead of a flatbed laser in the manufacturing of laser engraved stamps.

There are two characteristics unique to a die that has been rotary laser engraved. As stated in the chapter on manufacturing processes, the laser beam moves slowly right to left. When examining the die, the examiner will observe the right side of the letter to be convexed and the left side to be concaved, a trademark of the rotary laser.[19] Another characteristic that can be observed on the rotary laser engraved stamp die will be a "cup" on the left side of the letter where the shoulder meets the background (Fig. 4.32).[20] The exact cause is unknown, but the cup's presence does not interfere with the printing quality of the stamp and does not appear in the stamp's impression. A possible explanation for the cup's formation on the bottom left of the letter is that the rotary laser overcompensates for the power increase to create the shoulder.[21]

Characteristics of a Laserable Rubber Stamp Impression

The impressions produced by a laserable rubber stamp reflect most of the same characteristics as those observed in the vulcanized rubber and photopolymer stamp impressions. Due to the laser's ability to create a die with edge detail that is sharp and well-defined, the impression of a laserable rubber stamp can have square beginnings and endings of characters as opposed to the round beginnings and endings of characters found in vulcanized rubber impressions (Figs. 4.33A & 4.33B).

Potential Defects on a Laserable Rubber Stamp Die

Of all the manufacturing methods, laser engraving produces the fewest defects. Once the artwork has been perfected into a computer layout file and

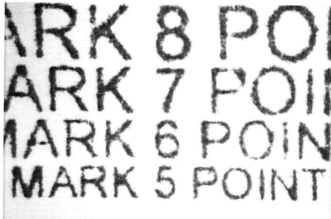

Figure 4.32. *Top left.* Shown here is laserable rubber engraved with a rotary laser. The examiner will observe a cup on the left side of the character if it was engraved with a rotary laser. The cup is located on the lower left side of the "N."

Figure 4.33A–B. (A) *Top right.* An impression from laserable rubber engraved on a flatbed laser is shown. In 4.33B *(lower center)* an impression from laserable rubber is engraved on a rotary laser is shown. The edges of the characters are sharp and well-defined on a laser engraved die.

the slab of material placed in the laser unit, the remaining steps in the production of the die are controlled by the laser engraver and not a human.[22]

- Poor shouldering is one defect that can occur and it can affect the quality of the stamp's impression. Poor shouldering is caused by the laser burning away too much of the shoulder's base, thereby not giving the letter or character the necessary support during printing.[23]

- Air bubbles caused by air pockets in compromised die material.
- Poor adhesion of the rubber die to the die plate could result in a portion of the rubber die being distorted as pressure is applied during stamping.
- Failure to horizontally align stamp die onto the die plate during gluing will create an impression out of alignment with the imagined baseline provided by the mount base.
- Dirt or debris causing a non-print area.

PHOTOPOLYMER STAMPS

Characteristics of a Photopolymer Stamp Die

The die of the photopolymer stamp is translucent, and can be clear, or reflect a tint of yellow, pink, or milky–white, depending upon the tint of the substrate used in the production process. The printed area will have a high relief and the stamp will have a hardness of approximately 40 durometer.

The appearance of the background is dependent upon the method used in the wash to remove the excess polymer. If the polymer was washed out by hand with a brush, the background will contain lines that, at first glance, may be mistaken for laser engraving lines. However, microscopic examination reveals that lines resulting from removing the excess polymer by hand brushing are not uniform in design or pattern (Figs. 4.34A & 4.34B). If an autobrush was used in the washout of the polymer, the lines more closely mimic those found in laser engraving because they are more uniform in size and spacing. However, the examiner will notice the shoulder of the character to be smooth and the background between the characters on the die itself will also be smooth (Fig. 4.35). If the auto jet action of the polymer machine was used to remove the excess polymer in the washout phase, the background will be smooth (Fig. 4.36). The excess background can also be removed by an ultrasonic wash that leaves the background with a bumpy or small pebble appearance (Fig. 4.37).

The photopolymer stamp cannot retain ink; therefore, it cannot be a pre-inked stamp. The photopolymer die can be mounted in a plastic self-inker as a self-inking stamp or it may be a hand stamp mounted on a handle using a separate ink pad. If the stamp is a hand stamp, the die may be attached to a wood or plastic mounting by a self-adhesive cushion or glued to a red or black rubber cushion that has a dipple or textured surface. If the stamp is a self-inking stamp, the stamp die will not be mounted on a cushion, but directly onto the die plate by a strip of two-sided adhesive tape.

Figure 4.34A–B. (A) *Top left* and (B) *Top right*. Pattern is observed on two areas of the background of a polymer die where a hand brush was used to remove excess polymer following the washout step in the ultraviolet process. Using an hand brush to remove excess polymer leaves a pattern or design that lacks uniformity.

Figure 4.35. *Center left*. Pattern is observed on the background of a polymer die where the autobrush is used during the washout step to remove excess polymer. The autobrush is part of the washout system and leaves lines that mimic laser engraving as they tend to be uniform. The examiner will observe the shoulders and background between the characters are smooth and free of lines.

Figure 4.36. *Center right*. A smooth background on a photopolymer die is a characteristic of the excess polymer being removed by an autojet action during the washout step.

Figure 4.37. *Lower center*. A background of a photopolymer die that has a texture or pebble appearance is indicative of the excess polymer being removed by the ultrasonic wash in the washout. Ultrasonic waves are used during the washout to remove the excess polymer.

Figure 4.38A–B. (A) *Left.* Burn lines can be observed in a laser engraved photopolymer stamp. This photo shows the lines as viewed with a microscope and oblique light. (B) *Right.* A weave pattern can be observed on the background of the same stamp using a microscope and transmitted light.

Characteristics of a Laser Engraved Photopolymer Stamp Die

The laser engraved photopolymer stamp has a basket weave pattern that can be observed using oblique or transmitted light on the background of the stamp (Figs. 4.38A & 4.38B). The laser burn lines are present on the shoulder of the characters and letters. With the exception of the weave pattern on the background, the laser engraved photopolymer stamp bears the same characteristics as the traditional type of photopolymer stamp.

Characteristics of the Photopolymer Stamp Impression

The appearance of an impression from a photopolymer stamp, or any stamp for that matter, is dependent upon the relationship of the ink to the paper as well as to the material used for the die. As a general rule, without the stamp, it would be difficult to make a definitive statement as to the type of stamp that made the questioned impression. With the use of a microscope, the document examiner will observe the following characteristics in the impression made by the photopolymer stamp (Fig. 4.39):

- Impression is not as even as that of a pre-inked stamp but similar to the vulcanized rubber. Ink saturation is usually even but may contain patchy areas.
- Squeegee effect is present. This effect, represented by the darker outer edge line, is caused by pressing the inked polymer stamp onto the surface of the paper causing the ink to squeeze out to the edge of the ink line.
- Feathering or "bleeding" around the edge of the letter may be present.
- Uneven outline of the letter.
- Ink filling in sharp angles and points of intersection between lines.
- Round beginnings and endings of letters of text on the die of a photopolymer stamp manufactured by the ultraviolet process.
- Sharp beginnings and endings of letters of text on a laser engraved photopolymer die.
- Absence of an impression (indentation) in the ink line.
- Varying type size and graphics (artwork) can be present in a single line on the die.
- Weave pattern may be present in laser engraved photopolymer (Fig. 4.40).

Photopolymer stamps made in the mid-1980s had difficulty in retaining ink coverage to produce a quality impression. In 1983, Herkt wrote that the plastic polymer had slightly less affinity for inks than rubber, which resulted in a more patchy stamp impression.[24] The combination of the poor quality polymer of the early 1980s and the incompatible inks contributed to the patchy impressions. Today's polymer stamps use quality photopolymer and inks that are more compatible to the polymer creating a stamp impression bearing characteristics found in a vulcanized rubber stamp impression.[25]

Potential Defects on a Photopolymer Stamp Die

The steps taken to produce a photopolymer stamp provide numerous opportunities for defects to occur. Even though the process of producing the photopolymer stamp is foolproof, an inexperienced or inattentive stamp maker can cause a defect in any or all of the steps in the manufacture of the stamp. The following defects may be found on a photopolymer die:

- A defect can occur if any of the materials used in the manufacturing process are compromised. For example, if there is a wrinkle in the plastic Mylar film, the wrinkle will cause a non-print area on the die due to the contact area being deprived of the same amount of ultraviolet light, thereby creat-

Figure 4.39. *Left.* This is an impression from the stamp illustrated in Fig. 4.36. Refer back to Fig. 4.36 and note that the debris outside of the character does not print in the impression.
Figure 4.40. *Right.* Weave pattern may be present in a lightly inked impression made by a laser engraved photopolymer die.

ing a more shallow relief than the rest of the die (Figs. 4.41A & 4.41B). The film must be smooth and free of debris and tears to ensure an adequate and even exposure of ultraviolet light to the photopolymer.

• Thin line strokes found in certain type styles will cause a non-print area in the letter as the thin stroke lacks the necessary density (thickness) to provide enough contrast from the negative to form an adequate amount of polymer in the print area.[26] The petite strokes may be removed with the excess polymer during the washing phase (Fig. 4.42).

• Bad spots or a defect on the negative will cause a non-print area (Figs. 4.43A, 4.43B & 4.43C).

• Air bubbles on the print area of the die will cause a non-print area (Figs. 4.44A & 4.44B). Air bubbles can occur if the liquid polymer is not allowed to settle in the container used for pouring during stamp production. The liquid polymer should be poured into a wide-mouth container the night before to allow the air bubbles to rise to the top and dissipate. Air bubbles can also occur when the liquid polymer is poured onto the plate prior to its curing under the ultraviolet light. The stamp maker must remove the air bubble prior to placement of the substrate in preparation for the curing process.

• The exposure time of the liquid polymer to the ultraviolet light affects the thickness of the relief. Overexposure to the ultraviolet light will produce an impression with a thinner relief. Even though a thinner relief might print, it usually is too shallow and causes a non-print area. If the thinner relief produces a complete impression, the life of the die is shortened because it is not

Figure 4.41A–B. Compromised materials can create defects in the photopolymer die. In 4.41A *(top left)* is a photopolymer die where the "C" does not have the same relief as the surrounding characters on the die. The Mylar plastic film was compromised by wrinkles forming in the film during its manufacturing process. The wrinkles prevented an adequate amount of ultraviolet light to that area of the die. As a result, the affected area has a shallow relief compared to the rest of the die. (B) *Top right.* Impression from the die demonstrating the effect of the wrinkle through the die. The "T" in "Notary," part of the "f" in "of" and the "C" in "Clark" did not print due to lacking the same relief as the rest of the text.

Figure 4.42. *Center left.* The ascending loop of the "J" and the top of the "A" did not form on the photopolymer die during the ultraviolet process. Lack of stroke density (thickness) is the cause for the incomplete stroke formation. The cured polymer in the lighter stroke area of the letters may not have the density and may be removed along with the excess polymer (Courtesy of Lamar Miller).

Figure 4.43A–C. (A) *Center right.* A negative with bad spots is shown. For some unknown reason, the negative failed in capturing the complete text from the vellum. (B) *Lower left.* The bad spots will be reflected in the photopolymer as non-print areas. (C) *Lower right.* If significant in size and location, the non-print area that is caused by any defect in the negative will appear in the impression.

Figure 4.44A–B. (A) *Top left.* This figure shows an air bubble located in the staff of the "L." (B) *Top right.* The air bubble is present in the impression and matches its source in size, shape, and location.

Figure 4.45A–B. (A) *Lower left.* Excess polymer not removed during the washout step will remain on the die and be reproduced in the impression shown in 4.45B *(lower right).* Also note the debris that extends outside of the characters "97" is not reproduced in the impression.

as sturdy as a properly exposed stamp die and is subject to breakdown due to wear.[27]

- Excess polymer outside of the character or text. The presence of the excess polymer is either due to not being removed during the washout or the area was exposed to the ultraviolet because of a problem negative (Fig. 4.45A & 4.45B).
- Poor adhesion of the polymer die to the die plate could result in a portion of the die being distorted as pressure is applied during stamping.

- Failure to horizontally align stamp onto the die plate during gluing will create an impression out of alignment with the imagined baseline provided by the mount base.

BATES NUMBER MACHINE

Characteristics of the Bates Number Machine Stamp Die

The Bates Number Machine is a manual paginator frequently used to number documents (Fig. 4.46). It is classified as a self-inking stamp since the ink pad is located in the chamber of the machine (Fig. 4.47). This machine is comprised of an oil-based ink cartridge and six independent rotating wheels of metal numbers each bearing the numbers 0 through 9 (Fig. 4.48). The rotating wheel can only rotate in one direction to position the desired number. Once the metal number is positioned properly, a click can be heard signaling that the number has locked into position. The printing area of this stamp always reflects the six positions. Therefore, if the user desires to stamp the number 300, the Bates Stamp rotating wheel will be set at 000300, which will be reflected in the impression.

Four numbering functions are present on the Bates Number Machine (Fig. 4.49). To achieve a numbering function, the user can choose one of the following: repeat position that allows the user to repetitively stamp the same number; duplicate position that allows machine to automatically advance to the next number after every set of two stamp impressions; consecutive position whereby the machine automatically advances to the next number following each stamping; and triplicate position whereby the machine automatically advances to the next number after every set of three stamp impressions.[28]

Characteristics of Bates Number Machine Stamp Impression

Conditions for producing impressions using metal stamps must be more rigid than those found in other types of stamp dies. The following characteristics can be observed in a properly executed impression from a Bates Number Machine (Figs. 4.50A & 4.50B):

- Even ink coverage.
- Clean and concise edge detail.

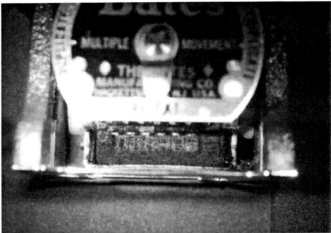

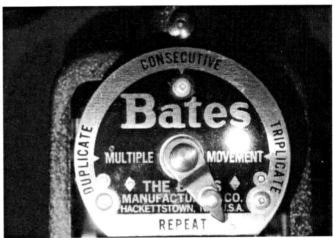

Figure 4.46. *Top left.* The Bates Stamp is a manual paginator used to number documents. This is the type of stamp generally used by attorneys and court reporters to number documents.

Figure 4.47. *Top right.* The Bates Stamp is a self-inking stamp that has a small ink pad containing an oil-based ink in the machine's chamber (Courtesy of Diane Tolliver).

Figure 4.48. *Lower left.* Six independent rotating wheels of metal numbers comprise the die surface of the Bates Stamp. Each wheel contains a set of numbers from "0" to "9" (Courtesy of Diane Tolliver).

Figure 4.49. *Lower right.* Consecutive, repeat, duplicate, and triplicate are the four numbering functions present on the Bates Stamp (Courtesy of Diane Tolliver).

- Bleeding of ink through the paper. This is due to an oil base ink being used with metal type.
- Absence of indentation.

The metal die by its very nature is not flexible, and therefore, the quality of the impression is affected by a number of factors. These factors are listed below, but should not be considered defects as the poor quality of the impression is due to the operator, and not a defect on the stamp die.

- Lack of cushioning underneath the document being stamped can create an incomplete impression (Fig. 4.51).
- Floor of the stamp not flush with the plane of the receiving surface of the document can create an incomplete impression. Improper seating of the individual wheels will cause a partial impression of the affected number (Fig. 4.52).
- Movement of the stamp during stamping can cause smearing of the numbers.

PRE-INKED STAMPS

Characteristics of a Pre-Mix Gel Stamp Die

The gel die is a high relief die and will be glued directly onto the stamp base mount. The container housing the die can be metal or plastic, and may or may not have an adjustable mount. The container will have a lid to cover the gel die to prevent undesired inking and to protect the gel die from debris or damage (Fig. 4.53). Oil-based ink is microencapsulated in the pre-mix gel, therefore eliminating the need for a separate ink pad.

The Apple Stamp

Stamp manufacturing is a thriving business worldwide. Even though the majority of cases submitted to an American document examiner will involve a stamp made in the United States, the author felt the Apple Stamp should be included in this book because of its differing characteristics.

Apple Stamp is a pre-inked gel stamp marketed by Lee Shing Stamp Limited in Hong Kong. The company started marketing their pre-inked system in 1992 with primary distribution to most Asian countries. Lee Shing Stamp Limited began marketing the Apple pre-inked stamp mount in 1998 and planned on distributing this stamp in North America in late 2000. Two physical characteristics separate this pre-inked stamp from those made in the United States: the first is the height of the relief is 1.58mm as opposed to the normal height of 1.43mm or less; the second most noticeable characteristic is that the die and die plate are the same size (Fig. 4.54).[29] A document examiner will notice that American stamps tend to be trimmed closer to the die than the Apple Stamp and the die plate is generally larger than the stamp.

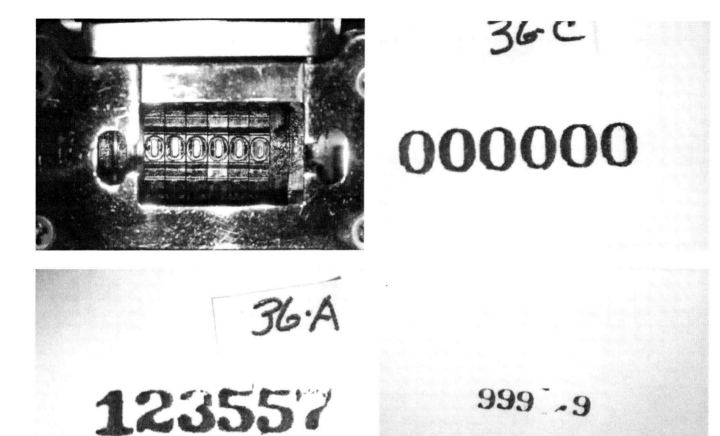

Figure 4.50A–B. (A) *Top left.* Setting of the rotating wheels on the Bates Stamp is shown. (B) *Top right.* This is an impression made from the Bates Stamp at the (B) proper setting (Courtesy of Diane Tolliver and Lamar Miller).
Figure 4.51. *Lower left.* Lack of a cushion underneath the document hosting the impression can affect the quality of a Bates Stamp impression (Courtesy of Diane Tolliver and Lamar Miller).
Figure 4.52. *Lower right.* Partial impression will occur if the six individual wheels of the Bates Stamp are not flush with the plane of the host material. A partial impression can be caused by a few of the individual wheels not being properly seated.

Lee Shing Stamp Limited manufactures pre-inked stamps made of pre-mixed gel and vulcanized rubber stamps for hand or self-inking stamps. All stamps manufactured will have a small sticker labeled "Ref. No." attached to the stamp container (Figs. 4.55A & 4.55B). The reference number will be assigned to one production run of stamps that may be comprised of twenty separate orders. This reference number can be used by the stamp customer to

Figure 4.53. Here are three different styles of containers for pre-inked stamps. Whether the container is plastic or metal, it will have a cover to protect the pre-inked die from contaminants and undesired inking.

reorder a stamp. It can also be used by the document examiner to determine who purchased the stamp and when it was made. The company only needs to know the text to determine which stamp the customer ordered.

Lee Shing Limited also uses a track and trace number system that records who ordered the stamp, the type of stamp, and the date of production. The track and trace number system uses a barcode to track the production of the stamp. Customers are given the barcode number on their invoice and can use the barcode number when reordering the stamp.[30]

Characteristics of a Gel Stamp Impression

The impression from a gel stamp will bear the following characteristics (Figs. 4.56A & 4.56B):

- Clean and concise edge detail.
- Even ink saturation throughout the individual characters.
- Absence of a heavier ink line on the inside or outside of letter form.
- Feathering or bleeding of ink may be observed on the edges of the letter.
- Rounded beginnings and endings of letters.

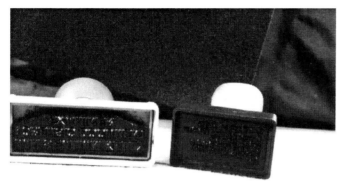

Figure 4.54. The stamp on the right is a gel stamp by Apple Stamp. The die and background fits the die plate. The stamp on the left is a gel stamp that has been trimmed and does not cover the die plate.

Figure 4.55A–B. (A) *Top right.* Stamps from Apple Stamp have a small sticker labeled "Ref. No." on the container or handle. (B) *Lower center.* The reference number is located on the top of the handle on the Apple pre-inked stamp. This reference number can assist in tracking down the individual who ordered the stamp and the purchase date of the stamp.

- An absence of an impression (indentation) in the ink line.
- Text with small type may be blurred and slightly distorted.
- Oil-based ink will bleed through the paper.

Potential Defects on the Gel Stamp Die

- Air bubbles can occur on the relief of the gel stamp die. This will cause a non-print area in the impression (Figs. 4.57A & 4.57B).

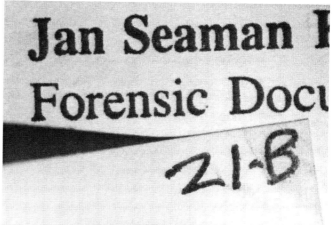

Figure 4.56A–B. (A) *Left.* An impression made from a pre-mixed gel stamp manufactured by a U.S. manufacturer is shown. (B) *Right.* This is an impression made from a pre-mixed gel stamp manufactured by Apple Stamp. An impression from a gel die stamp will have clean and concise edge detail, even ink saturation throughout the characters, and some feathering of ink may be observed (Courtesy of Lamar Miller).

- Letters can break off.
- Debris not removed from die can cause a non-print area (Figs. 4.58A & 4.58B).
- Poor adhesion of the die to the die plate could result in a portion of the die being distorted as pressure is applied during stamping.
- Failure to horizontally align stamp to the edge of die plate during gluing will create an impression that is out of alignment (Figs. 4.59A & 4.59B).

Characteristics of a Foam and Powder Stamp Die

The foam and powder pre-inked stamp has a high relief die with a clean and concise shoulder. The die and the background are saturated with either an oil-based or water-based ink. Since the background is viewed as an ink reservoir, it is usually not trimmed as close to the die (relief) as found in other manufacturing processes. The die is glued directly onto the die plate and the stamp has an adjustable mount.

Nitrile-butadine rubber (NBR) and PVC are the materials used in the foam and powder material of pre-inked dies. The nitrile-butadine rubber will be beige in color and is generally pre-inked with a water-based ink. The background has a shiny, grainy appearance resembling foam, and if the stamp is laser engraved, the characters are sharp with well defined shoulders.

The PVC material is blue in the United States, orange in Europe, and green in Canada. The PVC pre-inked stamp uses a fast drying or oil-based ink

Figure 4.57A–B. Air bubbles can occur in one of two stages in the vulcanization process of pre-mixed gel stamp dies. (A) *Top left*. An air bubble is located on the "O" of Metro on the gel die. (B) *Top right*. The air bubble created a non-print area in the impression.

Figure 4.58A–B. Debris such as a piece of fiber can cause a non-print area on the die if not removed. (A) *Center left*. This shows the placement of the debris and, in 4-58B *(center right)*, reflects the non-print area on the impression.

Figure 4.59A–B. (A) *Lower left*. This is an example of stamp die that is not horizontally aligned with the stamp mount. This misalignment causes the impression to deviate from the baseline. (B) *Lower right*. The impression produced from the stamp in (A) is shown. The right side of the text begins to move upward away from the baseline because it is aligned closer to the stamp mount than the left side of the die (Courtesy of Lamar Miller).

and does not lend itself to laser engraving.[31] Under magnification, the die has a shiny, grainy appearance and resembles foam or a cushion (Fig. 4.60).

Characteristics of a Foam and Powder Stamp Impression

The characteristics of an impression produced by a foam and powder die will bear the same characteristics as those found in the other pre-ink stamps with a relief die (Fig. 4.61).

Depending upon the type of material used for the foam and powder, the ink can be either oil-based or water-based. If the foam and powder material used is PVC, the ink will be oil-based. If an oil-based ink is used, feathering may be slightly heavier around the edges of the letter than that found in other pre-inked stamps.

If the die has been subjected to the extra step of laser engraving in order to produce the characters or artwork on the die, the edge detail will be sharp and clear.

Potential Defects on a Foam and Powder Stamp Die

The foam and powder material does not lend itself to many defects. Due to the nature of the materials used, air bubbles should not occur.

- A non-print or void area can occur if the slab is removed from the matrix board too soon.
- If the adjustable mount is not properly aligned, part of the background may print along with the relief of the die. Proper alignment of the adjustable mount allows for only the relief (die) to make contact with the printing surface.
- Poor adhesion of the die to the die plate could result in a portion of the die being distorted as pressure is applied during stamping.
- Failure to horizontally align stamp to the edge of the die plate during gluing will create an impression that is out of alignment.
- Debris on the die can cause a non-print area.

Characteristics of a Salt-Leached Rubber Stamp Die

Salt-leached rubber, also called salt-leached foam, is black in color (Fig. 4.62). Depending upon the manufacturer, a pre-inked die made from this material may be glued directly onto the die plate or secured by a retainer ring. Retainer rings are replacing glue as a means to secure the die to the base of the stamp mount. The retainer ring snaps inside the mount eliminating the need to glue the die to the die plate. X-Stamper[®32] and M & R Marking Systems are

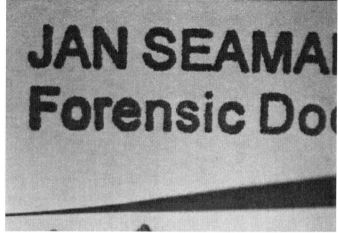

Figure 4.60. *Left.* The pre-inked die made from foam and powder has a shiny, grainy appearance and resembles a cushion (Courtesy of Lamar Miller).

Figure 4.61. *Right.* This impression from a foam and powder die made from PVC. The die from the PVC material is vulcanized and reflects the characteristics commonly observed in the pre-mixed gel die impressions (Courtesy of Lamar Miller).

two manufacturers that use retainer rings.[33] The stamp die will be housed in a plastic container with an adjustable mount and a cover to protect the die.

Microscopic examination reveals the burn lines left by the flatbed laser engraver on the shoulder of the character and the background (Fig. 4.63A & 4.63B). As we discussed in the Chapter 3, the burn lines of the laser are determined by the PPI. The laser burn lines are close giving the background of an X-Stamper stamp a textured appearance (Fig. 4.64). The background of the stamp can vary in thickness. For example, Trodat's salt-leached rubber stamp has a very thick background whereas the same type of stamp from M & R Marking Systems is thinner.

Characteristics of a Salt-Leached Rubber Stamp Impression

An impression made from a salt-leached rubber stamp has a few characteristics that separate it from an impression made by a vulcanized rubber or photopolymer stamp. The characteristics commonly observed in a salt-leached rubber stamp impression are (Fig. 4.65):

• Even ink saturation.
• Absence of darker outer edge line.
• Outline of letter is fairly even.

Figure 4.62. Salt-leached foam, also called salt-leached rubber, is black in color and used as die material for pre-inked dies.

- More feathering or bleeding of ink around the letters may be present than that found in the gel stamp impression or other pre-inked stamp impressions. This is due to the salt-leached rubber having larger pores than gel (Fig. 4.66).
- Sharp beginning and ending of letters. This is due to the laser engraving process as it is able to create images in fine detail.
- Absence of an indentation in the ink line.
- Bleeding of ink through the paper if oil-based ink is used.

Potential Defects on a Salt-Leached Rubber Stamp Die

- Poor shouldering caused by the laser vaporizing too much of the background material at the base of the letter or character. Poor shouldering will cause an impression that lacks clear definition.[34]
- If the ink was not vacuumed in and the excess ink extracted properly, the ink will not flow evenly. This will cause uneven ink coverage in the impression.
- Poor adhesion of the die to the die plate could result in a portion of the die being distorted as pressure is applied during stamping.
- Failure to horizontally align stamp to the edge of the die plate during gluing will create an impression that is out of alignment with the imagined baseline

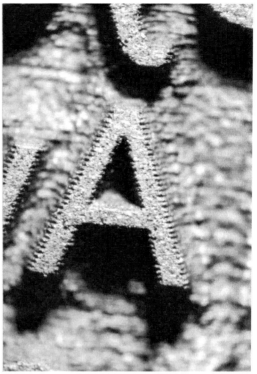

Figure 4.63A–B. (A) *Top left*. Burn lines created during the laser engraving process can be observed on the background of the die. (B) *Top right*. Burn lines are present on the shoulder of the die. Figure 4.64. *Lower center*. The background of an X-Stamper die has a textured appearance due to the close proximity of the burn lines to each other.

 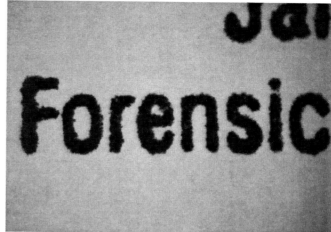

Figure 4.65. *Left.* The impression from a die made of salt-leached rubber will have even ink saturation, absence of the darker outline, sharp beginning and ending of letters, and ink may bleed through the paper since it is an oil-based ink.

Figure 4.66. *Right.* More feathering or bleeding of ink around the characters may be present than those found in a gel die stamp. The pores of salt-leached rubber are larger than the gel which can cause the additional feathering.

provided by the mount base. Stamp mounts using a retainer ring will not be misaligned.

- Defects resulting from compromised die material. For example, air bubbles caused by air pockets in the salt-leached rubber slab (Fig. 4.67A & 4.67B).
- Debris not removed from the die (Figs. 4.68A & 4.68B).

Characteristics of Light Burst Technology Stamp Die

The die of the light burst technology stamp will either have a low or no relief die (Figs. 4.69A & 4.69B). Due to exposure to the Xenon flash, the background is dry and free of ink. The ink is oil-based and exits the stamp through the relief (die) area only. Brother's Stampcreator Pro produces an image at 600 dpi using an oil-based ink that is pigment based instead of dye.[35] The ink was originally in three different colors, black, blue, and red. A fourth color, green, entered the market in mid-1999. Millennium's MaxLight uses an oil-based ink in five different colors, black, blue, red, green, and purple. The stamp die and background cover the die plate of the container (Fig. 4.70). The container will be plastic with a cover to protect the stamp, and neither manufacturer uses an adjustable mount (Fig. 4.71). The size of the stamp will vary among manufacturers. For example, Brother's Stampcreator Pro can make eleven different stamp sizes and Millennium's MaxLight initially could make six. As of

Figure 4.67A–B. (A) *Top left.* Air pockets exposed during the laser engraving of salt-leached rubber creates air bubbles that, if large enough, are reflected in the impression as shown in 4.67B *(top right).*

Figure 4.68A–B. (A) *Lower left.* Debris not removed during the wash of the salt-leached rubber creates a non-print area in the impression shown in 4.68B *(lower right).*

February 2001, Millennium's MaxLight pre-inked stamp is available in ten sizes.

Characteristics of a Light Burst Technology Stamp Impression

The characteristics of an impression made from a stamp manufactured using the light burst technology are the same as the other pre-inked stamps (Figs. 4.72A, 4.72B & 4.72C). The document examiner will find, depending upon the type style, the first stamps manufactured by light burst technology produce letters with round edges. The lack of sharpness of the character's edge

Figure 4.69A–B. A die manufactured using light burst technology will have a low or no relief die. (A) *Top left*. This is a flat die from Brother's Stampcreator Pro. Figure 4.69B *(top right)* is a flat die from U.S. Stamp/Identity Group's FlashStamp (Courtesy of Lamar Miller).

Figure 4.70. *Lower left*. The die and background of a flat die stamp covers the die plate and is secured by a retainer ring.

Figure 4.71. *Lower right*. The container of a flat die stamp will resemble a self-inking stamp container. The outside shell is plastic and a cover attaches to the bottom of the container to protect the die. From left to right, the first container is the FlashStamp from U.S. Stamp/Identity Group; the second is the MaxLight stamp from Millennium; the third is the first generation light burst stamp from Brother's Stampcreator Pro; and the fourth is the second generation light burst stamp produced from the revised Stampcreator Pro Unit. The second generation Stampcreator Pro stamp containers come in a variety of bright translucent colors. U.S. Stamp/Identity Group market the only containers of light burst stamps with adjustable mounts.

line is due to the strength of the light burst. The initial series of stamps made by Brother's Stampcreator Pro reflected this characteristic. Brother released an improved version of the Stampcreator Pro light burst unit on May 1, 2000.

The newer units contain an improved thermal ink ribbon that allows the unit to produce a stamp with sharper edges (Fig. 4.73).[36] The plastic housing of the improved stamp will differ from the original SC 2000 stamps because it is housed in a bright translucent color.

Oil-based ink is the ink media used to produce the light burst stamp impression. The ink reservoir can either be in the pad (FlashStamp and Max-Light) or is stored behind the die inside the mount base (Stampcreator Pro). In addition to total ink saturation in the text, the oil-based ink bleeds through the paper (Fig. 4.74).

All of the light burst stamps can produce approximately 50,000 impressions before requiring re-inking. A characteristic of the stamp running out of ink will be the lack of even ink coverage throughout the characters on the die. The examiner may observe one or two characters having diminished ink saturation while the surrounding characters are evenly and heavily saturated with ink (Fig. 4.75). Once the ink reserve has been replenished, the die will again produce impressions that are heavily and evenly inked throughout.

The text will appear round and lack sharp edges in smaller type sizes. The majority of stamps have difficulty producing a sharp image in an impression comprised of very small type.

Removal of unwanted characters or sealing micropores that should have been sealed during the production process can be achieved by using heat to seal the open micropores with a heat pen (Fig. 4.76).

Potential Defects on a Light Burst Technology Stamp Die

The defects are minimal in the light burst technology process. Possible defects that a document examiner might observe are:

• Inadequate pressure applied to the foam pad during the light bursting process causes blushing or shadowing in the background of the stamp. Blushing of ink occurs because the micropores in the background aren't sealed allowing ink to exit (Fig. 4.77).
• Overexposure causes a partially faded impression or a non-print area. The overexposure can be caused by too many light burst exposures or failure of the stamp maker to replace the acrylic plate (original MaxLight units). The acrylic plate retains heat after continuous use, i.e., three sets of exposures in five minutes, therefore, the stamp maker should change the plate frequently when making numerous stamps.[37] If the acrylic plate is hot, the heat from the acrylic plate will pre-heat the die prior to the light burst exposures, causing the toner to melt allowing the light burst to penetrate the toner area (Figs. 4.78A & 4.78B).

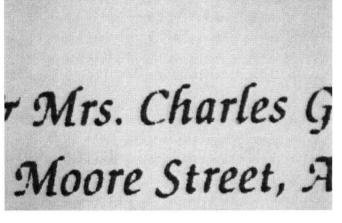

Figure 4.72A–C. Impressions made from flat die stamps manufactured using light burst technology bear the same characteristics of more conventional manufactured pre-inked dies. (A) *Top left*. This is an impression from U.S. Stamp/Identity Group's FlashStamp. Figure 4.72B *(top right)* is an impression from Brother's Stampcreator Pro. (C) *Center left*. An impression from Millennium's MaxLight is shown (Courtesy of Lamar Miller).

Figure 4.73. *Center right*. This impression is from Brother's second generation Stampcreator Pro. This impression contains sharp edge detail and the ink saturation is heavier (Courtesy of Lamar Miller).

Figure 4.74. *Lower center*. The backside of a sheet of paper reflects the bleed through of ink from an impression produced by the MaxLight pre-inked stamp. This light burst stamp uses an oil-based ink which bleeds through the paper (Courtesy of Lamar Miller).

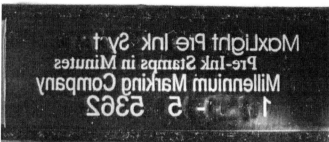

Figure 4.75. *Left.* Variation of ink saturation within the characters on a light burst die stamp is indicative of the stamp running out of ink (Courtesy of Lamar Miller).

Figure 4.76. *Right.* A hot pen can be used to seal areas on a flat die stamp to prevent the exiting of ink from the micropores that comprise undesired text. In this photo, the micropores comprising the hyphen between the "e" and the "I" in Pre-Ink on the first line as well as the two "e"s and the "m" in System have been sealed with a hot pen. Part of the phone number in the last line has also been sealed. With the hot pen, part of the text can be sealed eliminating its appearance in the impression (Courtesy of Lamar Miller).

- Debris extending from the character into the background on the die may print (Fig. 4.79).
- A defect in the master image on the draft sheet (the film positive) will be reflected on the stamp die (Figs. 4.80A & 4.80B).
- Use of positive film more than once. The positive film is designed for one use only. More than one use will cause the letter to bloat or fatten.
- Dirt or debris on the plastic film or the unexposed porous die will create an over-print area. The plastic film and the pad both generate static and should be checked prior to placement in the light burst unit (Figs. 4.81A, 4.81B, 4.81C & 4.81D).[38]

Characteristics of a Thermal Printer Stamp Die

The SC 300 PC and the SC 900 thermal printer stamps manufactured by Brother use a hard surface pad lapped by plastic film.[39] The die is a low or no relief die with the background dry and free of ink. Using oblique lighting, the examiner will observe small holes in the text area of the die (Figs. 4.82A & 4.82B). The thermal head uses silk screen technology by puncturing the pad

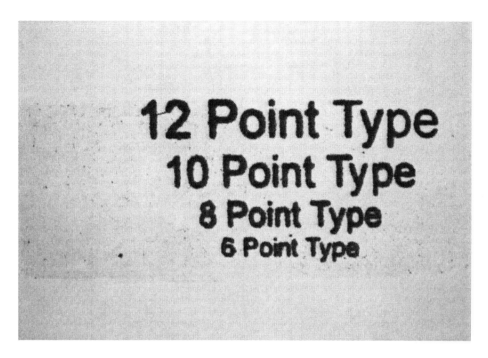

Figure 4.77. Blushing or shadowing is characterized by the presence of light inking in the background of the impression. Blushing in a flat die stamp is caused by inadequate pressure applied to the foam pad during the light burst process preventing the micropores from closing (Courtesy of Lamar Miller).

in the text area allowing ink to exit the pad only through the open micropores. The SC 300 PC has a 180 dpi thermal head and the SC 900 has a 360 dpi thermal head. The ink source is in a bag located inside the base mount. When the handle is locked into position, the bottom of the ink sack is punctured, allowing the ink to exit the open micropores in the pad. This type of stamp is considered a disposable pre-inked stamp. The stamp die is the same size as the die plate and can be found in five different sizes. The container is plastic, has a cover to protect the die, and the mount is not adjustable (Fig. 4.83).

The ThermalVision Printer by U. S. Stamp and Trodat's Stamp Printer produce a low or no relief stamp die with the background dry and free of ink (Fig. 4.84). Porous foam material is used as the material for the die. The thermal printer seals the micropores outside of the text area to create the background. The container is plastic with a handle that is round at the top. The stamp die and background are the same size as the die plate and with an adjustable mount.

Figure 4.78A–B. Overexposure of the flat die is characterized by a partially faded impression or a non-print area. This can occur in the MaxLight Light Burst Units that use an acrylic plate. Numerous stamp runs causes the acrylic plate to become hot. Failure to replace the overheated acrylic plate will cause the toner on the positive to melt which allows the light burst to penetrate that area of the die (Courtesy of Lamar Miller).

Figure 4.79. Debris extending from the print character into the background on a flat die stamp will appear in the impression.

Characteristics of a Thermal Printer Stamp Impression

The impressions produced from any of the thermal printer stamps reflect some of the characteristics commonly found in the more conventional pre-inked stamps. There will be some bleeding through the paper because the ink is oil-based. Due to different materials and mechanics each manufacturer employs in their thermal printer units, the characteristics of the impression differ depending on the unit used. For this reason, the characteristics of each impression are discussed below according to the type of thermal printer.

The Brother SC 300 PC stamp provides one of the most unique characteristics found in the impression. It is safe to say the pattern observed in a properly inked impression from the SC 300 PC is unique, at least at this writing, because it is the only hand stamp that makes the dot matrix pattern with no indentation (Fig. 4.85A & 4.85B). Even though it is the only hand stamp to produce an impression with a dot matrix pattern, the Reiner Multi-Printer is an electronic stamp unit that also produces a stamp impression in a dot matrix pattern. However, the dot matrix impression produced by a Reiner Multi-Printer is indented into the paper.

The dot matrix pattern observed in the SC 300 PC impression will vary according to the type size of the text. As the type size becomes smaller, the dot

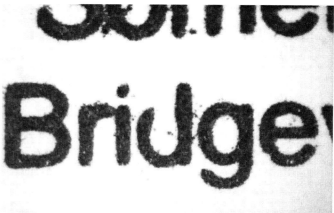

Figure 4.80A–B. (A) *Top left*. A defect in the master image caused a non-print area on the flat die. The top of the "b" did not close. (B) *Top right*. The defect is reproduced in the impression.

Figure 4.81A–D. An overprint area can be caused on a flat die stamp if there is dirt or debris on the unexposed porous pad or the plastic film. An example of this type of defect can be seen in 4.81A *(center left)* which is the flat die and 4.81B *(center right)* its impression. The circle above the "M" and the incomplete closure of the "a" in "Examiner" were caused by debris on either the pad or plastic film. Static causes the debris to gravitate to these two materials. A second stamp die shown in 4.81C *(lower left)* reflects a different defect caused by debris on the pad or plastic film prior to exposure to the light burst. (D) *Lower right*. The defect is reflected in the impression and is individual in nature (Courtesy of Lamar Miller).

Figure 4.82A–B. The thermal stamp printers manufactured by Brother International Corporation create the text of the die by puncturing the pad to allow ink to exit the open micropores. The die is flat and the text area resembles a dot matrix type pattern. (A) *(top left)* is the flat die of a Brother SC 300 PC which makes impressions at 180 dpi, and Figure 4.82B *(top right)* is the flat die of a Brother SC 900 which makes impressions at 360 dpi. The ink is stored in a sack above the mount. The SC 300 PC is considered a disposable pre-inked stamp while the SC 900's ink supply can be replenished.

Figure 4.83. *Lower left.* Containers for the thermal printer stamps are plastic and have a lid to cover the die plate protecting it from damage and debris. Beginning on the left side, the first container contains a Brother SC 900 stamp and the second container houses a Brother SC 300 PC stamp. Neither of these two containers have an adjustable mount. The third container contains U.S. Stamp's ThermalVision stamp and the fourth and final container houses Trodat's StampPrinter stamp. The containers for these two stamps have an adjustable mount that allows for height adjustment of the die.

Figure 4.84. *Lower right.* This is a close-up of a ThermalVision Printer stamp die. The die is flat as it does not have a relief. The ink is in the pad and exits through the open micropores.

Figure 4.85A–B. (A) *Left.* SC 300 PC stamp impression contains a dot pattern similar to those found in the dot matrix printing process. (B) *Right.* This is a close-up of the letter "m" and the characteristic dot pattern is present along with feathering of ink surrounding the outline of the letter.

matrix pattern evolves into a sawtooth pattern. Conversely, the larger stamp, the more dots in the impression (Figs. 4.86A & 4.86B). If the individual making the impression holds the stamp on the paper for a longer length of time, in essence overinking the impression, the dots may not be as noticeable or numerous. The remaining characteristics of the impression resemble those found in the pre-mix gel in the pre-inked stamp category.

The Brother SC 900 stamp will reflect a weave pattern if the impression is not heavily inked (Figs. 4.87A & 4.87B). The SC 900's weave pattern is the result of the SC 900 having twice the dpi (360) than the SC 300 PC (180 dpi).

Potential Defects on a Thermal Printer Stamp Die

- If small type is used, a portion of the letter or character may be absent. This creates a non-print area in the die (Figs. 4.88A & 4.88B).
- Text not centered on flat die causing part of character to not print (Figs. 4.89A & 4.89B).
- Image or artwork on computer screen not accurately transferred to thermal printer during the sealing of the die. Can cause extraneous print areas (Figs. 4.90A & 4.90B).
- Dirt or other debris on the die will create a non-print area.
- Dirt and debris extending from the print character into the background may print.

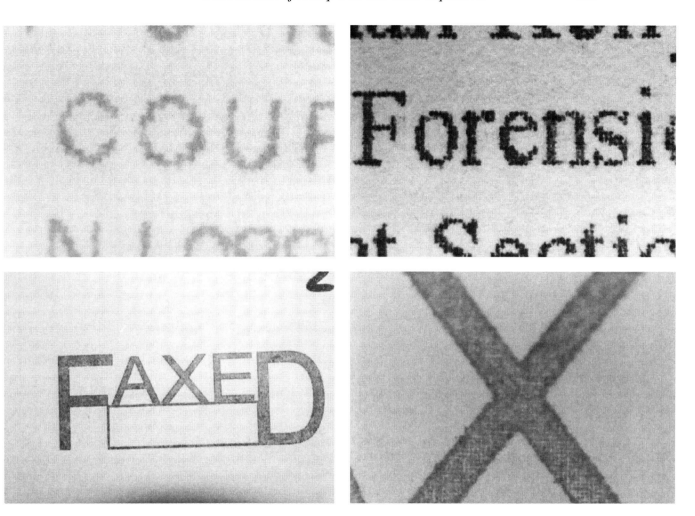

Figure 4.86A–B. The appearance of the dot pattern is dependent upon the size of the text. (A) *Top left.* An impression from the smallest stamp available from the SC 300 PC is shown. The sawtooth pattern is readily apparent. (B) *Top right.* This is an impression from a larger SC 300 PC stamp. The individual dots are not as apparent, but the sawtooth outline and the vertical line going through the middle of the character is still present.

Figure 4.87A–B. A lighter inked impression from an SC 900 stamp will reflect the weave pattern observed on the die in Figure 4.82B. The entire impression is captured in 4.87A *(lower left)* and the characteristics of a weave pattern inside the character and the outline of ink surrounding the character can be observed. (B) *Lower right.* This is a close-up of a portion of the "X" revealing the weave pattern.

AUTOMATIC STAMPS

Automatic stamping devices function to produce a consistent stamp impression with every use and are used by businesses to stamp multi-page documents. Different printing processes including ink jet and dot matrix are

Figure 4.88A–B. Non-print area can occur on the outline of the character because the thermal printer did not properly interpret the character from the computer. This situation tends to occur in the smaller size type. (A) *Top left.* Arrows point to the area on the "e"s that were sealed creating a non-print area in the letter's outline. (B) *Top right.* A non-print area is produced in the impression. This type of defect is classified as individual and permanent in nature.

Figure 4.89A–B. The "Y" on this flat die stamp is too close to the edge of the exposed pad as shown in 4.89A *(lower left)* and creates a partial impression in 4.89B *(lower right)* of the letter because it is not flush with the rest of the text.

used by various manufacturers in their machines to produce the stamped impression. This section will discuss a few of the machines in order to acquaint the document examiner with their method of operation and characteristics that can be observed.

Figure 4.90. Debris left on the porous pad prior to sealing by the thermal printer can create extraneous printing. (A) *Left*. This sample reflects a piece of debris to the right of the lower half of the staff of the "h." (B) *Right*. The extraneous area is reproduced in the impression. Note that debris extending past the outline of the characters "C" and "h" were reproduced in the impression.

The PowerMax Machine

The PowerMax machine was released in December, 2000 to be used as an automatic stamping machine using four (4) different sizes of the MaxLight pre-inked stamps and the MaxLight Dater. The MaxLight pre-inked stamp or MaxLight Dater is snapped into position in the PowerMax and accurate stamping is achieved with an adjustable activator that provides several different paper alignments.[40]

The Dorson Electronic Stamp

The Dorson Electronic Stamp is an automatic stamp machine marketed by Millennium Marking Company that can stamp a single document or a multipart carbon form (Fig. 4.91). This unit is comprised of metal type with the standard style being Gothic or Arial in a 10 point font to create the die of the stamp impression and uses an oil-based silk ribbon for the ink media. The paper is inserted onto the guide shelf of the unit to assure exact positioning of the documents. With insertion of the paper, an automatic trigger is released that causes the print mechanism to hit the paper creating an indented stamp impression. The stamping pressure is adjustable in order to assure a perfect impression. The print mechanism consists of bands numbering zero to nine in a position of right to left. The second band is a 12-character band and the third band is the AM or PM, which can be switched manually.[41]

Characteristics of a Dorson Electronic Stamp Impression

The impression made by a Dorson Electronic Stamp bears the following characteristics (Figs. 4.92A & 4.92B):

• Indentation of the impression into the paper is present.
• Complete ink coverage within the character.
• Pattern of the silk ribbon is present throughout the impression.
• Beginning and end border of plate present in the form of vertical line impression.

The Reiner Multi-Printer Electronic Stamp

The Reiner Multi-Printer is a multi-purpose electronic stamp machine that stores 35 selectable imprints of time, date, number, and test (Fig. 4.93).[42] The option of a custom imprint is also possible using a removable chip card. This printer can stamp single sheets up to a multi-copy form of six pages. A dot-matrix printhead using a ribbon cassette for the ink media creates an impression in either black or red ink. The Multi-Printer 780/785 uses three print styles: a standard style with ten characters per inch with a maximum of 23 characters per line; a condensed style with 15 characters per inch with a maximum of 35 characters per line; or, a wide style with seven characters per inch with a maximum of 16 characters per inch. The numbering function has an eight-digit maximum with the number range of 0 to 99.[43]

Characteristics of a Reiner Multi-Printer Electronic Stamp Impression

The Reiner Multi-Printer uses a dot-matrix-printhead to create the impression. The characteristics reflect those found in any printing process using dot-matrix and are as follows (Fig. 4.94):

• Light indentation of the impression into the paper.
• Individual dots are symmetrical.
• Tight dot pattern observed in the characters.
• White vertical band observed in the character.

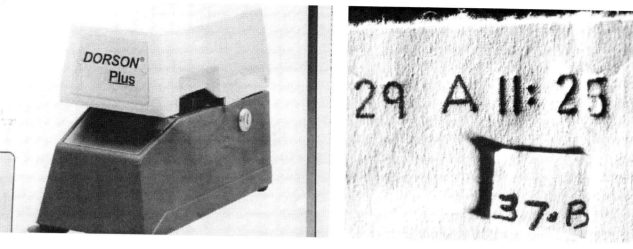

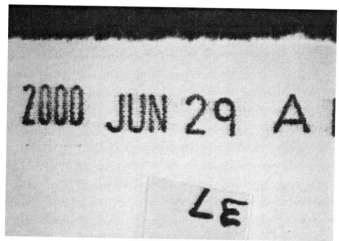

Figure 4.91. *Top left*. This is the Dorson Electronic Stamp marketed by Millennium Marking Company.

Figure 4.92A–B. (A) *Top right*. Impression produced by the Dorson Electronic Stamp as viewed using oblique lighting is shown. Indentation in the paper can be observed. (B) *Lower center*. This is the view of the same impression using direct lighting. This stamp machine uses a fabric ribbon as its ink source and the ribbon's pattern can be observed in the impression (Courtesy of Lamar Miller).

The Reiner JetStamp 790 Electronic Handstamp

The JetStamp 790 is a portable battery (rechargeable) operated handstamp that can stamp one or two lines of text, date, time, and numbers (Fig. 4.95). This unit has a repetitive numbering function of 0 to 99 and an automatic dater.[44] A standard feature of this unit is its memory capability of twenty standard selectable and four customized imprints. The JetStamp 790 uses inkjet

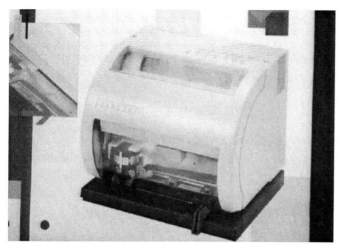

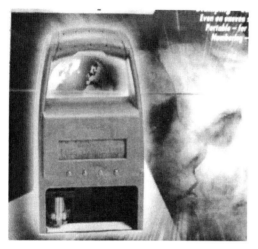

Figure 4.93. *Top left.* The Reiner Multi-Printer Electronic Stamp is shown.
Figure 4.94. *Top right.* This impression is produced by the Reiner Multi-Printer Electronic Stamp. This stamp printer uses dot matrix technology to produce its impressions (Courtesy of Lamar Miller).
Figure 4.95. *Lower left.* The Reiner JetStamp Electronic (Portable) Handstamp is shown.
Figure 4.96. *Lower right.* This shows the impression produced by the Reiner JetStamp Electronic Handstamp. This unit uses inkjet printing technology to produce its impressions in either black or red ink (Courtesy of Lamar Miller).

print technology to create an impression in either red, blue, or black ink. The print size is 3.2mm (inches) and the following three print styles can be produced by this unit: 12 characters per inch with a maximum of 20 characters per line; 10 characters per inch with 17 characters per line; and, six characters per inch with a maximum of 10 characters per line.[45]

Characteristics of a Reiner JetStamp 790 Electronic Handstamp Impression

The impression from a JetStamp 790 reflects the characteristics found in the inkjet printing process and are as follows (Fig. 4.96):

- Absence of indentation in paper.
- Individual ink drops are asymmetrical.
- Presence of light sporadic ink spray surrounding the character.
- White horizontal band present in character.

REFERENCES

1. Mauro, Mike: M & R Marking Systems. Piscataway, NJ.
2. Herbertson, Gary: *Rubber Stamp Examination.* Colorado Springs, Wide Line, 1997, p. 19.
3. Mauro, Mike: M & R Marking Systems. Piscataway, NJ.
4. Tanaka, Tobin: Interview.
5. Herbertson, Gary: *Rubber Stamp Examination.* Colorado Springs, Wide Line, 1997, p. 19.
6. Casey, Maureen A.: The individuality of rubber stamps. *Forensic Science International, 12:* 134–144, 1978.
7. Ibid.
8. Mauro, Mike. M & R Marking Systems. Piscataway, NJ.
9. Collins, William: Vice President of Indiana Stamp Co., Inc. and United RIBtype Company. Fort Wayne, IN.
10. Mauro, Mike. M & R Marking Systems. Piscataway, NJ.
11. United RIBtype product brochure. 1994.
12. Ibid.
13. Collins, William: Vice President of Indiana Stamp Co., Inc. and United RIBtype Company. Fort Wayne, IN.
14. United RIBtype product brochure. 1994.
15. Collins, William: Vice President of Indiana Stamp Co., Inc. and United RIBtype Company. Fort Wayne, IN.
16. Ibid.
17. Mauro, Mike. M & R Marking Systems. Piscataway, NJ.
18. Bosworth, Diane C.: Owner of Access Business Solutions, Inc., Hudson, WI.
19. Newger, Don: Louis Melind Company. Onarga, IL.
20. Ibid.
21. Ibid.
22. Bosworth, Diane, C.: Laser engraving to buy or not to buy. *Marking Industry Magazine, 94* (11): 30, 1999.
23. Mauro, Mike: M & R Marking Systems. Piscataway, NJ.
24. Herkt, A: Rubber stamp manufacture and identification. *Journal of the Forensic Science Society, 25:* 23–38, 1985.
25. Jackson, Chuck: Owner of ACT II Rubber Stamp. Las Vegas, NV.
26. Rowan, Kim: A1 Rubber Stamp and Engraving. Las Vegas, NV.

27. Hughson, Cliff: A1 Rubber Stamp and Engraving. Las Vegas, NV.
28. Tolliver, Diane K.: Indiana State Police Laboratory. Indianapolis, Indiana.
29. Chu, Rodney: Assistant General Manager. Lee Shing Stamp Limited. Hong Kong.
30. Ibid.
31. Lowrance, Kenneth: Superior Rubber Stamp & Seal, Inc.
32. Kirchner, Tom: X-Stamper® production part II; at long last, the arrival. *Marking Industry Magazine, 96* (8): 32–33, 2001.
33. Sculler, Steve: Pre-inks continue to emerge. *Marking Industry Magazine, 96* (8): 16–17, 2001.
35. Mauro, Mike: M & R Marking Systems, Piscataway, N.J.
35. Yuki, Eiji: Product Manager of Stamp-Making Devices. Brother International Corporation, Bridgewater, NJ.
36. Ibid.
37. Millennium Marking Company. MaxLight instruction manual. 2000.
38. Antonio, Ernie: Sales Manager. Millennium Marking Company. Elk Grove Village, IL.
39. Yuki, Eiji: Product Manager of Stamp-Making Devices. Brother International Corporation, Bridgewater, NJ.
40. Product Announcement. *Marking Industry Magazine 96* (4): 42, 2000.
41. Ryan, Bill: International Sales Manager. Millennium Marking Company. Elk Grove Village, IL.
42. Mear, Jeff: Interview and Reiner Multi-Printer product brochure.
43. Ibid.
44. Mear, Jeff: Interview and Reiner JetStamp 790 product brochure.
45. Ibid.

Chapter 5

THE EXAMINATION PROCESS

Mechanical device cases involve the examination of text or images produced by photocopiers, check protectors, printers, typewriters, and rubber stamps. Impressions, embossments, or text produced from mechanical devices lack variation among impressions because the impression is created by a mechanism of fixed elements. The net result is the repetitive presence of the same characteristics and defects in all the images created by these mechanical devices. The rubber stamp impression differs from other mechanical devices because the rubber stamp is influenced by a variable element absent in the other mechanical devices, that is, the individual producing the impression. Because the individual, referred to as the stamper, holds the stamp while producing the impression, variation in quality and appearance is apparent between impressions. Subtle characteristics and defects may not be present in all of the impressions due to variation created by the stamper's technique.

Even though rubber stamp impressions are categorized as mechanical impressions, the examination approach is not as straightforward as the approach in the examination of the other mechanical devices. The examination of rubber stamps or its impressions likens itself more closely to a handwriting examination. The justification for this statement is based on variation and other variable factors influencing the execution of both handwriting and rubber stamp impressions. However, the variation in stamp impressions will not be as extreme as that found in handwriting.

In any document examination, the examiner's consideration of the limitations inherent in the evidence is a basic requirement. Intrinsic limitations in the rubber stamp impression are determined by a combination of the following factors: the manufacturing process, the material used for the stamp, the type of ink, the type of material (paper, plastic, metal, etc) hosting the impression, and the stamping style of the individual (stamper) stamping the impression. Earlier research papers have addressed the importance of knowing not only the manufacturing processes and the different types of materials used in rubber stamps, but the application of this knowledge during the examination's assessment phase. Maureen Casey Owens wrote in her 1978 article, "In order to assess correctly the individuality of a rubber stamp, it is necessary to be aware of the different varieties of rubber stamps made and to understand the processes involved in the manufacture of each type of stamp."[1] The application of knowing the various die materials and understanding the manufacturing processes is the key to identifying the determinants of the defects with the ultimate goal of properly classifying the defects in order to assess their weight or significance.

THE DETERMINANTS OF DEFECTS

A critical step in the examination process is determining the source of the defect or anomaly observed in an impression or on a stamp die. Defects that occur in the manufacturing process are:[2]

- Damage to the original image.
- Defective die material, i.e., scarred rubber, poor quality plastic resin, cracked Bakelite.
- Poor quality control.
- Distortion or misalignment.
- Damage caused by cutting the stamp.
- Bubbles.
- Impurities such as dirt.

Identifying a defect or an anomaly as a manufacturing defect is the first step in a two-step process. Before the examiner can classify the defect as class, random, or individual, an attempt to assess the stage of occurrence in the manufacturing process must be made. From this assessment, the examiner is able to properly classify the defect by determining its significance based on the stage of its occurrence in the manufacturing process. For example, the frequency of occurrence for the creation of an air bubble in the vulcanization process is twice that of any other manufacturing process. In the vulcanization process of raw rubber, premixed gel, or laser foam, the air bubble would be classified as a random characteristic because it can occur in two different stages of manufacturing. The defect could be classified more specifically as class or individual if the stage of occurrence is determined. The ultraviolet process, however, has only one stage of occurrence for the air bubble. Therefore, an air bubble present on a photopolymer stamp would always be an individual characteristic.

Defects can occur through use of the stamp. These types of defects lend themselves to being classed as individual defects since their presence is individualized through the type of use, abuse and quality of care of the stamp. The defects or anomalies commonly caused through use of the stamp are:[3]

- Dirt, paper, fiber and ink accumulations.
- Nicks and cuts
- Edge wear and breakdown.
- Stamp distortion.
- Shrinkage over time.
- Cracks and splits resulting from dry and brittle rubber.

Each characteristic observed in the impression must be assessed in order to determine its source and value. In his 1985 article, A. Herkt wrote, "The document examiner not only needs to be aware of the individual or unique features in a rubber stamp and its impression, but also has to be able to interpret the significance of any particular feature, the relevance it has to the problem in hand, the weight of opinion that it merits and the depth of knowledge that can be gained from it."[4] Mr. Herkt's statement captures the essence of the examination process. Identifying the stage of occurrence provides an objective assessment of a defect's significance and the weight it should be given. The earlier example of the frequency and stage of occurrences of an air bubble in the vulcanization process stresses the necessity of proper interpretation of the individual feature. An air bubble on a vulcanized die is classified as a random characteristic because it is nearly impossible to determine the stage of occurrence without examining the mold. If the Bakelite mold is submitted along with the stamp, determination of the stage of occurrence for the air bubble is possible, thereby allowing the examiner to specifically state whether it is a class or individual characteristic. In summary, if the air bubble originated from the Bakelite mold, it is a class characteristic because every stamp made using that mold would contain the air bubble. The air bubble would be an individual characteristic if it originated from air being trapped between the Bakelite mold and the raw rubber prior to the rubber's vulcanization. This example is a classic illustration of a random characteristic whose classification status can be changed to a specific classification if the examination includes not only the known impression exemplars, but the stamp and the mold used to make the die.

Proper interpretation of the individual or unique features is achieved through understanding not only the manufacturing processes, but also to understand how the variable factors affect the quality of the impression. The variable factors[5] affecting the quality of the impression are as follows:

- Ink quantity and dispersion
- Type of stamp pad
- Pressure
- Angle of impact
- Characteristics of material receiving the impression
- Supporting surface
- Absorbency of stamp

The human being using the stamp to make the impression is the common denominator found in all of the above listed factors. The stamper influences how these factors relate to each other with the end result affecting the quality of the impression. The combination of factors such as heavy pressure and inking of the die when making the impression gives the impression a different look than one created with lighter pressure and inking. The relationship of these factors not only affects the physical appearance of the impression, but also determines whether the presence of the defect on the die will appear in the impression. The necessity of obtaining numerous sample impressions from a suspected stamp is obvious when considering these variable factors.

THE CLASSIFICATION OF DEFECTS

Past literature refers to features or defects in the image produced by a mechanical device as an accidental. An accidental characteristic is defined as a defect that occurs in the manufacturing process or individual usage.[6] This is an umbrella term since it is not specific in identifying a feature or defect as class or individual. If the examiner was able to specifically classify the defect, the report would indicate the observed feature or defect was a class accidental characteristic or an individual accidental characteristic.

Features or defects observed on the stamp die should be classified from a well-defined criteria based on objective evidence. Class, random, and individual are three primary classifications that have been defined in an effort to establish the criteria of each classification and to eliminate the confusion as to what justifies a feature as class or individual. In rubber stamp manufacturing, a class characteristic is a feature or defect specific to a production run rather than to a specific stamp.[7] A random characteristic is defined as a feature or defect whose origin cannot be determined because it has more than one possible stage of occurrence in the manufacturing process. An individual characteristic is a feature or defect that is unique to the one stamp.

Class characteristics include type style, design, spacing, size, and arrangement. Undesirable features or defects that would be classified as class would be the air bubble on the Bakelite mold in the vulcanization process or a spot on the negative preventing curing of the photopolymer during the ultraviolet process. In both examples, the occurrence of the defect is on the manufacturing material that acts as the negative for the stamp die in that particular process.

A random characteristic is defined as a feature or defect whose origin cannot be determined because it can occur in more than one stage of the manufacturing process. This classification assists in assessing proper weight to a feature or defect and clearly defines the primary classification by specifying the defect's origin as occurring in the manufacturing process, but its stage of occurrence is unknown. The earlier example of an air bubble is one example of a feature or defect having more than one stage of occurrence in the manufacturing process. Without examining the Bakelite mold used to produce the stamp, the examiner is unable to determine the air bubble's stage of occurrence.

An individual characteristic is a feature or defect that occurs through use or abuse of the stamp in the individual setting or poor quality control in the manufacturing process. Features or defects such as a cut or dirt and debris on a die are individual in nature, but their source of origin is generally unknown. Even though the source of origin is unknown, the proper classification remains individual instead of random because the feature or defect is unique to one stamp. Dirt or debris on the die causing a non-print area is an example of a feature or defect whose origin can either be the manufacturing process or individual usage. However, the form or shape of the non-print area would be individual to the one stamp and this would allow the examiner to classify the non-print area as an individual characteristic even though the debris's origin is unknown. Failure to protect the stamp die from dirt and debris, damage resulting from exposure to the surrounding environment, the technique of stamping used by the stamper, the frequency of use, and the use of the wrong type of ink on the die will produce defects that are individual to one stamp. Whether individually or combined, these external factors are created by the stamper who sets in motion the circumstances upon which the individual defects occur.

The three primary classifications of class, random, and individual characteristics have been defined in an effort to establish criteria based upon objective evidence. Class characteristics only occur in the manufacturing process and are not unique to one stamp. Random characteristics can occur in more than one stage of the manufacturing process and differ from class because the stage of occurrence or source of origin is unknown. An individual characteristic is a feature or defect that is unique to the one stamp and can occur in either the manufacturing process or from individual usage.

The examiner can further describe features or defects as permanent, progressive, or transitory. These three classifications describe the nature and permanence of the primary classifications and are considered secondary classifications. A permanent defect is defined as an anomaly that is part of the material used in the manufacturing process to make the stamp die. A progressive defect is one that is subject to change in appearance over time as a result of continued use. A transitory defect is an extraneous artifact that has attached itself to the die material.

A permanent defect will have the primary classification of class, random, or individual. Sources of permanent defects are damaged or excess die material and damage sustained from abuse. An air bubble on a vulcanized rubber die is a permanent defect with a random primary classification.

Progressive defects have the primary classification of individual. Wear patterns developed from use are subject to change in appearance as a result of continued use over time. Continued use of the stamp over time is the main cause of the progressive defect. Immigration stamps or a stamp used by a business marking an invoice "paid" are susceptible to wear patterns on the outer edge of the die. This wear pattern changes progressively due to the continued use of the stamp over time. The continual use of the stamp causes the wear pattern to progress to the point where that part of the edge of the die does not contain the necessary relief to print.

Transient defects such as dirt, hair, or paper fiber can occur in both the manufacturing setting and individual usage. Their presence on the stamp die can cause a non-print area that may be reflected in its impression. Primary classification of individual is given to these types of defects because their location, shape, and size are unique to one stamp. It is possible to dislodge and remove the transient defect either through use or cleaning. Upon removal of the transient defect, that part of the die will print since the die itself was not damaged (Figs. 5.1A & 5.1B).

The defect must be located in or on the intended print area (the die) in order to appear in the impression. An air bubble on the background of a vulcanized rubber stamp would be classified as a permanent random characteristic. However, it's significance is limited because it is located on the background which is typically a non-print area. Therefore, it would not be reproduced in the stamp's impression. Hand trimming of the die's background is a permanent individual characteristic and if the edge of the background is reproduced in the impression, it may have great significance in identifying the stamp as the source of the impression. Trimming the background too close to the shoulder of the die may affect the print quality of the impression since the letters in the die will not have the necessary support during stamping. Conversely, leaving excess background may print becoming a part of the impression during stamping (Figs. 5.2A & 5.2B).

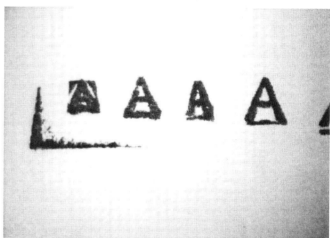

Figure 5.1A–B. Transient defects can be removed with usage or cleaning. (A) *Top left*. This illustrates the appearance of the die after the removal of debris next to the "h." (B) *Top right*. This illustrates the impression made from the this stamp. The appearance of the die and its impression prior to the debris' removal is illustrated in Figure 4.90.

Figure 5.2A–B. (A) *Lower left*. This is an example of a vulcanized rubber die that was not hand trimmed close enough to prevent the appearance of the background in the impression and, in 5.2B *(lower right)*, the impression containing the lower left corner of the background.

THE QUESTIONED IMPRESSION AND THE SUSPECTED STAMP

In the previous chapters, we have discussed the classifications of stamps, the manufacturing processes of stamps and seals, characteristics of stamp dies and their impressions and potential defects. Having an understanding of this information aids the examiner in the examination process by applying proper logic derived from a well-grounded knowledge base. This section of the chapter will discuss the examination process used in the comparison of a suspected stamp to a questioned impression and a questioned impression to known impressions. The reader should keep in mind this discussion primarily address- es rubber stamps for personal or non-industrial business use. Stamps used in the industrial setting have dies that are made of natural rubber, Buna, silicone, PVC, and other materials. The purpose of the stamp and the hosting material determines the type of die material and ink used to make the impression. The primary focus of this book limits the discussion to the description of charac- teristics and observations of personal and non-industrial business use stamps and their impressions. The examination procedures discussed in this chapter are not all-encompassing and do not have to be executed in the order they appear. The steps taken by the author are merely a guide for other document examiners and do not represent the only correct examination procedure.

It is an ideal situation when the stamp suspected of making a questioned impression is submitted for examination. Having the stamp available allows the examiner to microscopically examine the stamp's defects to determine whether they are class, random, or individual.

The first step taken by this author when conducting a document examina- tion of a stamp case is to examine the questioned impression to make sure it is an original stamp impression and not produced from a different printing process (Figs. 5.3A & 5.3B). The examiner should use a microscope to study the printing process characteristics observed in the questioned impression. If the questioned image is indeed a stamp impression, the examiner should observe the following general characteristics:

- Absorption of ink into the paper fibers.
- May be variation in the uniformity of the inking. Heavier inking of one area in the impression would be due to the application of uneven pressure of the stamp to the paper. Blotchy or patchy non-inked areas are caused by inad- equate ink coverage from that particular area of the die.
- Squeegee effect may or may not be present.
- Feathering of ink may be observed on some of the characters.
- Total saturation of ink through the paper (bleeding of the ink) if an oil-based ink is used.
- Lack of an impression or indentation in the paper.
- Absence of debris surrounding the individual letters that are commonly observed in inkjet or laser printer and photocopier processes.

If the microscopic examination reveals the impression image is a photo- copy, the examiner has to take into consideration the limitations posed by examining a photocopy of a stamp impression.

Herbertson comments on these limitations advising the examiner to con- sider the possibility of the image being a cut and paste insertion of a genuine

Figure 5.3A–B. (A) *Left*. This illustrates a photocopy of an impression made from a self-inking stamp. (B) *Right*. Offset printing process of text on a promotional envelope gives the appearance of being a hand-stamped impression.

impression on the original suspected document or created using another printing process.[8] Since the photocopy prevents the examiner from observing the characteristics of a rubber stamp impression, the examiner is limited to issuing a qualified conclusion stating the image on the questioned photocopy has the same general class characteristics as those found on the suspected stamp or in the known stamp impression exemplars. Under this scenario, the examiner is unable to state if the image examined on the questioned photocopy was produced from a rubber stamp or by another printing process.

Once it has been determined that the image is a stamp impression, consideration is given as to its purpose or function. The intended purpose of the stamp provides an indication as to the number of stamps bearing the same text and class characteristics that are possibly in existence. Is the impression a facsimile signature stamp used by one individual for personal use or is it used by the individual for business purposes? Even though the text may be customized with a business name, how many stamps with that text does the business use in conducting their business and how long has the business used a stamp with that particular text? Over-the-counter stamps with standard texts such as "Certified Copy," "Paid," "Past Due," etc. are sold by office supply stores, discount stores and stamp shops (Fig. 5.4). These generic text stamps are generally mass produced, but can be produced individually by a stamp maker. For the generic text stamps that are mass produced, all will share the same desirable class characteristics. A few may share the same random characteristics depending on how many stamps were made using a defective mold or negative. It is advisable to ask the investigator to inquire how many stamps the individual

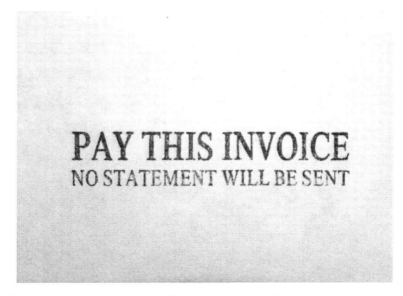

Figure 5.4. This impression was produced by a generic over-the-counter stamp purchased from a local office supply store. These types of stamps are mass produced.

suspect had access to and if it is a business, how many stamps of the same text exist and are accessible to employees or customers.

Before proceeding further into the examination process of the stamp, the author examines the questioned impression to note the general characteristics and assess if the characteristics observed are consistent with an impression that could have been made by the submitted stamp. The impression can contain evidence that may identify the type of manufacturing process and even the type of material used. For example, the examiner is asked to determine if the questioned stamp impression was produced by the submitted stamp which is a hand stamp. Visual examination of the questioned impression reveals it has heavy ink saturation that is even throughout the impression, the ink has bled through the paper, presence of some feathering of ink surrounding a few of the characters, and the squeegee effect is not present. These characteristics are indicative of a pre-inked stamp with the die material being either a pre-mixed gel stamp, laser foam rubber, or possibly a flat die, all of which use an oil-based ink. These characteristics are not in agreement with characteristics of impressions produced from a hand stamp, which typically has die material made of either vulcanized rubber or photopolymer.

The preliminary examination is a visual inspection of the stamp and provides the opportunity for the examiner to inspect it for permanent and transitory defects. In order to maintain the condition of the permanent and transitory defects on the stamp, care is exercised in handling the stamp upon its removal from the evidence package. Recording the visual inspection of the stamp and the stamp die will provide an accounting of the stamp's condition at the time of receipt by the examiner. Use of a microscope in the preliminary examination will assure the examiner that all anomalies, no matter how small, were observed and noted.

Following the visual inspection of the stamp, the next step is to compare the text of the questioned impression to the text on the stamp die. Are they in agreement in class characteristics? Class characteristics for rubber stamps, seals, or any marking device include the type style, design, spacing, size, and arrangement. If the type style, arrangement, and design are the same but the size and spacing are too close to call from a visual inspection, two acetate copies can be made bearing a photocopy image, one of an impression from the suspected stamp and one of the questioned impression. Overlay the two acetate images to determine if they are of the same size and spacing. If the class characteristics are in agreement, the examiner should proceed with a detailed examination to identify individual characteristics found on the questioned impression and the suspected stamp die.

The location of the ink source determines the classification of the stamp. Identifying the stamp as a hand, self-inking, or pre-ink provides objective evidence as to the choice of materials used for the stamp die, the type of ink used, and the potential defects that can occur in that particular classification.

The container housing the stamp die is examined to see if the product name used by the manufacturer and/or the name of the stamp maker are present. The majority of containers also have a plastic window attached to the outside that holds the index (title) of the stamp die. This information can provide investigative leads as to the customer who ordered the stamp, the stamp shop that made the stamp and the purchase date. For example, stamp makers conduct business with specific stamp manufacturers. The trade name is proprietary to the stamp manufacturer who may be able provide the list of stamp shops in the suspected purchase area. However, this is not as fool proof as it used to be due to increasing sales of rubber stamps over the Internet and by companies such as office supply stores who are not primary stamp making businesses.

Once the stamp shop has been identified, the investigator can contact the stamp maker and begin the process of ascertaining who ordered the stamp and the date of sale. A majority of stamp shops also maintain a file of proofs of the stamp dies prepared on a particular day. If the original proofs are available, they provide an excellent known exemplar reflecting the condition of the stamp impression when it was new.

Part of the examination of the stamp container includes the ink source. If the stamp is a self-inking stamp, the author visually inspects it to determine the ink saturation of the pad and also checks to see if the text of the die is recessed

Figure 5.5A–B. (A) *Left.* The text of the die is embedded into the stamp pad of a self-inking stamp. (B) *Right.* The impression is produced using this ink pad. Due to the severity of the indentations in the ink pad, even inking of the die is prevented causing patchy areas within the impression.

into the pad (Figs. 5.5A & 5.5B). The recessed text results from the die remaining in contact with the inkpad when not in use. If the text is deeply recessed into the ink pad, it can cause inadequate inking of the die between stamp impressions. A new ink pad will correct this problem.

Visual examination includes examining the index (title) to determine if the image is that of the rubber stamp or was created using a different printing process. The stamp maker makes numerous impressions with the newly created stamp. The stamp index is usually one of the first impressions made during this testing phase. Providing the index is an impression produced from the stamp, the die will probably be covered with ink even though it is a new stamp. Absence of ink on the stamp die can either indicate the stamp is new and has never been inked or it has been cleaned.

A microscope is the preferred instrument when conducting a detailed examination of the stamp. The ability to determine if the characteristic or defect is permanent or transitory is more easily answered viewing the die area at 10X to 30X magnification. The stamp needs to be secured to eliminate movement during the microscopic examination. To expose the die for microscopic examination, the stamp needs to be secured in an upside-down stationary position. A small inexpensive bench vise is an ideal tool in holding the stamp in this position (Figs. 5.6A & 5.6B). If the stamp is a self-inker, the container will need to be locked into position so that the cover is in the inking position exposing the die (Fig. 5.7). Most self-inker containers have a locking mechanism on the side. If the mechanism is broken or non-existent, the examiner can use rubber bands or tape placed on the far ends of the die plate in

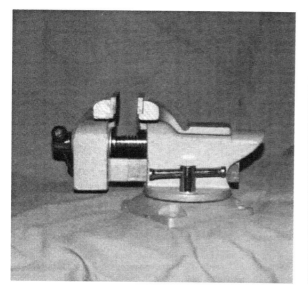 

Figure 5.6A–B. (A) *Top left.* A small bench vise can be used to secure the stamp in an upside down position for the microscopic examination. (B) *Top right.* A piece of cloth should be between the teeth of the vise and the stamp container. This will prevent damage to the container as well as provide a dark background when photographing the die.

Figure 5.7. *Lower center.* Most self-inking containers have a mechanism to lock the die in the open or printing position. The stamp on the left uses a "key" that inserts into the opening on the side of the container to secure it in the open position. The middle container and the container on the right use tabs on the side that can be pushed into lock the die in position.

order to keep the container open allowing for detailed viewing of the die and background.

The microscopic examination should include both direct and oblique lighting. Direct lighting provides even illumination of the area being examined microscopically, allowing the examiner to examine the die and background of the stamp to determine, when possible, the manufacturing process and the type of material used for the die. The information garnered from this part of

Figure 5.8A–B. Stamp dies are trimmed prior to mounting on to the mount base. (A) *Left*. Stamp die that has been hand trimmed using scissors. (B) *Right*. This pre-mixed gel die was trimmed using a cutter.

the examination will assist the examiner in classifying the defects as well as to determine the possible cause of each observed defect. Oblique lighting coupled with a higher magnification narrows the focus of the examination to detect even the smallest of defects and to determine whether they are permanent or transitory. Small particles of hair, dirt, and small air bubbles are more easily detected with side-lighting as it provides the necessary contrast as opposed to direct illumination.

Part of the examination of the stamp die includes the edge detail of the background (Figs. 5.8A & 5.8B). A cutter may have been used to trim the die if the edges are evenly cut or the edges reflect a rough cut which is indicative of a dull blade. If the trimming follows the contour of the text of the die, it is an indication the die was hand trimmed. However, there are cutters on the market that can be set to follow the contour of the die, so a closely trimmed die is not a definitive sign that it was hand trimmed.

To aid in the examination of the profile of the die's edge, the examiner inks the stamp die and immediately places it under the microscope. The inking provides easier visualization of the nooks and valleys that normally comprise the edge detail of older stamps. Including this step in the examination process is very beneficial when examining old stamps, but is of limited value if the stamp is fairly new.

Microscopic examination of the questioned impression follows the stamp examination. When possible, case notes should reflect the date of the questioned document. If the document is not dated, a notation of when it was first discovered and the suspected date of preparation are listed. Attention is then turned to comparing the corresponding area in the impression to that on the stamp die containing the class or individual characteristic. If a non-print area is present in the impression, its shape and size are compared to the defect on the stamp. This process continues until all the characteristics have been noted and compared from the impression to the submitted stamp.

Depending upon size and location, an individual defect may be present on the die but absent in the questioned impression. The defect's absence in the impression may be due to the person's method of stamping, different type of paper, fresh inking of the stamp source, or the defect was created after the date of the questioned impression. The final consideration as to why the defect is present on the stamp and not in the impression is that the submitted stamp did not make the questioned impression.

If the class and individual characteristics are in agreement thus far, the examiner might consider photographing the submitted stamp and die before using it to make known stamp impressions. Whether to take the photographs prior to making impressions with the submitted stamp or to wait until the known impressions have been made is a personal preference. The author chooses to photograph the stamp and its die in order to record its condition prior to making the known impressions. Additional photographs of the questioned impression and the known impressions are taken by the completion of the examination process.

IMPRESSION TO IMPRESSION COMPARISON

Once the stamp has been photographed, numerous stamp impressions are made on similar material as that used for the questioned impression. The material hosting the known impressions should be matched as closely as possible to the material hosting the questioned impression. In other words, if the questioned impression is on heavy bond paper, the known impression exemplars also need to be on heavy bond paper. The same rationale follows as that used in obtaining known handwriting exemplars using the same type of writing instrument as the one used in the questioned writing.

The amount of ink transferred from the stamp die to the material hosting the impression not only affects the physical appearance of the impression, it also affects whether a defect on the die will be reflected in the impression. Therefore, it is recommended that numerous impressions are made at varying ink saturations. Collecting a series of impressions without re-inking is the proper method of obtaining impressions from a suspected stamp.[9] The gradual decrease of ink saturation observed in successive stamping without re-inking exposes the subtle and minute characteristics in the impression that are often hidden due to heavier ink saturation.

The appearance of the impression from continuous stamping without re-inking is dependent upon the classification of the stamp. Impressions made from either a hand stamp or self-inking stamp will reflect dramatic changes in the impressions made by continuous stamping without re-inking the die (Fig. 5.9). Pre-inked stamps made from premixed gel or laser foam will reflect a subtle decline in ink saturation that becomes progressively discernable as successive impressions are made (Fig. 5.10). Obtaining progressively lighter impressions from a pre-inked stamp differs from a hand or self-inking stamp in that a greater number of successive impressions must be made to produce the lighter impressions. The reason for this is that the pre-inked stamps have their own ink source within the die itself. The impregnated and microencapsulated cell filled with ink will eventually deplete itself and will need a few seconds to draw replacement ink from the background to be filled to the level necessary to produce impressions that are evenly and heavily saturated. It is during the depletion state that the examiner will observe impressions becoming lighter during successive stamping. The die and background of a hand or self-inking stamp do not retain ink and the gradual decrease of ink saturation in the impressions made by continuous stamping is visually dramatic.

If the investigator submitted a stamp pad along with the hand stamp, a visual comparison of the color of its ink to the dried ink on the die and the ink color of the impression is conducted prior to inking the die. If the ink in the stamp pad is red and the ink in the impression is black, the examiner is safe in stating that the submitted pad is not the ink source for the questioned impression. Depending upon the owner's use of the stamp, the die can be cleaned and used to make impressions in any ink color. So, don't place a great deal of weight if the color of residual ink on the die differs from that of the submitted stamp pad.

When preparing to make known stamp impression exemplars, be sure to use a compatible ink for the die material on the stamp. If the stamp is a hand or self-inking stamp and functions as an office or personal use stamp, the die material most likely will be natural rubber or photopolymer. Oil-based inks are not compatible with these two materials and will ruin the die over time. The hosting material and the purpose for which the stamp is to function also determine the type of ink. The examiner should take these two considerations into account before obtaining a stamp pad for use in the examination. For example, if the investigator submitted a hand stamp with a natural rubber or photopolymer die and the questioned impression is hosted on plain white paper, use a stamp pad containing water-based stamp ink. If the stamp is used in an industrial setting and the die is made of Buna (synthetic rubber), the ink will be oil-based.

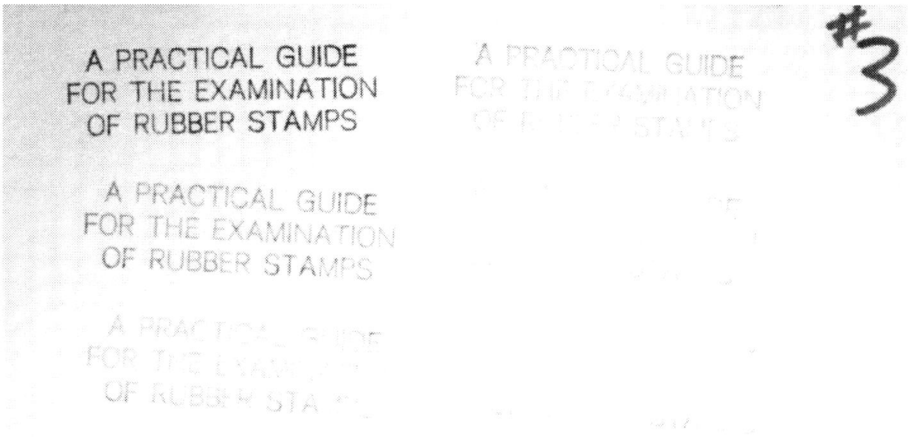

A PRACTICAL GUIDE
FOR THE EXAMINATION
OF RUBBER STAMPS

A PRACTICAL GUIDE
FOR THE EXAMINATION
OF RUBBER STAMPS

A PRACTICAL GUIDE
FOR THE EXAMINATION
OF RUBBER STAMPS

#3

Mara Beth Stevens
1234 West End Drive
Your Town, State
08855-6969

Mara Beth Stevens
1234 West End Drive
Your Town, State
08855-6969

Mara Beth Stevens
1234 West End Drive
Your Town, State
08855-6969

Mara Beth Stevens
1234 West End Drive
Your Town, State
08855-6969

Mara Beth Stevens
1234 West End Drive
Your Town, State
08855-6969

Mara Beth Stevens
1234 West End Drive
Your Town, State
08855-6969

Mara Beth Stevens
1234 West End Drive
Your Town, State
08855-6969

Mara Beth Stevens
1234 West End Drive
Your Town, State
08855-6969

Mara Beth Stevens
1234 West End Drive
Your Town, State
08855-6969

Mara Beth Stevens
1234 West End Drive
Your Town, State
08855-6969

Mara Beth Stevens
1234 West End Drive
Your Town, State
08855-6969

Mara Beth Stevens
1234 West End Drive
Your Town, State
08855-6969

Figure 5.9. *Top.* Continuous stamping of a vulcanized rubber hand stamp produces impressions with a noticeable decline in ink saturation in each successive impression.

Figure 5.10. *Bottom.* Successive stamping of a pre-mix gel stamp produces impressions that reflect a progressively lighter ink saturation with each successive impression.

Figure 5.11. *Left.* A standard ink pad is housed in a plastic container with a lid.
Figure 5.12. *Right.* Ink can be observed on the side of the background of a stamp die made of vulcanized rubber. The residual ink on the side is due to the die sinking into the stamp pad during the inking.

Stamp pads are resilient in nature with the most commonly used material being felt or cloth (Fig. 5.11). Ink coverage of the stamp die is achieved when the stamper presses the stamp die into the ink pad transferring ink onto the die. Because the pad has some pliability, it is not uncommon for residual ink to be observed on the mid to upper part of the shoulder of the die as a result of the stamp sinking into the stamp pad during inking (Fig. 5.12).

Stamp pads come in a variety of sizes and the pad chosen for the known exemplar needs to be large enough to accommodate the stamp, including the die, background and edge of the plate. If the stamp die is defective in such a way that the background will print while making the impression, the larger stamp pad will ensure ink coverage on what is normally a non-print area.

The self-inking stamp differs from a hand stamp by having the ink source housed in the same container as the die. It is worth restating that the material for the die of the self-inking and hand stamp will either be natural rubber or photopolymer or other materials commonly used in industrial settings that cannot retain ink. As stated earlier, the die in the self-inking stamp is in direct contact of the small ink pad in-between successive stampings and during non-use. Due to the pliable nature of the stamp pad used in the self-inking stamp, pressure points develop and the text of the die may be embedded in the pad. If the text is embedded deep enough, the die fails to obtain adequate ink coverage between successive stampings and the impression will be blotchy or patchy in areas. This uneven ink coverage is easily remedied by replacing the old ink pad with a new one. The examiner needs to keep this in mind when

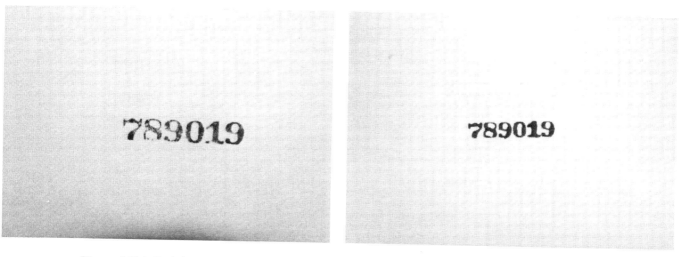

Figure 5.13A–B. (A) *Left*. Uneven ink saturation with patchy areas in this impression was caused by the deep indentation of the text in the stamp pad of a self-inking stamp. The deep indentation of the text prevents the corresponding area on the die to receive adequate and even ink coverage in between stampings. (B) *Right*. This impression was produced from the same self-inking stamp using a new stamp pad. Replacing the indented stamp pad with a new one dramatically alters the appearance of the impression since the die is now receiving an even application of ink.

checking the ink pad and noting its condition. If the ink pad was replaced between the date of the questioned impression and the seizure of the self-inking stamp, the dramatic visual difference between the unevenly inked questioned impression and the evenly inked known impression exemplars may well be explained by the presence of a new pad (Figs. 5.13A & 5.13B).

After checking the condition of the stamp pad inside the container of the self-inking stamp, one impression is produced on paper similar to a good quality copy paper. The stamp pad is removed and successive stamping begins immediately in order to obtain lighter impressions. Once the set of impressions reflecting the gradual decline of ink saturation is completed, the ink pad is returned to the self-inking container and additional impressions are made adding external variables to determine their influence on the submitted stamp. For example, successive stamping at high speed can cause a double impression or shadowing of some letters (Figs. 5.14A & 5.14B). Lengthening the time that the die remains in contact with the paper allows more ink to transfer to the paper. Another variable is incorrect positioning in the stamper's hand during stamping. The container is designed to assist the stamper in producing impressions that are consistent in quality and ink coverage. However, it is possible to influence the quality of the impression by applying more pressure on one end of the container or by failing to exert even pressure downward as the stamp die contacts the paper or hosting material. The application of the stamper's

Figure 5.14A–B. Successive stamping of a self-inking stamp can cause a doubling or shadowing of some of the letters in a few of the impressions. (A) *Left*. This illustrates a doubling of the letters "C" and "T" on page 5 of a multi-page document. (B) *Right*. This example illustrates an impression from the same self-inking stamp on page 2 of the multipage document. This impression is a true representation of the characters "C" and "T."

improper holding position of the self-inking container creates an uneven pressure that is evidenced by heavier inking in part of the impression or an absence of part of the text of the die.

The numerous known impression exemplars should exemplify a range of inking and stamping characteristics. Exemplar impressions are made on good quality copy paper and, if necessary, additional known exemplar impressions on similar material hosting the questioned impression. The author does not recommend obtaining impressions by twisting the stamp when in contact with the stamp pad or the paper (hosting material). The materials for hand and self-inking stamp dies are durable and are intended to endure a great deal of use. Stamps are designed to make impressions with the handle or container perpendicular and the die flush to the hosting material for even pressure throughout the impression. Rocking the stamp from side to side or front to back can cause transient characteristics directly attributable to the improper handling or method of stamping by the stamper (Fig. 5.15). Twisting the die while it is in contact with the stamp pad or the hosting material may damage part of the die due to cracks or other damage not detected during the stamp examination. In addition, the stamp pad may also be damaged from the pressure exerted during the twisting of the stamp. And finally, if the stamp is a pre-inked die made of pre-mixed gel or laser foam rubber, twisting the stamp while making an impression will destroy the die.

The ink for the pre-mixed gel die is microencapsulated into the material and the ink for the laser foam (salt leached rubber) die is impregnated into the

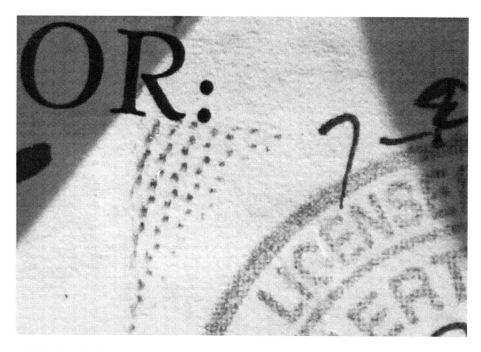

Figure 5.15. The dipple cushion on a vulcanized rubber hand stamp appears in the impression is a result of the stamper's improper handling of the stamp. The presence of the dipple pattern provides a clue to the document examiner as to the type of stamp used to make the impression.

material. Both of these materials are used for pre-inked stamps with heavy ink saturation in the die and background. Therefore, there is no need to have an external ink source since the die and the background are the stamp's ink source. The container housing this type of stamp usually has a cover to protect the die from damage, dirt, debris, and ink contamination to the surrounding environment during non-use. In order to achieve lighter inked impressions, the examiner will need to make numerous impressions without resting. Lighter ink impressions are possible as long as the continuous inking is performed in such a manner preventing the microencapsulated or impregnated ink cells from replenishing their ink reserve. The lighter impressions are achieved through depletion of the impregnated or microencapsulated cells. The lightness of the impressions will not be as dramatic as those impressions produced from the hand and self-inking stamps. Even though the gradation of lighter ink saturation is subtle, it still allows the examiner to observe characteristics hidden by the more commonplace heavier ink saturation of a pre-inked stamp. The pre-inked cells will replenish and fill with ink after the stamp has rested for a few seconds.

Obtaining lighter ink impressions from continuous stamping of a flat die stamp is difficult if not impossible. The ink is stored in a reservoir located behind the die and the ink can only exit through the open pores of the text on the die. Since the micropores are merely openings and are not impregnated with ink, their ink supply is not depleted and the stamp is able to produce heavily inked successive impressions. As a general rule, the first impression contains the same amount of ink saturation as the twentieth impression (Fig. 5.16).

The amount of padding underneath the paper or host material can affect the quality of the impression. Minimal padding underneath the host material provides a better quality stamp impression. A hand or self-inking stamp die has a tendency to bounce if there is no padding under the host material. Excess material allows too much flexibility resulting in an uneven stamping surface when downward pressure is applied to the stamp by the stamper. A pre-inked stamp with a relief die will compensate and still produce a properly inked impression even in the presence of excess padding under the host material. Flat die stamps must have a flat surface for the host material. If the host material is supported by excess padding, a partial impression made by a flat die stamp is the result (Fig. 5.17). The reason for the partial impression is that ink will only exit the micropores of a flat die stamp when it comes in contact with the material. An uneven surface prevents the necessary contact and because the die is flat, it cannot compensate because it does not have a relief.

Once the known impression exemplars have been made, the author examines the impressions to note the general and specific characteristics. Observations are made of the variation in ink coverage within the impressions and if the squeegee effect is present. Is the ink saturation even or patchy? Did the ink bleed through the paper? If defects were observed on the die during the examination of the stamp, did the defects appear in the impression and what affect did the external variables have on the presence of the defects?

The final phase of the examination process is to compare the questioned impression to the known impression exemplars. A side-by-side comparison of the two sets of impressions is conducted to determine if they share the same combination of characteristics or if each bears a different set. Observation and proper interpretation of what is observed are the two keys that provide the basis for a conclusion in a stamp impression case. As in all examinations, the examiner must be methodical not only in thought and reasoning processes, but must also exercise proper application of the knowledge regarding the stamp classifications, the manufacturing processes, and the stamp die characteristics. Why would the application of this knowledge be so important? In the examination of rubber stamps, the examiner must be mindful of the possibility of duplicate stamps. If the examination process yields a result that the questioned and known impressions reflect the same class characteristics but both are free of individual defects, the examiner would be hard pressed to state the

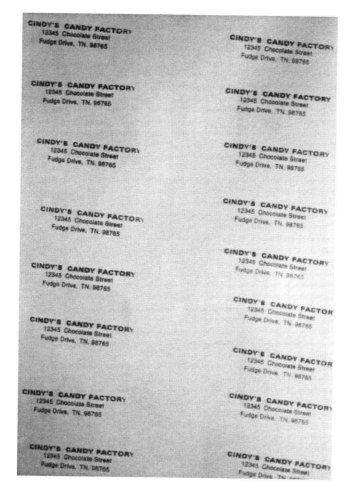

Figure 5.16. *Top*. These represent successive stamp impressions made by U.S. Stamp's ThermalVision flat die stamp. A progressive decline of ink saturation in each successive impression will not be observed in flat die stamps.

Figure 5.17. *Bottom*. Flat die stamps must have a flat surface to produce a complete impression. This partial impression was caused by an uneven host surface, thereby preventing the die from making contact with the envelope during stamping.

questioned impression and the known stamp impressions came from the same source. The final phase relies upon the application of the knowledge of the manufacturing processes and the materials used for the die in order to explain the observations.

DATING AN IMPRESSION

Over time, subtle changes occur to the stamp die. Defects can change in size and shape over time as a result of ink accumulation or continued damage (Figs. 5.18A, 5.18B & 5.18C). They may even disappear if the excess material has been removed by trimming or has endured wear to the point that it no longer prints when making an impression. Continuous use of the stamp creates progressive defects due to gradual wear on the relief of the die. The area of the die that is worn down as a result of continuous use lacks the initial relief height, thereby allowing either a non-print area or a distortion in that area of the die to print during the stamping process. Transient features such as dirt or debris may have been removed either through use or cleaning. Depending upon the environment, cracking or shrinkage of a vulcanized rubber die can also occur. These changes are of great assistance in dating a rubber stamp impression. Known exemplars spanning an extended time frame will allow the examiner to study the history of the defect to determine if it was initially present or developed over time. Chronological history of the stamp will also establish the progression of the change to the defect allowing the examiner to determine if the condition of the defect on the questioned impression is consistent contemporaneously with known course of business stamp exemplars.

Manufacturer improvements to the materials may provide additional evidence in dating a stamp. Introductory dates of the various sizes of stamp mounts, the design of the mount itself, use of pigments instead of dyes in inks, and improved die materials can aid the examiner in determining if the submitted stamp suspected of making the disputed impression even existed on the alleged date. For example, on November 15, 2000, Brother International Corporation released the improved version of their Stampcreator Pro light burst units. The newer units contain an improved thermal ink ribbon that allows the unit to produce a stamp with sharp edges. In addition to the improved ribbon, the container housing the second generation Stampcreator Pro stamp differs from the original or first generation stamp because it is available in bright translucent colors. Millennium's MaxLight Pre-ink Stamps originally made stamps in seven sizes. With the introduction of the XL-700 in February 2001, the available stamp sizes marketed by Millennium increased to ten.

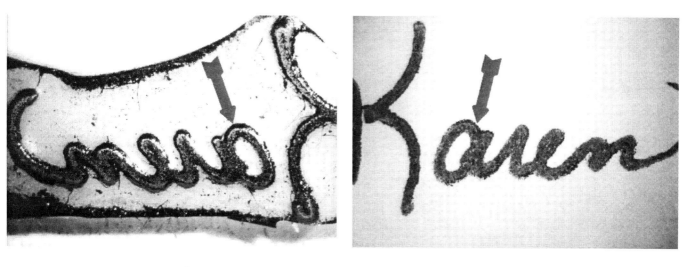

Figure 5.18A–C. (A) *Top left.* Residual stamp ink that has dried on the outline of the letters on a die may appear in the impression. This outline caused by the dried ink is a transient defect and mimics the outline caused by the squeegee effect commonly observed in stamp impressions produced from relief stamp dies as well as the letterpress printing process. (B) *Top right.* The impression was produced from the stamp die prior to cleaning. (C) *Lower center.* This impression was produced from the same stamp die after it had been cleaned removing the dried ink that was outlining portions of the individual letters in the name "Karen."

DUPLICATE AND COUNTERFEIT STAMPS

The contemporary stamp maker relies heavily on the computer in the manufacturing process of rubber stamps. The majority of stamps are made using one or more of the cold type processes such as ultraviolet (photopolymer), laser, light burst, and thermal. As a result, the computer with the appropriate software is used to design the artwork for the negative. A scanner is also used to scan a stamp impression or artwork that will be used for the new die.

Having to factor into the equation the use of the computer and scanner to create the image that will be used to make the negative, the possibility of a stamp having been duplicated or counterfeited is not as remote as it used to be. This one statement will be the most misunderstood by the layman and the most abused by opposing attorneys. The competent examiner, however, will remain focused on knowing and understanding the intrinsic limitations of the evidence: in the examination of rubber stamps, there is a possibility of the suspected stamp being a duplicate, or the suspected stamp is the original stamp and has been duplicated. Therefore, the author felt it necessary to make this statement since one of the limitations encountered by the document examiner in the majority of stamp cases will be the possible existence of a duplicate of the stamp suspected of making a questioned impression.

To illustrate the ease of making duplicate stamps, the author took an impression made from a pre-inked stamp having a pre-mixed gel die to Kim Rowan at A-1 Rubber Stamp & Engraving. The die on this stamp had numerous defects that were identified as air bubbles. Since the air bubbles could have occurred in one of two stages in the manufacturing process, their classification would be random. Kim Rowan made an impression from the gel stamp and scanned it so the image would appear on the computer screen. Within 30 minutes, four different stamps using the original impression from the gel stamp had been made. All four duplicates are photopolymer and were manufactured using the ultraviolet process.

The first stamp duplicated was a counterfeit of the original stamp impression (Figs. 5.19A, 5.19B, 5.19C & 5.19D). All of the defects that appeared in the original impression remained in the artwork. By comparing the original impression to the counterfeit impression, the edges surrounding the defect areas of the counterfeit are cleaner. The reproduction of defects in the artwork onto the die material is similar to the photocopy of an original signature lacking the reproduction of light tapering and connecting strokes.

Using the computer and Adobe Print Shop software, Kim removed the defects reproduced in the original impression and made the second stamp (Figs. 5.20A & 5.20B). This stamp and its impression are free of defects and reflects the class characteristics of the original impression. Even though the defects are gone, this stamp is still a generation of the original gel stamp.

The original defects were removed and new defects were incorporated into the artwork image for the third stamp. The result is a stamp impression whose original source remains the gel stamp but now has a different set of defects solely created on the computer and not a result of a manufacturing faux paux or individual use (Figs. 5.21A & 5.21B).

So far, all of the stamp impressions from the counterfeit or duplicate stamps have a slightly fuzzy look to them. The reason for the characters lacking crisp-

Figure 5.19A–D. (A) *Top left*. Air bubbles create void areas in the "O" and "S" on the pre-mix gel die stamp. (B) *Top right*. The impression is made from the pre-mixed gel stamp reflecting the presence of the two defects. (C) *Center left*. This is a duplicate stamp made from an impression produced from the original pre-mixed gel die stamp. The die was produced using the ultraviolet process and is made of photopolymer. (D) *Center right*. The impression was made from the duplicate stamp. Since the text is a copy, the defects tend to have more blunt endings as opposed to the tapering characteristic observed on the endings of the defects in the original stamp. Also note the ink coverage or saturation differ between the original and the duplicate stamps. The difference is due to the original stamp being made of pre-mixed gel that uses an oil-based ink. The duplicate is made of photopolymer that uses a water-based ink.

Figure 5.20A–B. (A) *Lower left*. This duplicate stamp was made from the impression of the original pre-mixed gel stamp. The impression was scanned into the computer and the operate removed the defects observed in the original stamp. (B) *Lower right*. The impression from this stamp contains all of the class characteristics of the original stamp minus the defects.

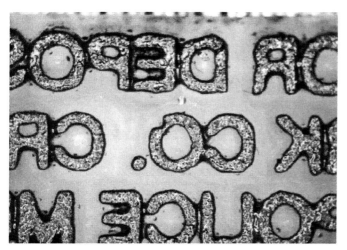 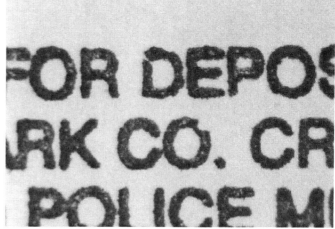

Figure 5.21A–B. (A) *Left.* This illustrates a duplicate stamp made from the impression of the original stamp with the defects removed and added new defects in the "O" of CO. and the "D" in Deposit using computer software. (B) *Right.* Impression produced from this stamp. The blunt endings on the defect areas are present indicating the defect was in the artwork for the stamp die and not part of the ultraviolet step in the manufacturing process (Courtesy of Lamar Miller).

ness is that the stamps are, in fact, a multi-generation copy of the original stamp. This same phenomenon is observed in multi-generation photocopies. The presence of thick or fuzzy characters is not sufficient evidence in and of itself to state the impression came from a duplicate or counterfeit of an original stamp. The fuzzy appearance may be a result of the quality of the paper hosting the impression.

The technique of overlaying was used to manufacture the fourth stamp that is free of the defects and this technique eliminates the fuzzy appearance of the characters. Kim types in the text from the original gel stamp and then pastes the new text image on top of the original image using the Adobe Photo Shop software. Once the two images overlay, she then commands the software to make the newer text the same size, spacing, type style, and arrangement of the original artwork. The result is a stamp that produces a well-defined and crisp impression reflecting all of the class characteristics of the original stamp impression minus the defects (Figs. 5.22A & 5.22B). Stamps produced using the overlay method will be free of the fuzzy appearance or thickening of characters since it is not a multi-generation copy of the original stamp impression.

The rationale for knowing the manufacturing processes of rubber stamps and being cognizant of the possibility of a duplicate stamp being in existence is obvious. The four different stamps created from the one original pre-inked stamp demonstrates the ease of taking an impression and manufacturing duplicate or counterfeit stamps using computer software and a scanner.

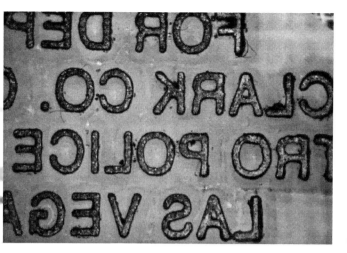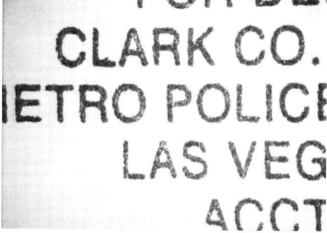

Figure 5.22A–B. (A) *Left.* The technique of overlaying the pasted image of the text onto the scanned image produces a duplicate die that makes an impression, shown in 5.22B *(right),* free of characteristics commonly associated with a multi-generation copy.

Another avenue the examiner can pursue in determining if a duplicate of a stamp exists is to find out the circumstances of how the stamp was produced. For example, if the stamp can be traced to the stamp maker, the examiner would know what was submitted for the artwork, i.e., an original artwork or a stamp impression from the customer's order form. The stamp maker's impression proofs would provide a known impression exemplar of the stamp. As stated earlier in the chapter, the retaining of this documentation varies among the stamp makers and manufacturers. Providing the stamp is submitted for examination and it contains information as to the identity of the stamp maker, taking the extra step to track down the stamp maker or manufacturer can provide a wealth of information that will aid the examiner in determining if the submitted stamp is the original or a duplicate.

REPORT OF FINDINGS

Due to the diversity of stamp manufacturing processes, materials used for the die, the stamp inks, and the variation introduced by the stamper while producing the impression, a definitive conclusion may be difficult to render except in certain instances. Jay Levinson, in his 1983 article, wrote, "Conclusions couched in such generalized terms as 'apparently,' 'probably,' or 'usually' are unfortunately very often the correct approach. And sometimes, even these terms must be rejected in favor of an honest assessment of even less certainty."[10] The inherent limitations in the evidence creates the difficulty for definitive conclusions, provides the justification for qualified conclusions.

Definitive conclusions of elimination are warranted when the suspected stamp bears class characteristics such as type size, style, or arrangement that differ from the questioned impression.

Definitive conclusions of identification, however, are not as common in the examination of rubber stamps. The possibility of a duplicate stamp being in existence is the primary reason for being unable to issue a definitive identification stating that the submitted stamp is the only stamp that could have made the questioned impression. The ability to issue a definitive conclusion is based on the following factors: the suspected stamp has to be examined; the questioned stamp impression has to be an original impression; the suspected stamp and the questioned impression have to be in agreement in class, random, and individual characteristics; the individual characteristics have to yield themselves to being unique in size, shape, and placement on the die or in a print area; and the feature or defect must be reproducible in some but not necessarily all of the impressions. All of these factors must also be in agreement contemporaneously to the date of the document.

The factors listed in the above paragraph set the stage for a definitive conclusion. Agreement in class characteristics is not enough to warrant a definitive conclusion, but rather, there must be individual characteristics or defects that would make the stamp that created the impression unique or one of a kind. The degree of conclusion is solely dependent upon the significance of the individual defects found in agreement between the questioned stamp impression, the known stamp, and the known stamp impressions. Without the presence of at least one significant individual characteristic or defect, a definite conclusion stating the submitted stamp is the only stamp that could have produced the questioned impression is not warranted.

The report that identifies the impression and the submitted stamp as having originated from the source not only acknowledges the possibility, no matter how remote, that a duplicate of the stamp could exist, but clearly states the questioned impression and the stamp are in agreement in class, random, and individual characteristics. Some examiners use the phrase, "the impression is a generation of the stamp" instead of stating "they originate from the same source." These two statements identify the impression as having been produced by either the submitted stamp or a duplicate of that stamp. Either way, the statements focus the basis for the identification on the random or individual defects present in both the questioned impression and the submitted stamp. Since the examiner knows an impression from the original stamp could have been used to make a duplicate, using this terminology allows the examiner to be technically correct in reporting the examination findings.

Qualified conclusions are the norm when the examiner must conduct an impression to impression examination because the suspected stamp cannot be submitted. Without the submission of a suspected stamp, it would be difficult for the examiner to state, without qualification, that the questioned and known impressions came from the same source. Since defects or features are not always reproduced in every impression, the examiner would never know if all the defects on the stamp die were reproduced in the questioned or known impressions. The type and source of the defect is much more difficult and may not be determined without examining the stamp. And finally, the known impressions may not reflect the variation in stamping and inking that are beneficial for the examination.

A no conclusion is issued when the examination reveals that the submitted stamp and the questioned impression lack random or individual defects even though there is complete agreement in class characteristics. The absence of any specific individual feature prevents the examiner from issuing even a qualified conclusion. The report can state that the stamp and the questioned impression are in agreement in class characteristics, but due to lack of individual features, a conclusion cannot be reached.

REFERENCES

1. Casey, Maureen A.: The individuality of rubber stamps. *Forensic Science International, 12:* 134–144,1978.
2. Lindblom, Brian S.: Handout. Examination Techniques in Rubber Stamp Cases. ABFDE Workshop, 1998.
3. Ibid.
4. Herkt, A.: Rubber stamps: manufacture and identification. *Journal of the Forensic Science Society, 25:* 23–38,1985.
5. Lindblom, Brian S.: Handout. Examination Techniques in Rubber Stamp Cases. ABFDE Workshop, 1998.
6. Hessler, R.W.: Identification of rubber stamp impressions *R.C.M.P. Gazette, 46* (1): 11–16, 1984.
7. Ibid.
8. Herbertson, Gary: *Rubber Stamp Examination.* Colorado Springs, Wide Line, 1997.
9. Ibid.
10. Levinson, Jay and Perelman, Benjamin: Examination of cachet impressions. *Journal of Forensic Science, 28:* 235–241, 1983.

Chapter 6

CLOSE-UP PHOTOGRAPHY OF RUBBER STAMPS

A. LAMAR MILLER

Photographs tell the story of what the forensic document examiner learned from the examination of evidence. All the subtle similarities or differences revealed in an examination can be demonstrated with close-up photographs. Photographs are demonstrative evidence to assist the court in understanding how the examiner reached his or her conclusion.

Forensic document examiners use photography as a tool to document their findings in a number of their examinations. Close-up photography is a useful tool to document rubber stamp evidence for the following reasons:

- Traditionally, it has been considered a good practice for forensic document examiners to pictorially record the evidence which has been examined.
- Photographs have the ability to record fine details which may not reproduce in photocopies.
- Creates a permanent record of the evidence because the original exhibits are often returned to contributors or introduced in court as evidence.
- Demonstrate examination findings in laboratory reports.
- An aid to prevent excessive handling of original evidence.
- Used as demonstrative evidence in support of expert testimony.

EQUIPMENT AND FILM

Cameras and Accessories

The same equipment used to photograph signatures, handwriting, fingerprints, and other forensic evidence may be utilized in photographing rubber stamps and impressions. Many document examiners now use a 35mm single lens reflex (SLR) camera and macro lens with a through the lens (TTL) light meter to photograph evidence. If a macro lens is not available, a series of close-up adapters which screw on the lens may be used. For on-film enlargements, a microscope, a bellows, or extension tube may be used.

Excellent photographs can be obtained with the use of a large format camera in the hands of a skilled photographer. The larger format cameras are expensive, require greater skill, and are not as readily available as 35mm cameras.

The use of digital cameras in photographing evidence has increased over the last few years. Digital cameras have the advantage of real time results. The images are immediately available providing the opportunity to adjust exposures and lighting to achieve proper photographs. Image quality from today's digital cameras surpasses those created by some consumer level printers.

Additional equipment to assist the examiner in photographing stamps and impressions includes a camera stand and a cable shutter release (Fig. 6.1). The purpose of the camera stand is to provide a secured mount for the camera to eliminate movement while the shutter is in motion. A cable shutter release will allow the examiner to trigger the camera's shutter without moving the camera. Using the camera's self-timer instead of a cable shutter release will also minimize camera movement during film exposure.

Film

To photograph a stamp or an impression with a 35mm camera, there are several types of film the examiner can use. The following types of film are available and suitable for close-up photography of rubber stamps and impressions:

- Conventionally processed black and white film is available in most emulsions and film speeds. Excellent results can be obtained from this type of film. However, this type of film requires darkroom skills and time to develop and print the photographs. If a darkroom is not available, the film will have to be sent to a custom photo laboratory for processing and developing.
- Process C-41 black and white film can be processed and printed at the local one-hour color photo labs. The one-hour color labs offer many services including the production of enlargements and digitizing the images onto a CD-ROM.
- Color film or color slides offer the advantage of recording the ink color of the impression. Color film can be processed and printed by the local one-hour photo lab and the images can be digitized onto a CD-ROM for use in computer applications. Kodak Ektachrome color slide film uses E-6 processing, which can be processed in about an hour. Accurate color reproduction in photographs will require control of lighting, exposure, and processing.

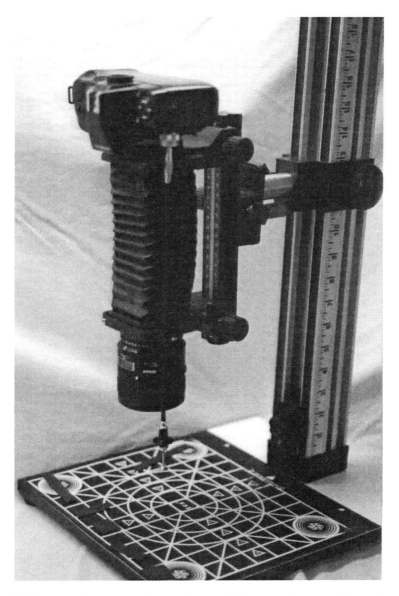

Figure 6.1. A bellows attachment may be used instead of a macro lens to achieve close-up photographs of a stamp die or an impression. A copy stand and cable shutter release are used to eliminate movement of the camera while the shutter is in motion.

Shutter Speed, *f* Stops, and Depth of Field

Light must reach the film in order to record the images. The amount of light reaching the film is critical for correct exposure and is controlled by the *f* stop and the shutter speed. The shutter speed is the time the shutter is open to allow light to reach the film and is measured in seconds or fractions of seconds from the slowest speed of 4 to the fastest speed of 1/1000 second. The examiner needs to keep in mind that each change to a slower shutter speed doubles the time the shutter is open, which doubles the amount of light reaching the film. For example, a shutter speed of 1/250 allows twice as much light to reach the film as a shutter speed of 1/500.

The *f* stop is a measure of the size of the opening through which the light passes to reach the film and is the second factor controlling the amount of light in the film exposure process. The numbers engraved on the barrel of the lens are the *f* stop numbers. Typical *f* stop settings on a modern macro or close-up lens will be *f*3.5, *f*5.6, *f*8, *f*11, *f*16, *f*22, and *f*32. The numbers are derived from a mathematical equation with the smaller numbers representing larger lens openings and the larger numbers representing smaller openings. For example, providing the shutter speed remains the same, an *f* stop setting of *f*3.5 allows twice the amount of light to reach the film than a setting of *f*5.6. Reversing the *f* stop setting, *f*5.6 allows half the amount of light to reach the film as an *f* stop setting of *f*3.5.

Depth of field is the area in a photograph that is in focus from the front to the back of the image. If the depth of field is shallow, the face of a character on a rubber stamp would be in focus while the shoulder is blurred. A greater depth of field would produce a photograph of the character and shoulder both in focus. The *f* stop controls the depth of field. The larger the *f* stop number, the greater the depth of field. For example, an *f* stop of *f*16 has a greater depth of field than an *f* stop of *f*5.6.

When photographing rubber stamp impressions on paper, depth of field is not a limiting factor. However, depth of field is a limiting factor when photographing the actual stamp. The modern single lens reflex (SLR) cameras usually allow the photographer to view what is being photographed with the lens at the lowest *f* stop (wide open).

EXPOSURE, LIGHTING, AND FOCUSING

Exposure Settings

In photography, the correct amount of light must reach the film to obtain a quality print. There are two types of light: reflected and incident. Reflected light is the light that bounces off an object into our eyes. Incident light is the light that falls on an object. The difference is not only one of perception, but measurement.

All objects absorb and reflect light. White objects reflect 100 percent of the light striking them and absorb 0 percent, while black objects reflect 0 percent of the light striking them and absorb 100 percent. Any object that is not pure white or pure black reflects some and absorbs some. For example, given the same light source striking two different objects, a white object and a black object, the white object will reflect all of the light striking it, while the black object reflects no light at all. Everything in between is gray and has a gray value, regardless of its color.[1]

Reflected light meters measure the light that reflects from the object the light is striking. They measure that light as 18 percent gray. This is a photographic standard and the 18 percent gray cards can be purchased at any quality photo store.

The meters built into SLR cameras are reflected light meters. They will try to see the subject, regardless of its actual gray value, as 18 percent gray, and whether you want it or not, will give you an exposure that will result in 18 percent gray. This will always result in either over- or underexposure. For example, when photographing a white object, the meter "sees" the white object as 18 percent gray, and tries to darken it. The final photo, therefore, is underexposed and comes out dark. Conversely, a black object will be overexposed (too light) as the meter reading will tell the camera to let in more light to render the black object lighter than it really is.

If relying upon the camera's reflected light meter, purchase an 18 percent gray card and place it in position to be occupied by the object to be photographed, set the lighting, then use the camera's built in reflected light meter to take the meter reading off the 18 percent gray card. Since the 18 percent gray card is reflecting 18 percent, the meter is getting what it wants, and won't yield false readings. Set the camera to the indicated settings, replace the 18 percent gray card with the object in question, and shoot the photo.

An incident light meter, however, will measure the amount of light striking the object in question. It is not trying to create 18 percent gray. Incident meters cannot be built into any camera. The meter is held in the same position as the object to be photographed, and pointed back at the camera. The lights are turned on, and the amount of light falling on the meter is measured, giving a correct exposure, regardless of the object's gray values.[2] Blacks will be black and whites will be white, and all gray values will appear correct.

Film is rated by an ISO film speed (formally known as the ASA rating) and the higher the number, the faster the film. Even though faster films require less light to properly expose the photographs, the photographic image may not be as sharp, thereby affecting the quality of the print.

To photograph rubber stamps and impressions through the microscope, the photographer can adjust the camera's built-in light meter to ISO 200 when using ISO 400 film. The lower setting will hopefully prevent overexposed images. If the prints are still overexposed (too light), then lower the setting to

ISO 100. If the ISO setting is changed on the camera, the examiner or photographer must advise the photo lab of the change. When submitting the film to the photo lab for processing, the examiner must advise the lab technician the ISO setting was adjusted to a different setting. If notification is not given, the lab technician will process the film at the ISO setting on the roll of film which will adversely affect the quality of the print.

Lighting

It is important to have even lighting when photographing rubber stamp impressions on paper. One method of providing even illumination is to focus two lights on the stamp impression from a 45 degree angle on each side of the camera. The angle may need to be adjusted to provide even illumination from edge to edge of the frame.

A second method of illumination is the use of tent lighting. A lighting tent is formed by making a cylinder from a sheet of white paper. The cylinder is placed over the rubber stamp or impression and the camera lens or microscope lens protrudes from the top of the lighting tent (Figs. 6.2A & 6.2B). The lights are on the outside of the cylinder and should be adjusted into a position to provide even illumination. This technique is especially valuable in photographing defects on the rubber stamp. The primary light is used to illuminate the tent from one side and a smaller maneuverable light, such as a fiber optic light source, can be adjusted to allow proper shadows and highlights to reflect the defect.

Focusing

Once the camera and lighting are in proper position, focusing the camera on the stamp or the impression is the next task the examiner must tackle. A good starting point for photographing rubber stamps and impressions is close-up photography in the range of $\frac{1}{2}$ X. This means the image on the film will be one-half life size. Additional detail may then be photographed at life size, or 1X.

It is difficult to accurately focus such close-up images by twisting the barrel of the camera lens in the manner one would use to focus the lens in a conventional snapshot. Focus is achieved in close-up photography by moving the entire camera to and from the copy (stamp or impression). This is one of the reasons a sturdy copy stand is needed. Fine control of moving the camera in and out of focus can be accomplished with the use of a focusing rail. The focusing rail has knobs which allow slow and steady movement of the camera, similar to the fine focus knob on a microscope.

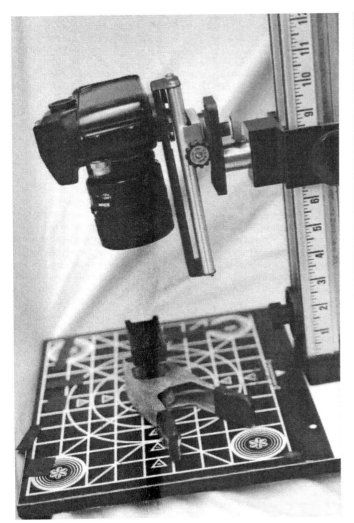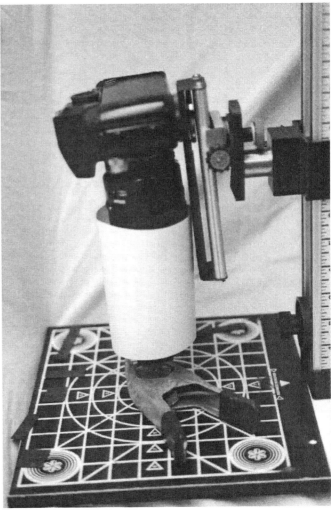

Figure 6.2A–B. (A) *Left.* The camera is securely mounted on the arm of the copy stand. The stamp die is held in an upright position. (B) *Right.* The lighting tent is placed over the stamp and the camera lens.

STEPS TO A QUALITY PHOTOGRAPH OF A
STAMP OR IMPRESSION

The forensic document examiner uses photographs to document characteristics or evidence deemed significant as well as to explain how he or she reached the conclusion. This section lists suggested steps the examiner can follow in order to obtain a quality close-up photograph of a stamp or an impression. The steps outlined in this section are merely a guide and do not reflect the only method used when photographing evidence.

Many of the items of evidence photographed by the forensic document examiner are two-dimensional and made under controlled laboratory conditions. Excellent close-up photographs of three-dimensional rubber stamps can be made in a laboratory with the camera equipment listed in this chapter and a little patience.

The steps to making a close-up photograph of a rubber stamp or an impression are as follows:

- Choose the type of film and load into the camera. The author recommends readily available film such as Kodak Black & White T400 CN, rated as ISO 400, or a similar Process C-41 film. The film box carries the warnings, "Process C-41 Only" and "Do not process in black and white chemicals."
- Mount the camera on a sturdy copy stand and attach a cable release or use the camera self-timer.
- Begin experimenting with close-up photography using printed text from a newspaper.
- Place the newspaper on the copy board and adjust the magnification settings on the lens barrel to $\frac{1}{2}$X.
- Focus the image by moving the camera slowly toward and away from the copy. A method of quickly achieving focus is to hold a pencil under the lens and move it back and forth between the camera and the copy until the pencil is in focus.
- The camera to pencil distance will equal the camera to copy distance for rough focus.
- Readjust the camera to this distance and use the focusing rail or copy stand to slowly move the camera to achieve critical focus.
- Some examiners use a ruler or scale in the photograph. This gives the viewer a frame of reference in which to judge the size of the object. The ruler can be a conventional ruler, printed tabs, series of lines, or rulers made by American Board of Forensic Odontology (ABFO). If a ruler is going to be used, position the ruler under the item to be photographed.
- Prepare a lighting tent and fasten the edges with staples or tape. Use a large diameter cylinder so it will not intrude into the photograph.
- Place the cylinder over the copy and adjust the length until it extends slightly above the bottom of the lens.
- Place two similar lights at equal distances from either side of the copy and at a 45 degree angle to the copy board. If the lights are not equal, place the largest light to one side and the smaller light on the other side of the cylinder, but closer to the copy.
- Adjust the positions of the lights by examining the image in the camera view finder.

- Adjust the lights until the copy is evenly illuminated from edge to edge. The paper cylinder diffuses the light and assists in achieving even illumination.
- Once the camera and lights are in position, set the exposure by adjusting the ISO setting, using an 18 percent gray card, or an incident light meter. If using the gray card or the incident light meter, place under the camera where the stamp die or impression will be placed and then set the camera to the indicated settings. If the camera is mounted on the microscope, adjust the ISO setting, set the lens f stop to the smallest number on the lens, usually $f2$ or $f3.5$. The smallest number means the largest lens opening and the greatest amount of light reaching the film.
- Adjust the shutter speed to bracket the exposures several settings above and below the light meter reading.
- Adjust the camera magnification to life size, 1X, and repeat the process.
- Have the film processed and critically examine the prints for proper lighting, focus, and exposure.

Photography of evidence can also be used to document and demonstrate our findings to the court. If the photographs are to be used for court exhibits, there should be a series of photographs beginning with an overview of the evidence. Subsequent close-up photographs should lead the viewer to the subtle characteristics of the evidence. The final photograph(s) should clearly demonstrate the basis of the opinion. Composite photographs depicting the questioned and known items are well suited for this purpose.

REFERENCES

1. Risi, Don. Interview. August, 2001.
2. Ibid.

Chapter 7

RUBBER STAMP INKS

JAMES GREEN

Preceding chapters have explored the construction techniques of various rubber and polymer stamps. Regardless of the construction type, the stamp's purpose or stamping medium, rubber stamps are obviously useless without compatible ink. After some interesting historical information, this chapter will cover some of the components used in the ink making process, as well as the results of using incompatible inks on stamps. This chapter also provides photographs from infrared examinations of various stamp inks and images from plates used in a Thin Layer Chromatography (TLC) comparison.

HISTORY

Prior to the development of inks for printing, the earliest inks known were used in writing. References to writing inks are made in China and Egypt around 2500 B.C.[1] These inks are believed to have been made from lamp-black mixed with gum and applied by brush or quill.[2]

Gutenberg has been credited with the development of moveable metal type and the press. In addition, he deserves recognition for his discovery of oil-based ink.

Joseph Moxon provides an interesting account of one of the ink making processes from the seventeenth century. He described how linseed oil is "heat-bodied" by boiling the oil until it catches fire. The flames are then extinguished by means of a metal cover and the fire rekindled until the oil has attained a satisfactory consistency. Moxon suggests testing the oils' viscosity, "to try if it be hard enough to put three or four drops on an oyster shell and when it be cold enough he touch it with his fore or middle finger and thumb,

181

for if it draw still like turpentine (meaning rosin) it be hard enough. If not he boyl it longer or burn it again till it be so consolidated."[3]

In addition, Moxon complained that other ink makers, ". . . used far too much rosin or train oil, that they bodied their oils insufficiently and used too little lampblack."[4] Moxon also mentioned the, ". . . placing of an onion in the oil during boiling to tell if it be hot enough—alternatively, an apple or crust of bread could be used."[5]

In the 1830s, another ink formula was utilized, following this simple process: "To Make Black Ink / 1 fi Galls 1 oz. Gum Arabick 1 oz. Sugar Candy / 1 fi oz. Copperas 6 Cloves 1 Drm. Indigo. / Infuse these in a Jug with 3 half pints Boilg. Water for 12 hours, stir(r)ing it occasionally." The sugar candy would make the ink glossy, the cloves would prevent molding, and the indigo was a provisional colorant (Fig. 7.1).[6]

During the 19th century, apothecaries provided much of the writing ink. It was more efficient for the apothecary to, ". . . prepare the fluid in quantity and pour it into standard bottles, which they sold with their own labels affixed."[7] Eventually, individual ink makers lost their share of the market due to the formation of large ink manufacturing firms such as Carter's, which was established in 1858.

INK COMPONENTS

In the last century, the ink manufacturing industry has developed into a highly technical field with numerous companies producing inks for specific applications. Yet, the development of rubber stamp inks has not been without challenges. Initially, some of the formulas used caused the stamp dies to delaminate from the handle, while other formulas caused the die to prematurely deteriorate through hardening or cracking.

Although similar components are used in the manufacturing process for pen inks and rubber stamp inks, the formula for stamp inks may be less exacting. Stamp inks may be much less viscous and do not require the concentration of dyestuffs, which are necessary in pen inks. In addition, rubber stamp inks require less engineering since the ink does not have to meet the exacting tolerances necessary for writing instruments, i.e., ballpoint pen mechanisms.[8]

Generally, there are a phenomenal number of inks that have been developed for use with polymer and rubber stamps. American Coding and Marking Ink Company, Inc., for example, utilizes over 6,000 different ink formulas.[9] These inks are tailored to match the intended use of the stamps. For example, the stamps used to imprint grades of meat carcasses have to meet stringent Food and Drug Administration requirements. Individual formulas

Figure 7.1. This is an example of an antiquated bottle of rubber stamp ink and pad (Courtesy of James Green).

are needed for stamping plastics and paper products, while another formula is utilized for metered postage stamp cancellations that are reactive to ultraviolet light (Fig. 7.2).[10]

Consumers will not find stamp inks marketed or labeled under the name of most major manufacturers in the industry.[11] Instead, manufacturers generally sell the ink by the gallon on a wholesale basis. The ink is typically packaged in two and four-ounce bottles by the distributors, and then labeled for sales at the retail level. Finally, the stamp ink is marketed through stationery or office supply stores (Fig. 7.3).

The basic components of stamp inks are similar to those used in writing inks. Two key components are "pigments" or "dyes" for coloration, and the "vehicle" which is the liquid portion of the ink. Dyes are used in the vast majority of stamp inks found in banking and other commercial industries.[12] Dyes, unlike pigments, dissolve in the liquid vehicle and can flow unrestricted in stamping mechanisms. In liquid form, dye inks appear very dark and transparent. The true color is apparent after the stamp is imprinted (Fig. 7.4).[13]

The dye, in a powdered state, is dispersed in a surfactant or "long chain fatty acid," which is the equivalent of liquid detergent.[14] Glycol is added to assist with the absorption of the dye into the surface of a paper substrate. Glycerin is also added to give body to the ink matrix.[15]

Figure 7.2. *Top.* A high-speed mixer in an ink vat is used to make dye-based inks. The mixer generates enough heat to totally dissolve the dye when blended with water, glycol, glycerin, and other components. This vat has a 1,000 gallon capacity (Courtesy of Gary Werwa).
Figure 7.3. *Bottom.* Automated filling machine fills stamp pad inks into re-inking bottles. The bottles are available as a roll-on, brush-on, or dropper tipped (Courtesy of Gary Werwa).

Unlike dyes, pigments are manufactured via a chemical process that forms a crystalline substance. Moisture is removed from the resulting mixture and the pigments remain as a solid, even after subsequent blending with a liquid vehicle (Fig. 7.5).

Normally, pigmented inks are found in the art stamp industry, since they provide more vivid coloration than dyes and are more colorfast. For the same reasons, pigmented stamp inks are utilized in the flexographic printing process on containers. However, pigments are avoided in most stamp inks because they remain as a solid, rather than dissolving in a liquid vehicle, which inhibits their ability to flow freely in stamp pads.[16]

The vehicle not only carries the colorant, but also acts as a mechanism to dry the ink. The drying rate is dependent upon the type of solvent selected by the manufacturer to use in a specific formula. The vehicle contains other chemical components, such as a "resin" or "binder" which serves two purposes. First, when pigments are used, it bonds the pigments to each other. Second, once the liquid vehicle has evaporated or has been absorbed into a paper substrate, the resin acts as a bonding agent to adhere the pigments to the paper or material stamped. Ink manufacturers have both natural and synthetic resins available for use during production. Each type of resin has properties suited for specific applications (Fig. 7.6).

Since all resins are solids, another necessary component in ink manufacturing is a solvent to dissolve the resin material. Depending upon the intended use of the ink, and necessary drying time, alcohol, water, or oil-based solvents may be utilized. For example, a high-speed stamping machine is commonly used to apply an expiration date or product code on cosmetics. This process may require the containers be stamped, released from the machine, and inserted into a box, all within 15 to 20 seconds. The stamped impression has to be scuff resistant within seconds.[17] In this type of manufacturing application, an alcohol-based solvent would be a likely choice. Contrary to a high production stamping process, a slower moving machine would require a correspondingly slower drying solvent to prevent the ink from drying on the die.

While alcohol-based solvents rely on evaporation to dry, inks intended for paper substrates will usually use an absorption process to disperse oil or water-based solvents. Castor oil is one type of solvent utilized during manufacturing. This oil-based solvent has the advantage of stability and also provides good saturation, which curtails oxidation. In addition, solvents that are oil-based have the advantage of a lubricating property, which is beneficial in high production stamping processes. A disadvantage of oil-based solvents is their tendency to bleed through to the backside of documents, as well as not drying quickly enough for some applications. Due to their impracticality, manufacturers have significantly reduced their use of true oil-based stamp inks.[18]

Figure 7.4. *Top.* An inventory of dye-based stamp inks is maintained in five gallon containers (Courtesy of Gary Werwa).

Figure 7.5. *Bottom.* A "three roller mill" is used to pulverize dry pigment into fine particles suitable for specific rubber stamp ink applications (Courtesy of Gary Werwa).

Figure 7.6. Blending process of stamp ink with the use of a high-speed mixer is illustrated (Courtesy of Gary Werwa).

In pigmented inks, glycol and glycerin components are added to prevent clumping. Drying oils, sometimes necessary in printing inks, are not used in rubber or polymer stamp inks due to their hardening effect on stamp pads. In most rubber stamp inks, wax components are not included except for special applications. For example, stamps used on paper exposed to petroleum products may require a wax additive to resist the corrosive effects.[19]

Just as the stamping process and the type of substrate influence the selection of a solvent type, the construction of the stamp also mandates a compatible solvent. The common "self-inking" stamp is self-sealing when in the stored position. Since the unit is essentially sealed, quicker drying ink may be used. However, a "pre-inked" stamp has pads that are heat cured at approximately 300°F. Therefore, special ink is necessary since many types of ink would dissipate when subjected to heat of this intensity.[20]

The question may be posed whether inks designated for rubber stamps may be used with polymer stamps, or vice versa. The answer is a solid maybe. True rubber stamps are less susceptible than polymer stamps to the effects of a wider variety of inks. Yet, the use of incompatible inks on rubber or polymer stamps may cause no noticeable difference, varying degrees of distortion of the die, or a complete delamination of the die from its handle.[21] The following photograph shows an endorsement stamp after regularly being subjected to incompatible ink. The die developed a distorted image and subsequently became completely separated from its holder (Fig. 7.7).

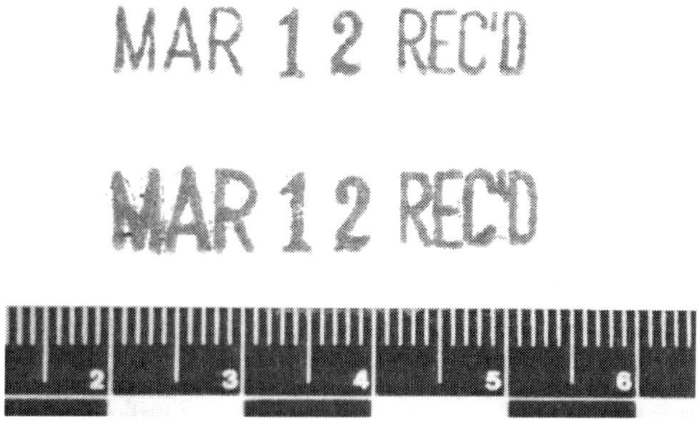

Figure 7.7. *Left*. This shows an endorsement stamp ruined by incompatible ink (Courtesy of James Green).

Figure 7.8. *Right*. The top date impression was made using ink compatible to the rubber stamp. The bottom impression was made eight months later, after incompatible oil-based ink was applied to the stamp (Courtesy of James Green).

Incompatible inks may cause the rubber, on a rubber stamp die, to absorb ink like a sponge. Figure 7.8 shows the effect on a rubber stamp after the application of incompatible oil-based ink. The top date impression was made using ink designed for the rubber stamp. The incompatible oil-based ink was then applied causing the die to swell over time. After several months, the die became distorted and enlarged 1mm both vertically and horizontally, thereby changing the stamped impression. The change in image size and quality could lead to an incorrect assumption that different stamps had been used for each imprint (Fig. 7.8).

Contrary to the previous incompatible ink example, the following photograph shows the results of using an alcohol-based ink to re-ink a pre-inked stamp designed for use with an oil-based ink. The less viscous alcohol-based solvent leaked through the ink pores of the die. The alcohol-based solvent dampened the non-image area of the die and caused the "ghost image" visible in the photograph (Fig. 7.9).

If a self-inking stamp is re-inked with an alcohol-based ink, the quality of print significantly degenerates as shown in Figure 7.10. The alcohol carrier, as in the preceding "Report filed" stamp photograph, has permeated the impression area of the die, causing interference as the oil-based ink is applied to the paper. The result is a mottled effect, rather than the solid image the stamp was designed to provide (Fig. 7.10).

As previously noted, not only must the stamp and ink be compatible, both of these elements must also be suited to the substrate. One problem encoun-

Figure 7.9. *Top left.* The alcohol-based solvent, mistakenly used on this stamp, caused a shadow around the image area (Courtesy of James Green).

Figure 7.10. *Top right.* An alcohol-based ink, used to refill a stamp designed for use with an oil-based ink caused a reduction in print quality on this stamp (Courtesy of James Green).

Figure 7.11. *Lower left.* The wrong choice of ink for this substrate resulted in the stamped image being easily smeared several hours after it was stamped (Courtesy of James Green).

Figure 7.12. *Lower right.* This illustrates an example of "set-off," the unintentional transfer of an image from one page to another (Courtesy of James Green).

tered by using inappropriate ink on a substrate is the failure of the ink to adequately cure. As shown in Figure 7.11, a substrate that prolongs the curing process makes the stamp impression susceptible to smudging. Eight hours after the stamp was applied to a cellophane substrate, the ink easily smeared. A rapid drying alcohol-based ink would be more appropriate than the oil-based ink used (Fig. 7.11). Another example of incompatibility between the stamp and the substrate is "set-off," which is the transfer of an inked image to another paper or material. Selecting a quicker drying solvent for the ink or providing ample time for the drying process can avoid this situation (Fig. 7.12).

Figure 7.13. A viscometer measures the viscosity of inks. Stamp pads must be a certain thickness in order for the ink to lay down on the stamp face and make a full imprint. This is especially critical in large stamps (Courtesy of Gary Werwa).

Obviously, great attention is given to the development of stamps and their compatible inks. Rubber stamp pads must also be engineered to maximize efficiency. Pads are made with a cotton fabric or synthetic material, such as rubber foam. Numerous factors are considered in pad development, including details such as the manner in which the fabric is woven. The weave is consequential for the efficient delivery of the ink to the stamp pad die (Fig. 7.13).[22]

EXAMINATION OF STAMP INKS

A document examiner has a professional interest in the information obtained through an analysis of rubber or polymer stamp inks. In reality, the examination procedures for stamp inks are the same as writing inks. Stamp ink dating may be available, on a limited basis, for government-employed examiners. Forensic ink chemist Larry Olson, of the Internal Revenue Service Laboratory, stated that two stamp ink libraries are maintained, one by the IRS, the other by the U.S. Secret Service. However, neither laboratory has a comprehensive collection of stamp inks. This is primarily due to the reliance on manufacturers to voluntarily submit their inks, and because of the greater demand for analysis of writing inks. Mr. Olson also commented that rubber stamp ink formulas are more simplistic than pen inks and do not seem to change as often.[23]

The same opportunity for ink dating does not appear to be available to document examiners in private practice. Although there are ink chemists in the private sector with writing ink reference libraries to facilitate the dating process, a comprehensive private stamp ink library is not known to exist at this time.

As with writing inks, a Video Spectral Comparator may be employed to compare stamp inks. To illustrate the similarity in the VSC responses between rubber stamp inks and writing inks, the black ink specimens listed below were applied to a Whatman filter. The inks were then examined with a Foster and Freeman VSC-2000, courtesy of Heather Carlson, a forensic document examiner at the Oregon State Police Crime Laboratory.

Pre-inked stamp inks:	*Rubber stamp inks:*
Brother	Sanford
Evermark	Fiskars
X-Stamper	Carter's
Stamp-Ever	Ancient Page
Self-inking stamp inks:	**Ball point pen inks:*
Ideal	Bic
Delmart	Montblanc
Trodat	Pilot
Stamp-Ever	Tombow

* The ballpoint pen inks were included for comparison purposes (Fig. 7.14).

When examined with the VSC-2000 using incident infrared light, differences between some inks are obvious (Fig. 7.15). In addition, differentiation may be obtained with the use of infrared luminescence (Fig. 7.16).

An infrared analysis of inks using incident light in conjunction with the inks' luminescence allows for further differentiation. For inks that do not readily differ, a Thin Layer Chromatography (TLC) process may be used to chem-

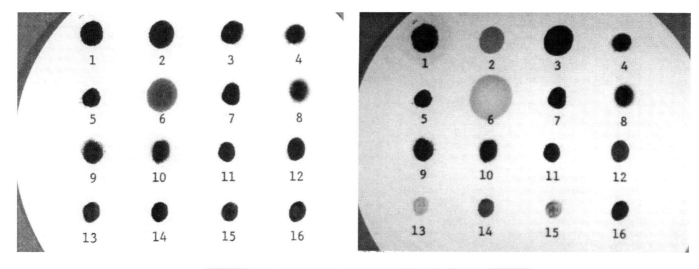

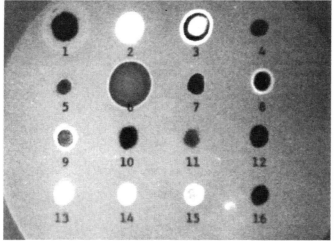

Figure 7.14. *Top left.* A Whatman filter with various ink specimens is used for Video Spectral Comparator (VSC 2000) examination (Courtesy of James Green).
Figure 7.15. *Top right.* VSC-2000 infrared examination results using incidental light are shown (Courtesy of Heather Carlson).
Figure 7.16. *Lower center.* This illustrates VSC-2000 infrared luminescence results. Note the luminescence property of some of the solvents (Courtesy of Heather Carlson).

ically determine their similarities or differences. Sue Fortunato, a senior document examiner with the U.S. Secret Service, stated that the TLC process examines the dyes in stamp inks. Other processes would be used to analyze the vehicles, resins, or other components of the stamp ink. Ms. Fortunato also mentioned the same ink used with rubber stamps may be used in roller ball or fiber tipped pens.[24]

The same inks previously examined utilizing the VSC-2000 were analyzed with the TLC process courtesy of Jane Lewis, an examiner with the Wiscon-

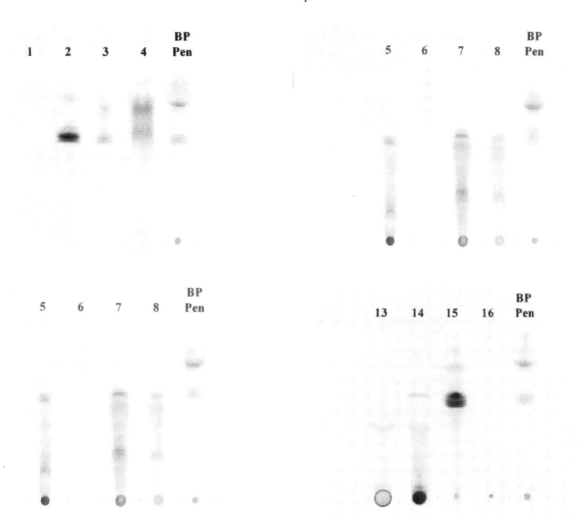

Figure 7.17. *Top left*. Thin Layer Chromatography comparison of pre-inked stamp specimens is shown (Courtesy of Jane Lewis).
Figure 7.18. *Top right*. This is an example of thin Layer Chromatography comparison of self-inking stamp specimens (Courtesy of Jane Lewis).
Figure 7.19. *Lower left*. Thin Layer Chromatography comparison of rubber stamp pad ink specimens is illustrated (Courtesy of Jane Lewis).
Figure 7.20. *Lower right*. This illustrates thin Layer Chromatography comparison of ballpoint pen inks (Courtesy of Jane Lewis).

sin Department of Justice. Photographs were made of the Thin Layer Chromatography plates after the tests were conducted on pre-inked stamp inks (Fig. 7.17), self-inking stamp ink (Fig. 7.18), rubber stamp pad inks (Fig. 7.19), and ballpoint pen inks (Fig. 7.20). The inks are identified by number in the same manner as in the VSC-2000 tests. (The ink sample identified as "BP Pen" on each of the following plates is a blue ballpoint pen, used as a standard.)

The information provided in this chapter should make it evident stamp inks have an effect on not only the stamp image, but also may change the integrity of the die itself. Because of these influences, inks should be given due consideration during an examination of rubber or polymer stamps.

REFERENCES

1. Finley, Charles, Ph.D., Printing Paper & Inks, Albany, 1997, Delmar, p. 238.
2. Printing Ink Manual, Commissioned by The Technical Training Board of the Society of British Printing Ink Manufacturers, W. Heffer & Sons LTD. 1961, Cambridge, p. 3.
3. Ibid. p. 5.
4. Ibid. p. 5.
5. Ibid. p. 5.
6. Nickell, Joe, Pen, Ink & Evidence, Lexington, 1990, The University Press of Kentucky, p. 37.
7. Ibid. p. 38.
8. Olson, Larry: Forensic Ink Chemist, Internal Revenue Service, Chicago, IL. From interview in May 2000.
9. Tracton, Art, Consulting Chemist, Research and Development, American Coding and Marking Ink Company, Inc., Plainfield, N.J. From interview in April 2000.
10. Ibid.
11. Sweet, Thomas, Owner of American Coding and Marking Ink Company, Inc., Plainfield, NJ. From interview in April 2000.
12. Werwa, Gary, Owner of Specialty Ink Company, Inc., Deer Park, NY. From Interview in May 2000.
13. Ibid.
14. Tracton, Art, Consulting Chemist, Research and Development, American Coding and Marking Ink Company, Inc., Plainfield, NJ. From interview in April 2000.
15. Werwa, Gary, Owner of Specialty Ink Company, Inc., Deer Park, NY. From Interview in May 2000.
16. Ibid.
17. Tracton, Art, Consulting Chemist, Research and Development, American Coding and Marking Ink Company, Inc., Plainfield, NJ. From interview in April 2000.
18. Ibid.
19. Doty, Charles, Development Chemist, Chicago Ink and Research Company, Inc., Antioch, IL. From interview in May 2000.
20. Tracton, Art, Consulting Chemist, Research and Development, American Coding and Marking Ink Company, Inc., Plainfield, NJ. From interview in April 2000.
21. Suo, Mike, Chief Chemist, American Coding and Marking Ink Company, Inc., Plainfield, NJ. From interview in April 2000.
22. Tracton, Art, Consulting Chemist, Research and Development, American Coding and Marking Ink Company, Inc., Plainfield, NJ. From interview in April 2000.
23. Olson, Larry, Forensic Ink Chemist, Internal Revenue Service, Chicago, IL. Interview in May 2000.
24. Fortunato, Sue, Senior Document Examiner, U.S. Secret Service, Washington DC. Interview in June 2000.

Appendix A

QUICK REFERENCE CHARTS

Kimberly Kreuz

(See pages 197 and 198.)

Manufacturing Processes of Stamps

Type of Stamp	Vulcanization	Laser Engraved		Ultraviolet	Lightburst/ Xenon Flash	Thermal Printer
		Flatbed	Rotary	Process		
Hand Stamp	X	X	X	X		
Self-inking	X	X	X	X		
Pre-inked	X	X	X		X	X
Pre-inked (gel)	X					
Materials						
Raw rubber	X	X	X			
Laserable rubber	X	X	X			
Foam & Powder NBR[1]	X	X				
PVC	X					
BUNA (Synthetic Rubber)	X					
Silicone	X					
Pre-mixed gel	X					
Salt-leached foam rubber (micro-porous)	X	X	X			
Photopolymer (soluble plastic/resin)		X[2]		X		

Notes
Brother Int'l Corp.'s SC-300 PC is a disposable pre-inked stamp (cannot be re-inked).

Footnotes
[1]NBR can be vulcanized or laser engraved
[2]Laser photopolymer (Merigraph Polymer) is manufactured by Stewart Superior Corp.

Types of Stamps and Their Materials

Materials	Type of Stamp			Relief Type
	Hand Stamp	Pre-Inked	Self-Inking	
Raw/molding rubber	X	never	X	High
BUNA (synthetic rubber)	X	never	X	High
PVC	X		X	High
Silicone	X		X	High
Laserable rubber	X	never	X	High
Foam & Powder: NBR or PVC		X		High
Pre-mixed gel		X		High
Salt-leached foam rubber (microporous)		X		High
Foam rubber – Thermal Process		X		None or flat
Foam rubber – "Lightburst" Technology		X		None or flat
Photopolymer (soluble plastic/resin)	X	never	X	High

Appendix B

MILESTONES IN THE HISTORY OF STAMPS AND MARKING DEVICES

1839   Charles Goodyear discovers vulcanization of rubber in his kitchen by accidentally dropping rubber mixed with sulphur on top of a hot stove.

1843   Jonathon C. Walker obtained the first U.S. patent for a hand stamp which was a rocker-bottom style wooden stamp with felt-covered letters.

1844   Charles Goodyear receives his patent for vulcanized rubber and uses his discovery in the manufacture of rubber overshoes.

1844   Horace Wells, a dentist, patented anesthesia. With anesthesia, tooth extraction could be painless, creating an increased need for false teeth. With the discovery of vulcanization, dental pots made of vulcanized rubber were used to make the molds.

Circa
1864   Invention of the vulcanized rubber stamp. The stamp industry credits James Orton Woodruff with the invention. L.F. Witherall and Henry C. Leland claimed to be the inventors of the first vulcanized rubber stamp and were given credit by at least one publication in the early 1900s.

Circa
1900s   Manufacturing process of seal dies and counters was manual. The letters and characters were hand punched.

Early
1900s   Metal self-inker used for self-inking stamps.

1906   Ludlow Typograph invented by Washington I. Ludlow.

1907   Leo "Doc" Bakeleton introduced a compound he called Bakelite. Bakelite is used those in the marking industry as the mold for vulcanized rubber.

Circa
1930s   Linotype and Ludlow machines began replacing handset moveable type in the manufacturing process of rubber stamps.

Mid 1940s	The matrix board replaced clay and plaster-of-paris molds in the production of vulcanized rubber stamps.
Circa 1940s	NCR and Barry Green patented the salt-leached technology used to manufacture pre-inked cash register dies and pre-inked marking stamps.
Mid 1950s	The Warner Model 46 vulcanizer was sold to budding entrepreneurs who could start manufacturing rubber stamps in their kitchens.
Circa 1955	Mechanical or machine engraving was implemented in the manufacturing process of seals with the introduction of the Pantograph machine.
1957	Harry Leeds and John Levey issued patent for manufacturing products with microporous resinous structures. S. C. Johnson & Son, Inc. acquired the patent and called the microporous material "Porelon."
1959	S. C. Johnson & Son, Inc. marketed the Perma-Stamp Pre-Inked Stamp and Porelon Ink Rollers. The first pre-inked gel stamp marketed.
1960	Invention of photopolymer.
1960	Swedpoint, a Swedish company, developed an adjustable mount to be used as the mount for gel stamps.
1960	Bakelite being used to form the counter for a seal die. Considered less hazardous than the previously used lead splash.
1964	Ludlow introduced the self-centering stick that automatically centered the line of type.
1964	Shachihata discovered the application of the salt-leached process for pre-inked stamps.
1965	The Faymus Stamp, a pre-inked stamp made of a cushion-type foam and a gel-type ink on a mount with spring feet, was marketed by Bankers & Merchants of Chicago.
1968	Shachihata marketed pre-inked stamps using the salt-leached process with the die mount being plastic.
Early 1970s	(A). Trodat developed the plastic self-inker, a small box containing a die plate that rotates inside and seats against a miniature stamp pad that allows for repetitive stamping. (B). M & R Marking Systems introduced an automatic "die sinking" machine.
1974	Stamp industry using photopolymer to manufacture photopolymer stamps. Graphic arts camera and photo typesetting machine used.
1980	Nitrile-butadine (NBR) foam and powder used as die material for stamps.

Early
1980s   (A). Manufacturing process of photopolymer stamps simplified when the process enabled the photopolymer machine to make its own negative in the open light. (B). Computerized engraving used in the manufacturing process of seals.

1981   Gene Griffiths invented the two-sided adhesive cushion used to secure the die to the stamp mount.

1983   Jeff Lovely, owner of Tacoma Rubber Stamp in Tacoma, Washington, introduced a plastic mount made of PVC to replace the wood mount.

1987   Polystyrene replaced the Bakelite as the material of choice for a seal die counter.

1985   Desktop publishing introduced and was integrated into the manufacturing process of photopolymer stamps.

1988   Gene Griffiths of Gregory Stamp, and M & R Marking introduced the plastic mount made of expanded extruded PVC in Montreal.

1989   Dave Hedgecoth discovered a method of self-stabilization of pre-inked gel.

Early
1990s   European rotary laser engravers initially used in the manufacture of pre-inked stamps.

Mid
1990s   Flatbed lasers were modified for use in the laser engraving of salt-leached foam rubber for pre-inked and laserable rubber for self-inking stamps. Also used in the laser engraving of seals using a hard plastic material called Delrin for the die and counter.

1995   Jackson Marking Products introduces the Ultrasonic Washout Unit that uses ultrasonic sound waves to remove excess photopolymer during the washout phase of the ultraviolet manufacturing process.

October
1996   Brother released the SC-300PC stamp machine that utilizes a thermal heating element to open micropores in the printing area of the die.

1996   Unigraphics introduced the FlashStamp in Europe. FlashStamp uses a Xenon flash and pressure to seal the background of an non-inked foam pad.

1997   Unigraphics introduced the FlashStamp in the United States through U. S. Stamp & Sign.

1997   SunStamp introduced by Elite Marking that uses a Xenon flash to seal the back of the rubber die in the non-print area.

1998   Stewart Superior Corporation introduces and distributes laser polymer.

1998   U. S. Stamp & Sign introduced the ThermalVision, which uses a thermal printer to seal the micropores on the pre-inked die.

November
1998   Brother introduced the SC-2000 Stampcreator Pro at Comdex. The Stampcreator Pro utilizes a Xenon flash to close the excess micropores in the non-print area of the die allowing the ink to exit through the open micropores in the print area.

March
1999   Brother releases the SC-2000 Stampcreator Pro.

August
1999   Brother discontinued the manufacture of the SC-300PC.

August
1999   Brother introduced the SC-900 utilizes the same technology as the SC-300PC, but at a higher dpi.

October
1999   Millennium Marking demonstrates the MaxLight, which uses intense light burst technology to make a pre-inked stamp with a flat die at the Marking Device Convention in Orlando, Florida. This machine was a prototype.

November
1999   Trodat's Stamp Printer released on November 11, 1999.

November
1999   Millennium Marking releases the MaxLight Light Burst Unit.

April
2000   Brother releases an improved version of the Stampcreator Pro that produces stamps with crisp edges and sharp corners. This newer version uses a faster drying ink and is contained in a plastic housing with a translucent top.

December
2000   Millennium Marking Co. releases the PowerMax machine that will convert four (4) different sizes of MaxLight pre-inked stamps as well as the MaxLight Dater into an automatic stamping machine.

January
2001   Millennium releases their second generation light burst unit, the MaxLight Ultra Exposures. This unit seal several different sizes of porous pads in one production run. The MaxLight Ultra Exposures employs a single light burst whose intensity setting is determined by the size of the production run.

February
2001   Millennium Marking Co. adds a larger size stamp mount to the MaxLight system The XL-700 mount measures 2 3/4 by 3 3/4 inches in size. MaxLight pre-inked stamps are available in ten sizes.

Appendix C

HUMAN RESOURCES: REFERENCES FROM THE STAMP INDUSTRY

To disseminate in-depth information regarding the classifications, the manufacturing processes, and the types of stamps based on die materials, the task of information gathering was conducted. The individuals listed in this section have a reputation of being knowledgeable sources in the marking industry. Each one graciously contributed their time and sharing of information making this book possible. Each manufacturer or stamp maker listed would be of assistance to a document examiner seeking additional information about a manufacturing process, die material, and introduction/discontinuation dates of product in the marking industry.

1. Diane C. Bosworth
   Access Business Solutions, Inc.
   523 Knollwood Drive
   Hudson, WI 54016

2. Sal and Janet Cannizzaro
   Cannizzaro Seal & Engraving Co., Inc.
   435 Ave. U
   Brooklyn, NY 11223
   1-718-627-5050

3. Rodney Chu (The Apple Stamp)
   Lee Shing Stamp Limited
   Kwai Chung, H.K.
   852-2544-3674

4. William Collins, Vice President
   Indiana Stamp Company
   1475 S. Calhoun St.
   Ft. Wayne, IN 46802
   1-219-424-8973

5. Gene Griffiths, Executive Director
   Marking Device Association International
   222 Wisconsin Avenue, Suite 1
   Lake Forest, IL 60045
   847-283-9810

6. Mike Han, General Manager
   Stewart Superior Corp.
   352 Fail Rd.
   LaPorte, IN 46350
   219-362-9921

7. John Houston
   Carolina Marking Devices, Inc.
   3405 South Tryon Street
   Charlotte, NC 28217-1349
   1-704-525-7600

8. Chuck Jackson
   ACT II Rubber Stamps
   1407 S. Commerce
   Las Vegas, NV 89102
   1-702-388-2098

9. Vicki Johnson
   Shoreline Rubber Stamps
   1747 Taylor Avenue
   Racine, WI 53401
   1-262-633-9033

10. Kenneth Lowrance
    Superior Stamp & Seal Co.
    P.O. Box 2258
    Wichita, KS 67201

11. Mike Mauro
    M & R Marking Systems
    100 Springfield Avenue
    Piscataway, NJ 08855-6969

12. Jeff Mear
    AMI
    605 N. Macquesten Pkwy.
    Mt. Vernon, NY 10552
    1-800-235-0060

13. Mollie Miller, Owner
    Cliff Hughson, Stamp Maker
    A-1 Rubber Stamp & Engraving
    3111 S. Valley View O-103
    Las Vegas, NV 89102
    1-702-876-1495

14. George Murphy; Bill Ryan
    Millennium Marking Company
    2600 Greenleaf Avenue
    Elk Grove Village, IL 60007
    1-847-806-1750

15. Cindy Thomas
    U.S. Stamp/Identity Group, Inc.
    1480 Gould Drive
    Cookeville, TN 38506
    931-432-4000

16. Gary Werwa
    Specialty Ink Company, Inc.
    P. O. Box R 20 Dunton Ave.
    Deer Park, NY 11729
    516-586-3666

17. Eiji "Eddie" Yuki
    Product Manager of Stamp Making
    Devices
    Brother International Corp.
    100 Somerset Corp. Blvd.
    Bridgewater, NJ 08807-0911
    908-704-1700

GLOSSARY

Adhesive Wafer: The backing applied to the die and counter of seals. The adhesive wafer's function is to standardize the gap between the die, the counter, and the space provided in the die holder.

Alphabet Stamp: The common term for a stamp assembled entirely with letter bands. Often used where coded lettering or complete words are to be stamped.

Alphanumeral Band Stamp: A band stamp with a full alphabet and number set on one band.

Amber Negatives: A yellowish negative that can be developed without chemicals using tap water. This is an alternative to the traditional black negative.

Anti-Tack Crystals: Used with water in post-exposure of liquid polymer plates to reduce tackiness.

Back Exposure: In the production of liquid polymer stamps, the light is briefly directed through the substrate to the resin, hardening the entire sheet at a shallow depth. This attaches the resin to the substrate and builds a background for the characters of the die.

Background: The non-print area of the stamp die.

Bakelite Matrix Board: Thermosetting wafer board, that, when subjected to heat and pressure in a vulcanizer, melts and hardens retaining a recessed image of a photopolymer or photo engraved image.

Bearer Bars: Precision ground steel bars used to regulate the distance between platens in a vulcanizer or used to regulate the distance between glass plates in a photopolymer process.

Bridge Dater: Die plate dater that has a separate die plate either above or below the date, or both. Typically 1/4" high and used for single line text.

Buna: Synthetic rubber used as the die material on hand and self-inking stamps.

Chase: A steel or aluminum fixture that regulates the amount of pressure applied between a type-high mounted photoengraving and the Bakelite matrix board. This type of chase is used in conjunction with a vulcanizer to make a matrix board. In the manufacture of pre-inked stamps, the chase is a metal frame used to form the mold in which a pre-ink mix (gel) is placed.

Class Characteristic: Feature or defect specific to a production run and not a specific stamp.

Cold Type: Term used when referring to any manufacturing process that uses computer software to make the negative for the stamp instead of typesetting material. Laser engraving ultraviolet, thermal printer, and light burst are examples of cold type.

Consecutive Action: Advancement of wheels on a numbering machine to the next number in sequence each time the machine is pressed once.

Counter: Part of the seal embossing assembly containing the indentation (female) of the seal text.

Counterfeit: A copy or simulation of a genuine stamp or seal used to deceive and defraud the public, the commercial sector and/or the legal community. Obtained without permission of the owner of genuine stamp or seal.

Cover Film: Thin plastic sheet material used to cover the negative in photopolymer processing. Prevents resin from contacting the negative.

Cushion: Part of the stamp assembly that is a foam material with a double adhesive backing is positioned between the stamp die and the mount.

Cut: An engraved block for printing. Materials used by an engraver were wood, brass, and zinc. A zinc cut, for example, would be used to print signatures, logos, or artwork for rubber stamps.

DPI: Dots per inch. Used to describe the clarity of images in desktop publishing.

De-Tack Powder: Used after post-exposure on drying polymer plates to lessen any remaining tackiness.

Delrin: Trade name for a hard plastic manufactured by DuPont used in the manufacturing of laser dies and counters.

Density: Refers to the ability of a black image to stop light from passing through it. When producing polymer plates, the images on the vellum paper must be very dense in order to produce a dense negative. Likewise, the images on the negative must be very dense in order to produce a good polymer plate.

Desktop Publishing (DTP): Typesetting and page set-up performed on a PC or a Macintosh.

Developer: A chemical used to wash away unexposed areas of emulsion from a traditional negative. It is always used with a fixer.

Die: The trimmed material bearing the printed text of the stamp. For embossing seals, the die contains the relief (male version) of the seal text.

Die Plate: Part of the stamp container where the stamp die is mounted.

Die Plate Dater: A marking device that includes a changeable date surrounded by a constant copy area. The date may be changed by rotating bands or by removing/inserting blocks of rubber type. Die plate daters are available in regular (requires use with a pad) or self-inking (with a pad in the unit).

Die Sinking Machine: A device that mechanically engraves a die. Known as the Automator, it has a typewriter keyboard and as the operator depresses each key, the machine stamps the proper characters into the die.

Double-Stick foam-backed tape: Mounting tape which is sticky on both sides of a foam strip. Invented by Gene Griffiths in 1981 and packaged in squares or rolls.

Duplicate: A copy of a genuine stamp or seal. The source of duplication can either be the matrix board allowing for the die text to be mass produced or a duplicate has been created using an impression from the genuine stamp. If duplicate produced from the genuine stamp impression, it is unknown if duplicate is produced with permission or knowledge of the owner.

Duplicate Action: Refers to a numbering machine action that imprints the same number twice, then advances to the next number.

Durometer: A hardness measure used to gauge the relative hardness of rubber, photopolymer, or other synthetic materials.

Emulsion: The light-sensitive material applied to one side of a piece of film. When exposed to light, this material hardens and will not wash away with developer (when using traditional negatives) or water (when using amber negatives).

Engraving: The art of cutting or carving grooves or characters into a surface. The more common forms of engraving are hand engraving, mechanical engraving, and a variety of photographic and chemical etching processes.

Exposure Pad: Dark foam pad, generally used to create proper surface contact between negative film, vellum paper and glass plate during exposure process. Eliminates need for a vacuum frame.

Feathering: Bleeding of stamp outside the letter in a stamp impression.

Felt Stamp Pad: A stamp pad that uses linen covered felt to hold ink.

First Generation Stamping: The first impression made with the stamp after inking.

Fixer: A chemical in processing traditional negatives halting the action of the developer.

Flat Band Dater: A marking device using thin, continuous rubber belts with months, days and years that can be changed by advancing the belts.

Flat-Bed Laser: Laser engraving process used in stamp manufacturing to burn away the non-print areas, leaving the printed image with a relief. The flatbed laser leaves a series of parallel grooved lines on the non-printing area of the die.

Flexographic Printer: A printer that uses an engraved roller to control the amount of ink used for printing.

Fluorescent: Special formulations of ink that will become visible only under ultraviolet light source. Under normal lighting, the image can be "invisible" or incorporated as part of the color design of the document.

Font: An assortment or set of type all of one size and style.

Frame: The outer metal parts of a self-inking stamp.

Front Exposure: In liquid polymer stamp production, the light is directed through the negative to harden the polymer only where the light hits, forming the characters of the die. This exposure also hardens the characters deep enough to attach them to the background.

Gel: A microporous material saturated with ink that is microencapsulated in the material. Also known as Pre-Mix.

Gravers: Hand tools used by engravers to chisel the features into the seal die.

Gum Rubber: Unvulcanized rubber compound molded in a vulcanizer to form stamp dies.

Hand Engraving: The art of engraving done freehand using specially shaped and contoured hand-held tools and requiring a considerable degree of artistic talent.

Handle: The part of a hand stamp or marking device that is held while making the impression.

Handpunched: A technique for engraving dies by hand. Also referred to as die sinking or hand stamped.

Hand-Stamp: A stamp that requires a separate ink pad when making impressions. The hand stamp may or may not have a handle on the stamp mount.

Hobbed: Trade term for machine stamping generic data such as "Notary Public" or "Corporate Seal" into a batch of dies.

Holland Cloth: Protective sheet of material placed between platens and back of rubber die to protect rubber during the vulcanizing process. May be attached to gum rubber or provided in roll form.

Hosting Surface: Surface used for the impression. The hosting surface can be paper, plastic, windows, cardboard, photographs, etc.

Hot Stamping: Manufacturing process using heat transfer and plastic (no ink) to place an image on a document or item.

Hot Type: Term used when referring to any manufacturing process using to make the negative for the stamp. Examples are lead type used in handset type, Linotype, and Ludlow.

Index: The label that indicates the text on the stamp. Also known as the title.

Individual Characteristic: A feature or defect that is unique to the one stamp and can occur in either the manufacturing process or from individual usage.

Justification: Refers to the arrangement of the characters on a line. The three types of justification are: right justification, center justification, and left justification. Also called Quadding.

Kerning: In typesetting, adjustment of spacing between pairs of characters by subtracting space making them closer together.

Keylining: In polymer production, fitting artwork as closely together as possible on a plain white piece of bond paper.

Laser Cut: Process of stamp manufacturing using "laser rubber" (pre-vulcanized natural rubber) and laser engraving to cut the image to form the "die" of the stamp. Laser dies can reflect greater detail as the laser dies stay straighter and crisper in small detailed areas.

Laser Printer: A printer used with a desktop publishing system to output artwork for proofing and/or for use in producing a negative to make polymer or rubber stamps.

Light Burst Technology: Use of Xenon flash in the manufacturing process of flat die stamps. Numerous light bursts are used to seal the background of the stamp pad, leaving only open micropores in the area of the flat die to print the text.

Line Dater: A date stamp showing the month, day, and year.

Liquid Photopolymer: A liquid form of plastic that is sensitive to ultraviolet light. When exposed to UV light, the liquid hardens. Also known as liquid polymer.

Liquid Polymer: See Liquid Photopolymer.

Local Dater: A flat band dater with a small die plate space either before or after the dates so the wording can be put on the same line. The wording appears like a regular rubber stamp (Example: SHIPPED APR 1987).

Marking Device: Tools with which people add marks of identification or instruction to their work or product.

Mat: Abbreviation for matrice.

Matrice: The individual type used in the Linotype or the Ludlow that was placed in the composition stick to form the type slug.

Matrix Board: Thermoplastic board that hardens to approximately 90 durometer with heat and pressure. The matrix board is used as the mold for rubber and photopolymer stamps. Also known as Bakelite or engraved phenolic material.

Merigraph Process: Brand of photopolymer that is hardened to 95 durometer. This hardened sheet replaces the lead slugs used by Linotype and Ludlow machines in the vulcanization process of raw rubber stamps.

Metal Self-Inker: A self-inking stamp where the container is metal instead of plastic.

Mirror Image: A stamp or type that is itself right reading so that it prints a "mirror" image (an image that is backward) of its message on an opaque surface. These are usually used in printing devices that have an "offset" roll, or on the inside of clear packages so the message is "right reading" to the customer.

Mold: The form in which the pre-ink mix is cast to make pre-ink stamps.

Molding Strip: A rubber stamp mount that does not require a handle.

Mount: The plate in the stamp assembly that holds the die.

Natural Rubber: Term used by stamp printers to separate gum rubber from synthetic materials that are also vulcanized and used for stamp dies.

Negative Image: Artwork that is in a "reverse" state (black background with white or clear artwork). Also called "inverse" in some desktop publishing programs.

Neoprene: A black, vulcanized rubber that is more impervious to solvents than natural rubber.

Non-Porous: Indicates a surface that has no openings to absorb ink. Therefore, marking requires an ink that will air dry.

Numbering Machine (Manual/Non-Electric): A hand-held, automatic stamping device, which imprints numbers and/or letters, or dates consisting of metal wheels in Roman or Gothic. These machines are capable of several movements: consecutive, duplicate, etc.

Offset Printer: A printer that transfers an image to the surface by means of an intermediate roller, which is normally of softer rubber and will conform to curved surfaces.

Pantograph: All-inclusive term that is used to describe a wide variety of machines ranging from very small, two-dimensional, fixed ratio non-motorized machines to large, free standing three-dimensional, variable ratio ones. The pantograph traces a template with a stylus attached to the arms of the machine, and through a reduction ratio, produce a mark on or into a surface of the material being engraved.

Permanent Defect: An anomaly that is part of the material used for the stamp. The anomaly can develop during the manufacturing process or from individual use. The anomaly reflects an area of the material that has been damaged. If it is located on the stamp die, it can cause a non-print area in the impression.

PPI: Pulses per inch. Unit of measurement of the number of times the laser fires per inch during the engraving process of stamps. The setting is in the driver.

PMT: Photo Mechanical Transfer, which is used to reproduce a high contrast black and white image.

Phenolic Engraving Stock: A heat resistant paper-based laminate that can be engraved for use as a matrix board.

Photoengraving: A chemical etching process used on magnesium and zinc. Commonly used for making rubber stamp dies or hot-stamping dies. Also called "photoetching."

Photoetching: See Photoengraving.

Photopolymer: A photosensitive plastic that hardens when exposed to ultraviolet light.

Photosensitive: Sensitive to light (in this case, ultraviolet light). Many of the materials used in the photopolymer process are photosensitive and should be kept in protective packaging until needed for use.

Pica: A unit of measurement used in typesetting. There are ten characters to an inch.

Pitting: Void or non-print area in the character.

Plastic Mount: Introduced by Gene Griffiths and M & R Marking in 1988. The material is expanded extruded PVC with a blowing agent added to make it lightweight. The plastic mount replaced the wood mount in hand stamps.

Plastic Self-Inker: Small plastic box featuring a die plate that rotates inside and seated against a miniature stamp pad, allowing repetitive stamping. The standard container for self-inking stamps in the mid-1970s.

Platens: Heating surfaces of a vulcanizer. The platens are mounted in parallel alignment, one above the other.

Point: A unit of measurement used in typesetting. There are 72 points to an inch.

Polymer: See photopolymer.

Porous: Indicates a surface with openings that will accept ink.

Positive Image: Artwork in its "normal" state (black artwork on a white or clear background).

Post Exposure: Refers to a period of exposure of the washed out plate to UV lights for final hardening of the polymer. When producing liquid polymer, this is done immediately after washout with the plate immersed in a mixture of water and anti-tack crystals. When producing from sheet polymer, this is done on the glass, after the plate has been dried and allowed to cool from room temperature.

PostScript: Term used in desktop publishing to describe a format for fonts, files, and makers. Allows type to be resized without losing clarity.

Pre-Inked Stamp: The ink is in the die of the stamp; therefore an ink pad is not required. Gel stamps and laser foam rubber stamps are pre-inked.

Pre-Mix: The raw, viscous liquid material that is cured under heat and pressure during manufacture to produce pre-inked dies. The ink is microencapsulated. Also known as "gel."

Progressive Defect: A defect or feature whose appearance and presence changes with continual use over time.

Proof: A single hand printing from the original die or printing plate to ascertain image development quality and accuracy prior to production.

Quadding: Refers to the arrangement of the characters on a line. The three types of quadding are: right quadded, center quadded, and left quadded. Also called justification.

Quadruplicate Action: Refers to a numbering machine action that imprints the same number four times, then advances to the next number.

Ramping: One of the factors controlling the smoothness of the laser cut on the background of a stamp. The ramping method reduces the laser power as the beam reaches the edge of the character, giving the character a shoulder. If ramping is turned off, the edge of the character is almost straight.

Random Characteristic: Primary classification of a defect or feature whose origin is unknown due to possibility of occurrence in more than one stage of the manufacturing process.

Raster: Raster engraving is used to create detailed graphic images using a high resolution dot matrix styled printing. In laser engraving, the laser head moves back and forth, left to right, engraving a series of dots one line at a time. As the laser head moves down, line by line, the dot pattern begins to form the image that was "printed" from the computer. The DPI of an image that has been raster engraved can be as high as 1200 DPI resolution.

Reciprocating Coder: An air-actuated printer with a printhead that moves back and forth.

Reduction: A photographic method used to make images smaller.

Release Agent: Silicone or graphite aerosol used to minimize sticking of the matrix material to other surfaces during the molding cycle.

Repeat: Refers to a numbering machine action that stays on the same number constantly.

Retainer Ring: A ring that snaps inside the mount to secure the die, eliminating the need to glue it to the die plate.

Reverse Image: The text is clear or "white" and the background is black or colored.

Reverse Tie Knot: On ribbed rubber type, the ribs or "tie knots" normally run the same direction as the text. Reverse tie knots run at a right angle to the text (vertical ribs).

Rib-Base Stamp: Type of stamp with a ribbed rubber base that has grooves or ribs that fit onto a ribbed or grooved mat.

Ribbed Rubber Type: A form of rubber type that interlocks with matching ribbed holder. The ribbed back rubber type comes in sets of the alphabet and numbers.

Right Reading: Refers to positioning the negative in the position where you can read the copy.

Riser: Transition between the mat and the printing surface of the die. The riser is the outline of the type on the lead slug. It is usually coarse and is not a straight line, but in a wave formation.

Rocker Mount: A wooden rubber stamp base with a curved bottom, to which the rubber die is glued. The stamp impression is "rolled" onto the surface being marked. Used mainly for large rubber stamps to help give a better impression.

Roll Coder: (Also known as "friction-driven coder"). A machine with a print wheel and cylindrical ink roll used with rubber type to mark "codes" or other information on products and packages. Roll coders that are "continuous," "random," or "non-indexing" and have free print wheels that continue to revolve as long as they are in contact with a printing surface. "Indexing" coders have a spring that returns the print wheel to the starting point after printing. This ensures that only one imprint is made each time.

Rotary Engraving: Engraving that is done with a rotating tool or cutter in a motorized spindle. The process is similar to routing and is used to produce cuts of specified widths and depths in a wide variety of materials.

Rotary Laser: Type of laser used in the manufacturing of stamps. The laser light removes the non-print area by burning away the background, leaving holes in the mat surface.

Rubber Die: Relief letters or image in a rubber material in reverse of the message to be conveyed. The part of the rubber stamp that actually prints the message.

Seal: An impression, mark, or a device with a cut or raised emblem, symbol, or word which can be impressed in relief upon a soft tenacious substance, such as clay, wax, or paper to certify a signature or authenticate a document.

Seal Die: The round metal part of a seal embosser in which the message is inscribed.

Seal Embosser: A marking device that uses pressure to leave a relief image of a seal on paper.

Sealer: A clear liquid that is applied to the face of the pre-ink die to block the ink from printing on blank areas.

Second and Third-Generation Stamping: Succeeding impressions after the first impression made without re-inking the stamp.

Self-Inking Stamp: A stamp in a container, usually plastic, that houses a rotating die plate seated against a miniature stamp pad. The die plate rotates to the enclosed ink pad to re-ink after every impression. This action allows for repetitive stamping and a separate ink pad is not needed.

Shim Plate: Precision ground flat plate used in the molding process to adjust thickness of finished mold.

Shim Strips: Thin metal strips placed on top of the bearer bars. Used to increase the distance between platens or glass plates in very small increments.

Sorts: Individual letters, numbers, or other single characters. Often used in relation to ribbed rubber type.

Sponge Cushion: Rubber or foam material used between the mount block and the stamp printing die. Facilitates the quality of the stamp imprint.

Spray Release Solution: See Release Agent.

Stamper: The individual holding a stamp producing an impression on the hosting surface.

Stamp Maker: The local stamp shop or stamp business whose business is primarily making rubber stamps.

Stamp Resin: Liquid polymer in its uncured state (before it is exposed to ultraviolet light).

Stencil: Sheet of material, such as wax-coated paper, cardboard, or vinyl, which does not allow moisture to pass through it. Text or designs are created by cutting through the stencil so that a substance such as ink or paint can be forced through the openings onto a surface to be printed.

Substrate: In liquid polymer production, it is the rigid plastic with an adhesive on the side that meets the resin, and becomes part of the plate during the back exposure. In sheet polymer production, this refers to either the Mylar or metal backing already applied to the polymer.

Tang: A projecting shank, fan, tongue, or the like as on a knife, file, or chisel to connect with the handle. In the marking industry, it refers to the projecting piece of the backside of the mold to anchor it to the hobbing machine.

Tenon: The protruding portion at the base of a stamp handle which is inserted into a hole drilled in the mount block.

Thermal Transfer: A type of print technology that uses a heated printhead to form the printed area of the die on the stamp.

Traditional Negatives: Negatives traditionally used in the graphics industry which require chemical developer and fixer.

Transitory Defect: An anomaly such as dust, hair, dirt, or fiber that attaches itself to the material of the stamp. If the anomaly is on the stamp die (print area), it can create a non-print area in the impression. A transitory defect is not a part of the material and therefore can easily be removed from use or cleaning.

Triplicate Action: Refers to a numbering machine action that imprints the same number three times, then advances to the next number.

Type Band Dater: Same type of dater as flat band dater, only these dates are raised about 1/4" and are a continuous belt. The die plate holds them in place firmly.

Type High: The standard thickness measuring .918 inches used in letterpress printing. This standard was developed for hand-set type.

Ultraviolet Light: Radiation waves just beyond the visible spectrum at the violet end which may be harmful to your eyes.

Ultraviolet Process: Process of curing materials sensitive to ultraviolet in the manufacturing process of stamps. In stamps, photopolymer is the most common material.

Vector Cutting: A continuous path that follows the outline or profile of an image. Normally used to cut completely through materials in laser engraving and can also be used for marking of characters and geometric patterns.

Vellum: A fairly translucent fine-grained paper that is used as the negative in the photopolymer process.

Vulcanizer: Pressurized heat press used for molding of matrix materials, rubber, and pre-inked gels.

Vulcanized Rubber: Raw, opaque rubber that has been pressurized with heat to harden sufficiently for use as a stamp die.

Washout: Process of washing unexposed polymer away leaving the hardened characters on the plate.

Wrong Reading: Placement of negative in a position where it is backwards and cannot be read "left to right."

Xenon Flash: Used in the light burst manufacturing process of flat die stamps. See Light Burst Technology.

INDEX